Christianity in Review

Christianity in Review

A History of the Faith in Fifty Books

Anthony Kenny

DARTON·LONGMAN + TODD

First published in 2015 by
Darton, Longman and Todd Ltd
1 Spencer Court
140 – 142 Wandsworth High Street
London SW18 4JJ

ISBN 978–0–232–53172–5

A catalogue record for this book is available from the British Library

Phototypeset by Kerrypress Ltd, Luton
Printed and bound by Scandbook AB, Sweden

Contents

PART SIX: THE DEBATE BETWEEN THEISTS AND NATURALISTS

PART SEVEN: MODERN MORAL THEOLOGY

Foreword

The reviews collected in this volume were written for various periodicals over a period of more than fifty years. Some of them date from a time when I was a Roman Catholic priest. Most were written during the course of an academic career, after I had been laicised and left the Church, while I was an Oxford don, first as Fellow, then as Master, of Balliol College. The most recent ones belong to the years since my retirement, as Warden of Rhodes House, in 1999. Looking back over them from the perspective of the present, I can claim that they add up to a coherent, if highly selective, history of Christian thought. They are presented here not in the order in which they were written but grouped according to the period or aspect of church history to which their subjects belong.

Anthony Kenny
September 2014

PART ONE

THE EARLY CHURCH

Introduction

Christianity, like Judaism and Islam, is a 'religion of the book'. Each of the three monotheistic religions possesses a text, or set of texts, that it regards as its foundation charter. The books of the Torah, the histories of Israel, and the writings of the prophets and psalmists provide the bedrock of Jewish religion. The same books are accepted by Christians as the word of God: an Old Testament, to find its culmination in the New Testament unfolded in the Gospels, and the Acts and Epistles of the apostles. Christianity and Islam both recognise the Hebrew Scriptures as inspired texts, bearing a message from God that has been superseded by a later, definitive, revelation – in Islam that contained in the Quran. Members of all three faiths appeal to their own sacred texts to guide or justify their actions at the present day, and within each tradition there are many different methods and procedures by which the ancient sayings are linked to the conditions of modern life.

The authority of sacred texts, if they are to be taken as guides to practical life, is inseparable from the authority of the religious communities and officials whose role is to interpret them.

In the Judaeo-Christian tradition, for instance, the very notion of 'the Bible' as a single entity depends on the various authorities throughout history who have established the canon. However impressive individual books of the Bible may be, to see them as being elements of a single revelation that contains also some or all of the other books is already tacitly to accept a religious authority which defines a canon. One might gather together the works of Homer, Hesiod, Aeschylus, Sophocles, Euripides, Herodotus and Thucydides into an epitome of Greek thought. The books would share a common cultural tradition and cohere with each other as well or ill as the books of the Old and New Testament do. But we do not treat them as a single book, to be treated differently from all other books, because there has never been a Hellenic rabbinate or episcopate to adjudicate on their canonicity and impose them as authoritative.

Christianity differs from the other religions of the book in an important respect. Christians do not believe that Jesus himself wrote any book, in the way that Jews have believed that Moses wrote some or all of the Torah, and Muslims believe that Muhammad committed to paper the words dictated by the Angel Gabriel. We know the teaching of Jesus only at second hand, from the accounts of his life given by the evangelists. Consequently it is important for Christians to form an opinion of the value of the Gospels as records of historical truth. In recent years even many conservative scholars have come to accept that the gospel narratives bear the marks of literary artifice as well as of historical record. For the most authentic account of primitive Christian thought many now prefer to focus on the letters of St Paul – the earliest surviving documents – rather than on the sayings attributed to Jesus in the Gospels.

When we consider the reliability of the New Testament record, we find that St Luke, the third evangelist and the author of the Acts of the Apostles, occupies a unique position. On the one hand many passages in the Acts that describe the journeys of St Paul are accepted even by atheist historians as likely to be eye-witness accounts. On the other hand the infancy narrative in the Gospel is treated as fiction even by some conservative Catholics. Scholarly debate on these topics is far from concluded.

For centuries Christians were divided on the relationship between the Church and the Bible. Should one accept the Church's teaching only in so far as it accorded with the Bible (as Protestants claimed)? Or should one accept the Bible only because it was authenticated by the Church (as Catholics claimed)? Secular critics complained that all Christians were guilty of reasoning in a circle, giving authority to the Church on the basis of the Bible, and accepting the teaching of the Bible on the authority of the Church. Christians in response tried to show that there was no circularity, only symbiosis.

During the first three centuries after the death of Jesus Christianity was a minority sect, generally tolerated but occasionally persecuted by the Roman imperial authorities. The Emperor Constantine (274–337) transformed it into an established church ruled by a hierarchy of bishops who often enjoyed temporal as well as spiritual power. A series of councils of bishops in the fourth and fifth centuries hammered out the formulation of the central Christian doctrines. Nicaea (325) proclaimed that Jesus was the son of God, coeternal with God the Father. Ephesus (431) declared that Jesus, a single person, had two distinct natures, one divine and one human. Chalcedon (451) affirmed that he was both perfect God and perfect man, with a human body and a human soul, sharing divinity with his father and sharing humanity with us.

The decisions of these councils henceforth provided the test of orthodoxy for the great majority of Christians. But the person who brought Christian doctrine into the shape which was to dominate the thinking of Western Europe for a millennium and more was St Augustine, who became a Christian convert in Milan in 387, and went on to become Bishop of Hippo in North Africa, where he died just too soon to attend the Council of Ephesus. Augustine presented an elaborate narrative of world history, from the original sin of our first parents Adam and Eve to the declining years of the Roman Empire. He devised an elaborate system to establish the role of divine predestination in the salvation and damnation of frail individual humans. His teaching on grace and freedom provided the background to controversies which rumbled on centuries after consensus had been reached on the doctrines of the incarnation and the

Trinity. The greatest classics of Christian literature – from Dante's *Divine Comedy* to Milton's *Paradise Lost* – owe as much to St Augustine as they owe to the Bible.

The New Jerusalem Bible
Darton, Longman & Todd, 1985

The New Jerusalem Bible is not a Bible for the New Jerusalem. It is the revised English version of the *Bible de Jerusalem* made in the 1960s by the Dominican Fathers of the École Biblique in Jerusalem, and first translated into English under the general editorship of Alexander Jones in 1966.

The purpose of producing an English version of the Jerusalem Bible was originally to make available the careful notes provided by the Dominicans. The translation of the text – mainly from the original languages, but with an eye on the French version – was, as it were, to be a peg to hang the notes upon. It was a surprise to the editor and translators when the English Jerusalem Bible became a popular version in its own right and was approved for liturgical use both in the Roman Catholic Church and in the Church of England

In 1973 a new edition of the *Bible de Jerusalem* was published, taking account of recent scholarly trends, and incorporating substantial changes in the introduction and notes. The new general editor, Dom Henry Wansbrough of Ampleforth Abbey, tells us: 'The biblical text of the first edition was occasionally criticised for following the French translation more closely than the originals. In this edition the translation has been made directly from the Hebrew, Greek or Aramaic.'

Many readers of this journal will no doubt be familiar with the Jerusalem Bible in its first version. I shall not attempt to evaluate its merits. It has often been compared unfavourably with the Authorised Version. Of course it lacks the archaic splendour of that version, but it was never intended to compete with it. The way to judge a new version of the Bible is not to look at the passages one knows by heart – any alterations there will seem an alteration for the worse. The fairest method is to look at an unfamiliar passage in Chronicles or Deuteronomy and see how much sense it makes at first reading.

In this review I wish simply to compare the old and new Jerusalem Bibles. I should here declare an interest: I was myself one of the original translators. However, my contribution was restricted to the book of Job, the Epistles to the Romans and the Galatians, and the Petrines. In sampling the difference between the two versions I will concentrate at this Christmas season on the gospels of the infancy in Matthew and Luke.

Placing the old and new texts of these chapters side by side, the reader notices that the changes in the text are comparatively small: by my count 95 per cent of the words are the same in both versions. In the first chapter of Matthew, where the old version began 'A genealogy of Jesus Christ', the new one begins 'Roll of the genealogy of Jesus Christ'. Where the old version had 'Abraham was the father of Isaac' and so on through the generations, the new has 'Abraham fathered Isaac'. The general effect of the small differences is to make the text read less smoothly in English while presenting a more literal version of the Greek. Thus, a Greek particle, frequent in Matthew, was left untranslated in the old version; it appears constantly in the new, translated sometimes by 'suddenly' and sometimes by 'look!' In one place the return to a more literal translation is clearly an improvement: in the old, Mary replies to the angel's annunciation, 'How can this come about, since I am a virgin?'; in the new version it is 'How can this come about, since I have no knowledge of man?'

The new version makes a conscientious attempt to render the same Greek word by the same English word. The Greek word *dikaios* appears several times. In the old version we are told, for instance, that Joseph, when he found Mary with child, 'being a man of honour and wanting to spare her publicity decided to divorce her informally'. The word translated 'man of honour' appears, when later used to describe Simeon, as 'upright'. The new version uses 'upright' in both places: Joseph's decision to divorce as attributed, more elegantly, to his 'being an upright man and wanting to spare her disgrace'.

There are two changes which will take some readers by surprise. One concerns a single passage, the other is a recurrent issue.

The newborn Jesus was laid in a manger, the old version tells us, 'because there was no room for them in the inn'. The new version says instead, 'there was no room for them in the living space'. A note suggests that Joseph actually lived in Bethlehem, but that his house was too crowded for there to be room for the newborn. But if a house is overcrowded, surely a newborn and a new mother are the last who are likely to be turned out of doors. So far as I am aware there is no scholarly objection to the tradition which would necessitate such a brutal destruction of a well-loved story.

When *The New Jerusalem Bible* was launched emphasis was placed on the fact that the text had been vetted to see that it would give no offence to feminists. Critics objected that a fair translation of a chauvinist text would itself have to be a chauvinist version. But the matter is more complicated than that. The nature of English idiom has sometimes ensured that in the past chauvinist features were introduced into translations which were not in the original Greek. For instance, Greek has two words, one meaning 'human being' and the other meaning 'human male'. Both have traditionally been rendered into English by the word 'man'. *The New Jerusalem Bible* seeks to avoid offence by avoiding the use of 'man' to mean 'human being'. Thus, for 'the humiliation I suffered among men' we now read 'the humiliation I suffered in public'. For 'Jesus increased in wisdom, in stature, and in favour with God and men' we read 'with God and people'. It is difficult to carry out such a strategy consistently, and the new version, wisely, has not attempted to substitute 'Son of Person' for 'Son of Man'.

The problem here, of course, is not one that is created by, or can be solved by, any single Bible translation. It is indeed a defect in the English language that there is only a single word for the gender and the race, and it is wholly understandable that feminists wish to remedy this defect. But in my view they have chosen the wrong target, and in doing so distorted the sense of volumes of past English literature. They should have insisted that 'man' be reserved for its major use as the name of the race, and forced those who wished to refer to the masculine gender to use 'male' or some marked expression such as 'he-man' or 'gentleman'.

When one turns from the text of *The New Jerusalem Bible* to the notes, one discovers many more substantial alterations and additions, covering, I should guess, about one-third of the whole. In addition to incorporating recent archaeological or literary discoveries, these notes show two very perceptible concerns: first, to avoid anything that may appear sectarianly Catholic, and, second, to put a greater distance than hitherto between the sacred text and the historical facts.

In the infancy narrative, the first concern is most manifest in the treatment of the Virgin Mary. According to Catholic doctrine, Mary was not only a virgin when she gave birth to Jesus (as is unmistakably suggested in the text); she also vowed and kept perpetual virginity. In the note to Mary's words, 'I have no knowledge of man', the new version says, 'nothing in the text suggests a vow of virginity'. In the older Jerusalem Bible we read, '[Joseph] took his wife to his home and though he had not had intercourse she gave birth to a son'. The new text reads, 'he had not had intercourse with her when she gave birth to a son'. We are told in a note, 'the text is not concerned with the period that followed, and, taken by itself, does not assert Mary's perpetual virginity. This is assumed by the remainder of the gospel and the tradition of the church.' The hymn Magnificat which the text attributes to Mary is withdrawn from her by the notes which read, 'Luke must have found his canticle in the circles of the "poor" where it was perhaps attributed to the daughter of Zion. He found it suitable to bring into his prose narrative and put on the lips of Mary.' Indeed the notes now tell us that none of the canticles of the infancy narrative are genuine: two of them are pre-Christian writings and the third is an invention of Luke himself. No doubt this accords with the consensus of contemporary New Testament scholars.

Altogether the notes imply that the infancy narratives should be taken with a pinch of salt by serious historians. Already, in the earlier version of the Jerusalem Bible we were told that though the Synoptic Gospels set out to give us historical fact 'that does not mean that each of the events or discourses which they record corresponds exactly to what in fact took place'. We are now invited in the footnotes to regard the infancy narratives as midrashic. This word – it is explained elsewhere – indicates that liberties have been taken with the historical events and sources.

It is an irony of the present day that those parts of the Bible that are regarded as most dispensable by the theologians are those that are most precious to the simple faithful – and indeed to agnostics and sceptics. Theologians who have soaked themselves in the evangelical discourses or in the Epistles of St Paul can feel free to regard the infancy stories, or the story of the empty tomb, as legendary embroideries on a message which is essentially moral and spiritual. But for most people the birth and death and resurrection of Jesus are the most vivid, memorable and important events in his story – whether the story is, as it stands, fact or fiction.

It seems to me that it is time for agnostics and sceptics to stand up for the reputation of St Luke. At a time when most Christians took the infancy stories as the literal truth, Luke could be regarded as a faithful journalist committing to paper what his sources had told him. If the angel's visit to Mary and the birth in the manger never happened, as bishops and theologians are now happy to tell us, then Luke is something much greater: he is a creative writer of genius, one of the best storytellers ever to have lived. No other story has so gripped the imagination of the Western world; no other story has so often been echoed by poets, embroidered by painters and adorned by composers. No other story has been so often repeated and has brought tears to so many eyes and joy to so many hearts. When Christmas comes, whatever we think of theologians and translators, let us give thanks to St Luke.

The Listener, 19 December 1985

Jaroslav Pelikan
Jesus through the Centuries: His Place in the History of Culture
Yale University Press, 1985

There is a prayer that used to be popular among Roman Catholics called 'the Litany of the Most Holy Name of Jesus'. The priest would recite, one after the other, various titles of Christ: 'Jesus, Son of the Living God', 'Jesus, splendour of the Father', 'Jesus, brightness of eternal life', 'Jesus, King of glory', and so on through some fifty designations. After each, the congregation would respond 'Have mercy upon us'.

Pelikan's book is a history, not a prayer, but in structure it is very similar to the Litany. Each chapter is a historical meditation on a particular title of Jesus, or a particular concept of his role, or a particular image of his significance. The actual titles chosen as the chapter headings differ, to a greater or less degree, from those that figured in the Litany. 'The Light of the Gentiles' and 'The King of Kings' would fit harmoniously with the ancient titles in the prayer. Some of the later chapter headings, however, would make an uncomfortable fit: 'The Universal Man', 'The Teacher of Common Sense', 'The Poet of the Spirit'. This is because Pelikan is interested in the perception of Jesus not only by orthodox churchgoers but also by marginal and heterodox Christians and by those who might not call themselves Christians at all.

In a work of many volumes, *The Christian Tradition*, Pelikan has already described the history of the significance of Jesus for the faith and teaching of the Christian Church. In this book he sets out to tell the story of his place in the general history of culture.

Reading the book is a rich and rewarding experience. At the most basic level the book serves as an anthology of thoughts about Jesus by diverse thinkers of many ages and cultures, from St Augustine to Mahatma Gandhi and from the Emperor Constantine to Thomas Jefferson. It reminds the reader of many of the great books of the Western world and introduces a number of fascinating out-of-the-way texts. In both cases it whets the appetite to follow up the references in the extensive but unobtrusive footnotes. Well-chosen illustrations help to trace the visual image of Jesus in painting and sculpture through the centuries.

Each chapter deals with a single historical period, though of necessity there is overlap between one period and the next, as the waves of history rise and fall in the rolling tide. The best way for the reviewer to communicate the majestic sweep of Pelikan's narrative is to set out in order the themes of his successive chapters.

We are introduced first to Jesus the Jewish teacher, who instructs by parable and question, who is given in the New Testament the Aramaic names of 'rabbi', 'amen', 'messias' and 'mar'. From the beginning of Christianity Jesus is revered not only as teacher, but also as saviour: the notions of 'Lord' and 'Christ' lose their Semitic context and Jesus is seen as significant for the wider world. His first coming is the turning point of history, and his second coming its hoped-for, but ever-delayed, ending. The pagan theory of cycles in history is replaced by the linear, pointed, time that runs through Augustine's *City of God*. The significance of Jesus for the Gentiles is read not only forwards but backwards in time: like the Hebrew prophets of old, the pagan sibyls and Roman Vergil himself were held to have predicted the new age of the Virgin's child. Odysseus and Socrates, no less than Moses and David, were regarded as foreshadowing types of the wisdom and sufferings of the Christ who was to come.

When, in the age of Constantine, Christianity was transformed, with remarkable speed, from a persecuted sect into an established religion this could be seen as the triumph of the heavenly King Jesus over the Caesars who had ruled over the darkness of this earth. But under the sign of the King of Kings the Christian political order made room for a terrestrial monarch of unique significance: the sacred emperor, first of Byzantium, and then of the Holy Roman Empire in the West. The Emperor's power was the temporal sword of Christ, wielded sometimes in uneasy harmony, sometimes in open conflict, with the spiritual sword of the Pope who also claimed to be the Vicar of Christ.

Among Christians, Jesus was seen as transcending not just Judaism or the Roman world, but the cosmos itself. The doctrine of the cosmic Christ as incarnate Logos is described by Pelikan in the words of A. N. Whitehead as 'a combination of the personal energy of Jehovah with the rationality of a Greek philosopher'. The title Logos had consequences that were as momentous for the history of thought as were those of the title King for politics. The modern scientific conviction that the universe is an orderly system exemplifying general principles discoverable by the mind grew, if Pelikan is right, from the belief in the Logos as the rational instrument of the creation of the structure of the universe out of nothing.

Jesus' own favourite title for himself, however, had nothing to do with the creation of the cosmos: he spoke of himself, by preference, as the Son of Man. Pelikan shows how reflection on the person and mission of Jesus led Christians into a new conception of human nature itself: in particular to the vision of the human race as accursed by an inherited, original, sin. Logically, perhaps, the doctrine of the creation and fall of man should come first, to be followed by the doctrine of the person and work of Christ as the divine answer to the human predicament. But historically the doctrine of Jesus had to be elaborated first: Christian thought measured the gravity of the original sin by the dignity of the redeemer who set it right. The crime was, as it were, tailored to fit the punishment, the diagnosis devised to fit the prescription.

Consideration of the iconoclast controversy gives Pelikan an opportunity to reflect on the attitude of Christians to literal images of Christ. Did his special role as the unique image of God rule out the attempt to portray him in his turn by material icons? Or did the Eucharist, as the unique way of recreating the presence of Christ, preclude every other so-called image?

Beyond all representations of Jesus, the cross, as the special emblem of Christianity, pervaded the culture and folklore of the nations of medieval Europe as no other symbol had. Poems were written in cruciform shape, the cross figured in sacral and secular uniforms, and it was used in almost magical ways for military and medical purposes. Behind this imagery lay changing theories of the significance of Jesus' death on the cross. The most influential was that propounded in Anselm's *Why God Became Man*. Only one who was both human (and therefore a representative of sinful humanity) and divine (and therefore capable of infinite satisfaction) could repay the debt of man's sin. Many Protestants, Pelikan observed, have paid Anselm the ultimate compliment of not even recognising that their version of the wisdom of the cross comes from him, but attributing it to the Bible itself.

The cross is above all the symbol of the discipline and self-denial involved in the discipleship of Christ; and in his chapter 'The monk who rules the world' Pelikan traces the monastic ideal and the regime of poverty, chastity and obedience which gave structure to the religious orders. St Francis of Assisi and the Franciscan tradition is singled out for separate treatment in the chapter 'The divine and human model' because Pelikan believes that Francis embodied the life and teaching of Jesus more fully than anyone else during the past two thousand years. The mystical strand that was powerful in many of the monastic or mendicant traditions is studied in a chapter 'The bridegroom of the Soul', which, as its title suggests, lays special emphasis on epithalamic mysticism, uneasily poised between the dangerous aberrations of pantheism and eroticism.

With the coming of the Renaissance the development of philology allowed the study of the sources for Jesus' life to be pursued with ever greater enthusiasm. The flowering of representative art gave a new exuberance to the portrayal of Jesus' humanity in all its aspects. In spite of their enthusiasm for pre-Christian antiquity, many of the humanists retained an intense personal devotion to Jesus.

In describing the characteristic contribution of the Reformation to the appreciation of the personality of Jesus, Pelikan singles out, a little surprisingly, the concept of Christ as the mirror of the eternal. More expectedly, he associates Reformation theology with the musical setting of the biblical texts by Johann Sebastian Bach, the 'fifth evangelist'. The wars of religion that succeeded the Reformation present an opportunity for reflection on changing Christian attitudes to peace and war: first holy wars, or crusades against infidels, then just wars between Christian princes, and finally pacifism gradually resurgent in the Quaker tradition.

In the last four chapters of Pelikan's book we move further and further away from mainstream Christianity. We meet the demythologised Jesus of the age of Enlightenment, shorn so far as possible of the miraculous element that embarrassed Reimarus, Lessing and Strauss. We meet the romantic Jesus of Schleiermacher and Coleridge, the Jesus presented in the most famous of all post-biblical lives, that by Renan. And in the twentieth century we are presented with the figure of Jesus the liberator, the Tolstoyan Jesus who inspired Mahatma Gandhi and Martin Luther King. With this final stage we reach a point where, in Pelikan's words, we can see that there is far more in Jesus than is dreamt of in the philosophy and Christology of the theologians: a person and message that belongs not only to the Churches but to the world.

F. Van der Meer
Augustine the Bishop
Sheed & Ward, 1962

Augustine the saint is not so well known as Augustine the sinner. We all remember the cauldron of unholy loves at Carthage; few of us know much about the houseful of ascetic priests at Hippo.

This magnificent book takes up St Augustine's story where the *Confessions* leave off. In its pages, the bishop becomes as familiar to us as the worldling; his sermons are made as fascinating as his sins.

Basing himself mainly on the saint's own letters, homilies and pastoral tracts, the author gives us a vivid picture of his life from the day on which, as an alleged adulterer and dealer in love potions, he was refused consecration by the Primate to the day on which he died penniless with the seven penitential psalms nailed above his bed.

We are told little about the Father of the Church, or the polemical writer on grace; instead we read of the asthmatic preacher telling his boisterous congregation how to give up swearing in three days; of the reluctant administrator, bothered over the betrothal of one of his wards; of the admired spiritual director accepting the gift of a handwoven tunic from a pious woman.

The church of Hippo was not an easy one to govern. Many of the townsfolk were pagan, and many heretical. The Catholics had vinegar thrown at them by the Circumcellions, and the sermons were sometimes drowned out by noise from the Donatist church next door. The Catholics themselves were an unruly lot, given to strange practices that Augustine could never decide whether to condemn as superstitious. They would throw coins into the baptismal font, sew the Eucharist into their clothes while seafaring, and place porridge on the tombs of the dead. But they knew large portions of the Bible by heart.

Augustine himself emerges from the narrative as full of contradictions: so tender in his imagery, so puritanical in his advice; so rational, and yet so credulous; now ecumenist, and now intransigent; so masterly in his description of the human condition, so childish in his obsession with mystic numbers; so consoling in his vision of the City of God, so terrifying with his conviction that the mass of mankind is hurtling to hell. It is no wonder that he has been admired by men very different from each other, such as Aquinas and Pascal, or Calvin and Wittgenstein.

Catholic Herald, 19 April 1962

Henry Chadwick
Augustine
Oxford University Press, 1986

It is a daunting task to write an intellectual history of Augustine, for the saint's own *Confessions* set such a high standard: they are the description, by a biographer nearly as gifted as Boswell, of a mind more capacious than Johnson's. Henry Chadwick warns at the outset that a short introduction to Augustine's thought cannot also offer a biography. Nonetheless he manages, while writing tightly packed intellectual history, to bring the narrative alive with telling and fascinating detail.

It was sixteen hundred years ago this July that Augustine became a Christian at the age of 32. He was the last really great writer of classical antiquity, and his influence through succeeding ages was gigantic, even if much of it was indirect. He saw himself as expounding a divine message which had come to him from men much greater than himself: Jesus, Paul and Plato. But the way in which succeeding generations have conceived and understood the teaching of Augustine's masters has been in great part the fruit of Augustine's own work. Only Aristotle had a greater influence on human thought.

Chadwick helpfully summarises Augustine's legacy in seven points. He set the curriculum for the medieval universities; he inspired generations of Western mystics; he was the arbiter to whom both sides appealed in the Reformation and Counter-Reformation debates about grace and merit. In the eighteenth century, because of his emphasis on original sin, he was the target of Enlightenment preachers of human perfectibility. By contrast his exploration of the human heart – and it was he who first thus spoke of 'the heart' – endeared him to Romantic thinkers. He was a Platonist, but also a critic of Platonism. He has fascinated philosophers in many different traditions: he was an inspiration to Kierkegaard, the bête noire of Nietzsche, an anticipator of Freud, and one of the very few philosophers whom Wittgenstein could bear to read.

Chadwick writes:

> He was the first modern man in the sense that with him the reader feels himself addressed at a level of extraordinary psychological depth and confronted by a coherent system of thought, large parts of which still make potent claims to attention and respect ... The modern scientist's assumption that mathematical order and rationality are the supreme features of the world had no more eloquent advocate than he.

Augustine was the most prolific writer of antiquity. When he wrote the *Confessions* much of his output was still in the future. Chadwick's book brings out brilliantly the breadth and depth of his interests, and the varied strands of classical culture that were woven into the rich texture of his thought. He also shows how dynamic an intelligence Augustine possessed, forever a critic of his own thought, always revising his philosophical preconceptions and experimenting with different interpretations of the Bible.

Chadwick takes us through the stages of Augustine's *oeuvre*. First come the philosophical dialogues of his first Christian period; his treatise on the origin of evil and on free choice, still used as a text in a number of university philosophy departments; the donnish, Platonic *83 Questions*, the energetic, imaginative work *The Teacher*. All these and the tract *On True Religion* were written before he became a priest in 391. Afterwards there comes the great corpus of sermons, letters and biblical commentaries. Among these Chadwick singles out Augustine's expositions of Genesis and creation (a topic that he treated at length no less than five times) and the 15 books *On the Trinity*, completed at the age of 65. Crowning the theological treatises is the great *City of God*, his 'large and arduous work', a Christian meditation on the tragic course of history as the Roman Empire passed away.

Chadwick expounds Augustine briskly, clearly and respectfully. Inevitably he sometimes has to simplify things in a drastic manner; but he never does so in a way which is unfair or partial. He knows that many admirers of our current secular mores regard Augustine as symbolising all that they find repellent in Christian theology. He defends Augustine against some of the exaggerated abuse that has been heaped on him in connection with his treatment of sexuality and femininity. But he does not conceal the fact that the saint's works contain bizarre as well as endearing elements. He is clearly less comfortable with the late polemical works which spell out a profoundly pessimistic theory of grace, sin and damnation, worked out in controversy with the British heretic Pelagius, champion of free will.

Chadwick ends by inverting Gibbon's scornful verdict on Augustine, 'His learning is too often borrowed, and his arguments are too often his own.' Augustine's arguments, Chadwick says, were often borrowed, but his learning was largely his own. He could draw on a fine library, but one detail recorded by Chadwick brings out how lonely a genius he must have been. In the port of Hippo, where Augustine lived for the last 40 years of his life (for most of the period a bishop), he was the only person in town to possess any books at all.

The Listener, 15 May 1986

PART TWO

THE MIDDLE AGES

Introduction

The Emperor Constantine moved the capital of the Empire from Rome to Constantinople, and Greek Christian culture survived there until the fifteenth century. In the Latin West, however, from the sixth to the ninth century Christianity suffered a dark age. Outside the Empire the world was transformed beyond recognition by the life of the prophet Muhammad. Within a century of his death the religion of Islam had spread throughout North Africa and into Spain. Muslim military expansion was halted only in 732 at Poitiers by the Frankish leader Charles Martel.

Charles' grandson Charlemagne drove the Muslims back to the Pyrenees and established his own rule through large portions of Italy and Germany. On Christmas Day 800 he was crowned Holy Roman Emperor by the Pope in St Peter's Church in Rome. He inaugurated a revival of Christian scholarship, bringing scholars from various parts of Europe to his capital Aachen. But for three centuries more the centre of civilisation was not in Christian Europe but in the capitals of Islamic states. It was there that the treasures of Greek science and philosophy were preserved and studied.

By the twelfth century Christendom was in a position to take over the torch of culture from Islam.

The Christian thinkers Abelard and Anselm were of the same calibre as their contemporaries, the Muslim Averroes and the Jew Maimonides. The works of Aristotle were translated into Latin and after an initial period of disapproval became important items of study to Catholic philosophers and theologians.

The thirteenth century was a time of uncommon intellectual energy and excitement. The context for this ferment of ideas was created by two innovations that occurred early in the century: the new universities and the new religious orders.

The university is, in essentials, a thirteenth-century innovation, if by 'university' we mean a corporation of people engaged professionally, full-time, in the teaching and expansion of a corpus of knowledge in various subjects, handing it on to their pupils, with an agreed syllabus, agreed methods of teaching and agreed professional standards. Universities and parliaments came into existence at roughly the same time, and have proved themselves the most long-lived of all medieval inventions.

A typical medieval university consisted of four faculties: the universal undergraduate faculty of arts, and the three higher faculties, linked to professions, of theology, law and medicine. Students in the faculties learnt both by listening to lectures from their seniors and, as they progressed, by giving lectures to their juniors. A teacher licensed in one university could teach in any university, and graduates migrated freely in an age when all academics used Latin as a common language.

For the intellectual life of the age, the foundation of the religious orders of mendicant friars, the Franciscans and the Dominicans, was no less important than the creation of the universities. St Francis of Assisi secured papal approval in 1210 for the rule he had laid down for his small community of poor, wandering preachers. St Dominic, a tireless fighter for orthodoxy, founded convents of nuns to pray and friars to preach against heresy: his order was approved by the Pope in 1216. Like the Franciscans ('Friars Minor', 'Grey Friars'), the Dominicans ('Friars Preachers', 'Black Friars') were to live on alms, but at the outset their ethos was less romantic and more scholarly than that of the Franciscans. However, after the first generation of wholly other-worldly friars, the Franciscans became just as successful academically as the Dominicans. By 1219 both orders were established in the University of Paris. The Black Friars arrived in Oxford in 1221 and the Grey Friars in 1224. By 1230 each order had founded a school there.

The roll call of the great medieval philosophers is largely drawn from these two orders. Five thinkers of great distinction are St Albert, St Thomas Aquinas, St Bonaventure, John Duns Scotus and William Ockham. Of these, the first two are Dominicans and the last three Franciscans. Only in the fourteenth century, with John Wyclif, do we meet a philosopher of comparable talent who was a member of the secular (parish) clergy rather than a friar. Wyclif's eventual lapse from orthodoxy made him, in the minds of ecclesiastical historians of philosophy, a doubtful exception to the rule that it was thinkers of the religious orders who enjoyed the pre-eminence.

The most powerful intellect of the Middle Ages was St Thomas Aquinas, who was both a university professor and a member of the Dominican order. It was he who, more than anyone else, made Aristotle respectable in Christian eyes. He was not only a most perceptive commentator on the works of that philosopher, but was an original thinker in his own right: a theologian to rival St Augustine and a philosopher of the same calibre as Descartes or Kant. His surviving works add up to nearly 9 million words. Best known are his two encyclopaedic syntheses, the *Summa contra Gentiles* (Against the errors of the Infidels), some 325,000 words long, and the *Summa Theologiae*, which, in a million and a half words, expounds his mature thought at even greater length.

By making a distinction between matters of faith, which can be learnt only through a divine revelation such as the Bible, and matters of philosophy, which can be reached by the unaided operation of the human reason, Aquinas achieved a working relationship between Aristotelianism and Christianity. Within the area of philosophy itself he developed and modified

Aristotle's ideas, and while his treatment of logic and physics has been antiquated by later progress, his contributions to metaphysics, philosophy of religion, philosophical psychology and moral philosophy are still valuable today.

Christopher M. Cullen
Bonaventure
Great Medieval Thinkers series,
Oxford University Press, 2006

The city of Paris in the 1250s housed a remarkable trio of saints. In the university St Thomas Aquinas held the chair of theology assigned to the Friars Preachers, the order of begging friars founded a generation earlier by St Dominic. The head of the school belonging to the other mendicant order, the Friars Minor of St Francis, was another Italian theologian, St Bonaventure. Presiding over the city and nation, the King was St Louis IX, founder of the Sainte Chapelle, and recently returned from a crusade. St Louis entertained St Thomas at his table, and became a lay member of St Bonaventure's order.

The lives of Aquinas and Bonaventure were closely intertwined. The two were exact contemporaries, born within a few years of each other in the twenties of the century. They took their master's degree and were installed in their Paris chairs on the same day in 1257. Both were to die in the same year, 1274, each a delegate to the Council of Lyons which, it was hoped, was to reunite the Greek and Latin Churches. They differed, however, on important philosophical and theological issues. The disagreements arose from divergent attitudes to Aristotle whose works had just, in the 1250s, become obligatory texts in the Paris Faculty of Arts.

Bonaventure knew Aristotle well, as Christopher Cullen brings out in this book, but he regarded him as inferior to Plato. Aristotle was wrong, Bonaventure believed, to reject the transcendent Ideas of Plato's system: and from that initial mistake many other errors followed – that the world is eternal, that there is no providence, that there is only a single intellect, and that there is no personal immortality. The Platonic Ideas, however, should not be conceived as existing independently of any mind; rather, they should be regarded, as St Augustine had shown, as eternal ideas existing in the mind of God.

Aristotle was correct, Bonaventure conceded, to deny that the Ideas were the *only* objects of knowledge. In a passage quoted by Cullen, Bonaventure summed up the relationship between the two pagan philosophers thus: 'Aristotle provided a firm foundation for the way of science while neglecting the way of wisdom. It seems, therefore, that among the philosophers, the word of wisdom is to be granted to Plato, and the word of science to Aristotle.'

Bonaventure was sufficiently empiricist to agree that we acquire genuine knowledge from the changeable and perishable objects of self-perception, but he insisted that such knowledge was subject to doubt and error. If we are to acquire certainties, we need assistance from the unchangeable truth that is God. The Ideas in God's mind exercise an invisible causal influence on our thought: this is the divine illumination that enables us to grasp the stable essences that underlie the fleeting phenomena of the world. Here Bonaventure differs from Aquinas, who saw no need to invoke the supernatural to explain how the human mind works.

Bonaventure accepted the Aristotelian distinction between form and matter ('hylomorphism'), but he applied it in novel ways by associating it with a metaphysics of light. 'Let there be light' had been God's first command in Genesis, and this means, according to Bonaventure, that light was the first form given to prime matter. Light is present actually in the celestial bodies, and virtually in terrestrial bodies, as a disposition to become coloured when illuminated. Bodily creatures possess other forms in addition to the form of light. Human beings, for instance, have a form that makes them living creatures, another one that makes them animals, and a final supreme form that is their rational soul. Here Bonaventure once more took issue with Aquinas, who thought that the rational soul was the one and only form of human beings.

Again unlike Aquinas, Bonaventure believed that hylomorphism applied in the spiritual as well as the terrestrial sphere. Everything other than God, he maintained, is composed of matter and form. Even angels who lack bodies contain 'spiritual matter' – a notion that might appear to the uninstructed to be self-contradictory.

Christopher Cullen's book is a learned and judicious introduction to the philosophical and theological thought of Bonaventure. It will interest and inform those who are already familiar with Roman Catholic theology, or with the philosophy of Aquinas; but other people may find it hard reading. From time to time the reader encounters, without explanation, sentences such as the following: 'Bonaventure defends the Scholastic view that within the Godhead are two modes of emanation, three hypostases, four relations, and five concepts.'

The book, however, also brings out more accessible features of Bonaventure's style. We observe his partiality for triads: there are three kinds of moral philosophy, for instance (individual, domestic and political); there are three ages of history (the ages of nature, of law and of grace); and there are three classes of society (rulers, ministers and plebs). We notice, too, his fondness for erotic imagery in describing the relation of humans to God: the sinner who prefers creatures to the creator, we are told more than once, is like a bride who prefers the wedding ring to the bridegroom.

If Bonaventure was more mystical than Aquinas, he was also ruthlessly practical. Appointed Minister General of the Franciscans in 1257, he put an end to the disarray which had threatened to dissolve the order, with different factions claiming to be St Francis' sole authentic heirs. He reformed and reorganised the constitution, and wrote the official life of St Francis, ordering all others to be destroyed. In 1265 he rejected an invitation to become Archbishop of York, but in 1273 he was made Cardinal Archbishop of Albano. The Pope's letter of appointment brooked no refusal: but Bonaventure, before receiving it, made the papal messengers wait until he had finished the washing-up he was doing when they arrived.

Times Literary Supplement, 2007

Denys Turner
Thomas Aquinas: A Portrait
Yale University Press, 2013

Professor Turner believes that Aquinas was one of the few minds in history large enough to contain a coherent universe of thought. 'Thomas', he says, 'is in that company to which Dante, Plato, Shakespeare, Homer, and perhaps a few others belong.' Turner's enthusiasm for his subject infects the reader, and the vivacity of his style makes the reading easy. He brings out the contemporary relevance of Aquinas' thought, and he avoids encumbering his text with scholastic terminology.

Not that Turner ignores the medieval context of Aquinas' ideas – far from it. He constantly contrasts the saint's thought with that of his Christian contemporaries. While others, Platonically, regarded human beings as souls imprisoned in bodies, Aquinas, materialistically, insisted that human persons were animals of a particular kind, and that a disembodied soul would no longer be a person. While other theologians, following the Song of Songs, described the relationship between God and man in erotic terms, Aquinas, following Aristotle's *Ethics*, took friendship as the guiding concept.

Turner sums up accurately key elements of Aquinas' philosophy, wisely avoiding the topic of Being. In theology he is not afraid to present a full-frontal view of the most difficult theses, such as the claim that the persons of the Trinity are subsistent relations (pure relations that are not relationships *between* anything) and the claim that divine grace, though irresistible, does not constrain human freedom. Despite the genius of Aquinas and the skill of Turner, only those who are already believers are likely to find these sections convincing.

Turner is at his best when discussing Aquinas' character. He points out that the great *Summae* are completely devoid of ego. In other philosophers (such as Descartes and Kant) and other saints (such as Augustine and Bernard) the author's personality constantly intrudes. Not so with Thomas: he is a teacher invisible, standing out of the light so that others may see. It is no accident that he was canonised not for working miracles but for writing the *Summa*. The saint's sanctity shows itself above all in his silence about himself.

Common Knowledge, January 2015

Ralph McInerny
Characters in Search of Their Author
Gifford Lectures, Glasgow, 1999–2000,
University of Notre Dame Press, 2001

John Milbank and Catherine Pickstock
Truth in Aquinas
Routledge, 2001

The thought of St Thomas Aquinas continues to fascinate many minds. After the Second Vatican Council, Thomism lost the commanding position it had occupied in the training of Catholic clergy, but in compensation many philosophers outside the Roman fold began to study Aquinas' two great *Summae*. The seminary manuals had, in any case, functioned at some distance from Thomas' actual writings, and the disrepute that overtook manual Thomism has in the long run served the saint's reputation well.

In the English-speaking world there are three different schools among contemporary admirers of Aquinas. First, there are the conservatives who prolong the neo-scholastic tradition of Gilson and Maritain, albeit in a chastened and less triumphalist form. Second, there are the so-called 'analytical Thomists', who interpret Aquinas in the light of recent advances in philosophy of language and philosophy of mind. Third, there are those who follow an agenda drawn from postmodernism, among whom are the proponents of the theological movement that styles itself 'radical orthodoxy'.

Professor Ralph McInerny of Notre Dame is a doughty exponent of the first school of thought. His Gifford Lectures are a popular defence of traditional natural theology, written in a clear and lively style. In his account of natural theology in its relation to theoretical and practical reasoning he draws on Reid, Kierkegaard and Newman, as well as on St Thomas. He attacks various forms of irrationalism that underpin contemporary atheism, and remarks that nowadays it is often the proponents of faith who are loudest in their defence of the rights of reason. His criticisms of nihilism and positivism are convincing; less so is his attempt to reinstate, in spite of the centuries-old collapse of Aristotelian physics, the proof of God as the unmoved mover of the universe.

McInerny urges that theism has a better claim than atheism to be the default position of the human mind. He writes explicitly as a Christian philosopher, and admits to an antecedent expectation that natural theology can be successfully completed. This is no lapse in philosophical integrity, he claims. Every philosopher, atheist as well as theist, brings to his task antecedent convictions, and neither side can claim a monopoly of willingness to follow the argument where it leads.

There is, however, an important difference here between the believer and the unbeliever. An unbeliever can contemplate without guilt the possibility of changing his mind and accepting belief; the believer, on the other hand, holds that it would be sinful for him to change his mind and lose his faith. This does not, in itself, make faith irrational: after all, a secular liberal must surely believe that it would be wicked for him so to change his own mind as to become a Nazi. It does, however, nullify McInerny's claim that the believing philosopher is as open-minded as the unbeliever.

McInerny sees it as a merit of St Thomas that his philosophical thought is anchored in the ordinary thinking of the ordinary person. Many philosophers in the analytic tradition would make a similar claim for the later philosophy of Ludwig Wittgenstein. Wittgenstein, like Aquinas, stands at the opposite pole of philosophy from the Cartesian tradition that sees epistemology as the basic philosophical discipline and private consciousness as the fundamental datum of epistemology. This is one reason why several thinkers have combined an admiration for both philosophers. There is by now an impressive corpus of works of analytical Thomism. Some of the leading practitioners are Catholics, such as Peter Geach and John Finnis; some indeed, like the recently deceased and much lamented Father Herbert McCabe, were members of St Thomas' own Dominican order. But there are other influential writers of this school who – like Norman Kretzmann – have never been Catholics or – like Alasdair McIntyre – have held varying religious allegiance.

Very different are the writings of the radical orthodoxy school, of which John Milbank and Catherine Pickstock are celebrated exponents. In *Truth in Aquinas* they start from a crisis in philosophy which they describe as 'the death of realism', and they offer a reconsideration of Aquinas' thought as a way of surmounting this crisis. Unlike the analytic Thomists, who address a secular audience no less than a believing one, and beg no theological questions, the radically orthodox assume from the outset the validity of doctrines such as the Eucharist and the Trinity.

The title of the book may mislead. Truth, Aquinas tells us at the beginning of his *de Veritate*, is primarily to be found in the mind 'combining and dividing', that is, forming affirmative and negative propositions. Propositional truth of this kind has been the main concern of contemporary philosophical discussions of truth. Milbank and Pickstock, however, have little interest in this topic. After a brief and misleading discussion of the work of Donald Davidson in their first chapter, they turn their attention elsewhere, devoting their second chapter to the relationship between reason and faith, their third chapter to the sense of touch, and their fourth to the doctrine of transubstantiation.

The authors would claim, however, to have kept their eyes on the same topic throughout, because the final, astonishing, claim of the book is that only belief in transubstantiation will resolve the crisis of postmodernity. 'Outside the Eucharist', we are told, 'it is true, as postmodern theory holds, that there is no stable signification, no anchoring reference, no fixable meaning, and so no "truth".' Before assessing the manner in which this remarkable conclusion is reached, something must be said about the book's general approach.

The authors are very familiar with the works of St Thomas and have read widely among his commentators. Unfortunately, being well read is insufficient to make a good writer, and the style these authors adopt makes it extremely difficult to follow their thought or evaluate their arguments. On almost every page there are problems of vocabulary, syntax and logic. Jargon and neologisms abound, and pages are sprinkled with words like 'modus', 'chiasmus', 'linguisticality', 'discursivity', 'theoontology' and 'fetishisable'. Adjectives are regularly made to do duty as nouns: we are introduced to various problematics and thematics, and we are invited to digest sentences such as, 'For Aquinas, the real is identified in the meaningful, just as the semantic is identified in the ontological.' Contorted clauses are so interlinked that often the sense of a sentence emerges only like Laocoon striving amid smothering snakes.

Obscurity so dense does not come about by negligence or incompetence: it must surely be the work of conscious art. Perhaps the authors see themselves as addressing a small coterie of Gnostic initiates. Or perhaps the reader is meant to respond, 'This is all too difficult for my poor brain, but doesn't that just show …' Many a sentence would find itself at home in Pseud's Corner. The authors ask, for instance, 'What is it that we are

knowing when we discern the treenesss of a tree?' They offer
the answer:

> In knowing the treeness of a tree, we are knowing a great
> deal more besides. Since the tree only transmits treeness
> – indeed only exists at all – as imitating the divine, what
> we receive in truth is a participation in the divine. To put
> this another way, in knowing a tree, we are catching it on
> its way back to God.

The book is full of sophistical legerdemain. Take the following
argument, which is intended to dispose of Hume on causality:
'a cause does not really "precede" an effect, since it only
becomes cause in realizing itself as the event of the giving of
the effect.' One might as well argue that a mother could not be
older than her child, since she only becomes a mother when
the child arrives. Or consider this sentence, which I leave as an
exercise for the reader to construe: 'nothing is more identical
than nothing is to nothing.'

The authors frequently quote St Thomas, but often, rather than
getting to grips with his text, they skim above it like a hovercraft.
It would be easy to cite many cases of misunderstanding: I will
focus on a few that occupy significant positions on the main
line of the book's argument.

In the second chapter the authors attack on the common
(and correct) view that Aquinas drew a sharp distinction
between reason and faith, and similarly between philosophy
and theology. One strand in their attack is the claim that
reason requires faith because knowledge of God is impossible
without grace. To prove this impossibility they cite the *Summa
Theologiae* (Ia, q 8 a3) as stating that God is present to our
intellect. It is made clear, they say, 'that this presence is only
by grace'. But in the passage quoted, the word 'only' does not
appear; and the interpretation given contradicts many texts

that distinguish between natural knowledge of God and the acquaintance obtained by faith through grace (e.g. ScG III, 37–9).

A principal theme of the third chapter is that Aquinas assigns to the sense of touch such a fundamental role in sensation that all the other senses are really modes of touch. This claim is based on a passage in the commentary on Aristotle's *De Anima*, which is paraphrased as 'since touch is diffused over the whole surface of the body, all the senses partake of touch and are, indeed, variants of touch'. In fact what Aquinas says is that all the *organs* of the senses are also *organs* of touch – that is, the ears and nose and eyes can also *feel* things as well as, respectively, hearing, smelling and seeing things. On the basis of this misread text, the authors erect a massive metaphysical structure that they call a 'new ontological exaltation of the sensory over the intellectual'.

This fantasy is taken to further lengths in the final chapter, which exploits the idea that the most intimate and discerning touch of all is that of the tasting tongue. It is this that leads to the happy ending to the postmodernist predicament. 'There is no induction of God *a posteriori*, and there is no deduction of God *a priori*, and yet, in the Eucharist, there is a tasting of God through direct physical apprehension, conjoined with a longing for the forever absent.'

Once again, there is a misrepresentation of Aquinas' doctrine. For Aquinas, there is no non-metaphorical tasting of God in the Eucharist. According to his doctrine of transubstantiation, after the consecration in the Mass, bread and wine are no longer present on the altar; only their appearances, miraculously sustained. A communicant does not taste the body of Christ, still less the intangible Godhead; he does not even really taste the bread, for the bread is no longer there.

Milbank and Pickstock, however, say such things as, 'the sense and reference of this bread and wine is the Body and Blood of Christ'; they even attribute to St Thomas the idea that it is permissible 'to adore a mere piece of bread'. They know, to be sure, that the only sense in which St Thomas is willing to call what is on the altar 'bread' is if one means by this 'what is contained under the appearances of bread'. But the taste of bread – the only taste involved in the Eucharist – is itself one of the 'appearances of bread'. There is, therefore, no basis in Aquinas for the privileged place that our authors give to the sense of taste in their great 'ontological revision' of the relation between sense and intellect.

Those who do not believe in transubstantiation may well feel untroubled by all this. But we must recall that transubstantiation was supposed by our authors to provide the solution to fundamental philosophical problems about the relationship between appearance and reality. The Eucharist, we are told, provides the most absolute guarantee of the reliability of appearances, 'for now, it is held that certain sensory phenomena mediate, and are upheld by, a divine physical presence in the world'.

This is surely to turn Aquinas on his head. He held that, in general, appearances are a reliable guide to reality but that in this one exceptional case, they are not. In the Eucharist the appearances of bread do not indicate bread but are miraculously held in existence by divine power. This book's radically orthodox proposal is that those of us who have been cast down by the demise of realism should be reassured by the thought that *all* appearances may be held in existence in a similar manner.

This suggests that transubstantiation may be not an exceptional but a universal phenomenon. To me it seems to increase, rather than diminish, any temptation to scepticism to be told that the socks I am wearing may, for all I know, be Queen Victoria transubstantiated.

However, since I have never myself been cast into the abyss of postmodernism, it may be churlish of me to sniff at any crumb of comfort that may be offered to those who have suffered that misfortune. But one thing I do know: *Truth in Aquinas* is far from being the truth on Aquinas.

Times Literary Supplement, 5 October 2001

Robert Pasnau
Thomas Aquinas on Human Nature
Cambridge University Press, 2002

Aidan Nichols OP
Discovering Aquinas
Darton, Longman & Todd, 2002

According to Robert Pasnau, 'Aquinas remains the most underappreciated and misunderstood of the great philosophers.' According to the blurb on Aidan Nichols' book, 'recent years have seen a new Thomistic renaissance'. The two books under review illustrate, in different ways, both of these judgements.

Pasnau's book is a study of 15 questions in the first part of the *Summa Theologiae* (qq. 75–89), which he calls Aquinas' Treatise on Human Nature. It may seem odd to base a philosophical study on a text that is a work of theology. This is easy to justify by pointing out that amid theological discussions Aquinas often engages in analysis within the bounds of what we now call philosophy. But Pasnau goes further and claims that 'philosophy today actually has more in common with medieval theology (that is, theology as then practised) than it does with medieval philosophy (that is, the part of the arts curriculum that was referred to as philosophy in the medieval university).' Thus medieval theology, not medieval philosophy, is the closest medieval precursor to the core subjects of modern philosophy.

In practice, Pasnau makes full use, in an exemplary way, of both the theological and the philosophical works in the corpus.

His book is structured round the *Summa* not because it is the summit of Thomas' achievement, but because it is a summary of his system. In his close reading of individual passages of the *Summa* he draws on the often more subtle treatments of the same topics to be found in the Disputed Questions and in the Commentaries on Aristotle.

In the first section of his book Pasnau gives a lucid exposition of Aquinas' thesis that the human soul is a subsistent form, and takes pains to set out what lies behind Aquinas' use of the weasel word 'subsistent'. He shows how Aquinas' account differs from the dualism of Plato in holding that the capacity for sensation is an essential part of being human, and differs from the dualism of Descartes in holding that sensation is impossible without the body. For Aquinas, Pasnau argues – controversially but correctly – sensation is a wholly corporeal activity. In the case of the intellect, however, Aquinas rejects materialism on the basis that thought is an activity impossible for a corporeal agent. Pasnau is not alone in finding his arguments to this effect unacceptably weak.

Nonetheless, Pasnau argues, Aquinas' account of the soul is an internally coherent doctrine: it is not simply an ad hoc combination of the Aristotelian theory of matter and form with the Christian doctrine of the soul's survival of death. This defence is supported by a novel account of the Aristotelian theory. While most exponents of Aristotle will say that the material world is full of substances composed of matter and form, Pasnau maintains that at the level of experience the only true substances are living beings. Moreover, he maintains – with only minimal support from either Aristotle or Aquinas – material substances do not contain matter but are organised bundles of actuality (whatever that may mean).

The second, central, section of the book is entitled 'Capacities'. It deals principally with human sensation and with human freedom, but it also extracts illuminating material from Aquinas' discussion of the abstruse question whether the soul's capacities are identical with its essence. The teleological elements in Aquinas' account are well brought out and related to his theory of the appetites of natural agents.

The book gives an admirably clear and convincing account of the cluster of concepts connected with voluntary agency: rational choice, free decision, weakness of will.

Aquinas' account of the rooting of freedom in reason shows him to be a compatibilist, that is to say, a philosopher who sees no necessary contradiction between free choice and determinism. 'Perhaps we too', Pasnau says, 'do not escape the chains of causal necessity. But if we are determined, we are determined by our own beliefs and values, not simply by the brute design of nature and the happenstance of events. This difference, for Aquinas, makes all the difference.'

The third and final section of the book, entitled 'Functions', deals with the operation of the intellect, and the mind's relation to reality. Pasnau sets out Aquinas' distinction between the agent intellect and the possible intellect, and does his best to make sense of his mysterious account of abstraction. Aquinas' generally empiricist account of human knowledge, he maintains, is tempered by his appeal to a form of divine illumination. This leads to an interesting, if debatable, conclusion:

> Aquinas represents the end of a long tradition in Western philosophy. All the great philosophers had seen no way to explain the workings of mind without appealing to the supernatural ... at least until the end of the thirteenth century when John Duns Scotus would propose a thoroughly naturalistic account of the workings of the mind ... Scotus's thoroughly naturalistic account of the human intellect represents a turning-point in the history of philosophy.

Pasnau presents, and ably defends, some of Aquinas' more surprising theses about the mind: for instance, that we have no direct access to our own minds, and that the intellect has no immediate understanding of its own nature. Sometimes he saddles Aquinas with untenable philosophical baggage, such as a belief in mental acts that take place in a mysterious medium somewhere between the realm of conscious thought and behaviour and the physical system of the brain. This is not so much because of the demands of Aquinas' text as because of Pasnau's own questionable philosophy of mind.

The book ends with a chapter devoted to the survival of the soul after death, which gives due emphasis to Aquinas' insistence that a disembodied soul is not a human person. Even though Abraham's soul survives, Aquinas believed, Abraham does not. But Pasnau qualifies this doctrine: 'When I die, I cease to exist, as a whole, but part of me continues to exist, and hence I partly continue to exist.' But for both Aquinas and Pasnau the important issue is to establish whether one and the same person can both die and be resurrected at the last day. Pasnau believes that a careful analysis of the notion of personal identity can enhance the plausibility of the resurrection.

Pasnau's general approach to Aquinas is a balance of respectful admiration and critical caution: the appropriate attitude to take towards a great philosopher of the past. When he believes that Aquinas has erred, he is never afraid to say so, and he does not downplay unfashionable parts of Aquinas' system such as the role assigned to angels in the management of the world. Yet, as the book progresses, he shows a tendency to be too charitable to his subject. He perseveres in trying to make sense of some of Aquinas' less successful projects – such as his theory of phantasms – when it might have been wiser to give up. The overindulgence is particularly noticeable in the chapter on life after death, where some arguments that deserve more severe scrutiny are waved through.

All in all, however, the book is a remarkable achievement. It is written in an energetic and imaginative style, which constantly engages the reader's attention and curiosity. It raises questions about Aquinas' treatise that take by surprise even those well acquainted with its content. No matter whether one agrees or not with the answers Pasnau gives, the familiar texts will never look quite the same again.

When we turn to Aidan Nichols' *Discovering Aquinas* we find a book of a very different kind. Whereas Pasnau writes for the general philosophical public (including, explicitly, materialists and 'Humeans'), Nichols seems to have in view readers that are exclusively Christian – and indeed devout, since on the first page they are assumed to know what is meant by 'oblateship' and 'simple profession'. He is anxious to convince his readers that Roman Catholic decline in interest in Aquinas after the Second Vatican Council has been, and ought to be, a merely temporary phenomenon.

Discovering Aquinas is subtitled 'An Introduction to his Life, Work, and Influence', but the book is not really introductory, except in the sense that it is brief and selective. The themes chosen for discussion, such as Trinity, Angels and Grace, are among the most difficult topics Aquinas ever dealt with. There is frequent use of unnecessary technical terms, such as 'apobatic' for 'upward' and 'katabatic' for 'downward'.

In his Preface Nichols distances himself from English Dominicans such as Herbert McCabe and Brian Davies who chose to discuss Thomas 'in a way well suited to the Anglophone philosophical climate of our time'. His own work, he tells us, 'owes more to the French-language reception of Thomas in the twentieth century'.

This contrast needs to be qualified. During the last half-century the work of McCabe and Davies, and still more of lay philosophers such as Geach and Kretzmann, has placed the work of Aquinas firmly on the philosophy curriculum in many a secular university. There has not been a comparable 'reception' of Aquinas into the philosophical mainstream of non-Catholic French universities. The French authors favoured by Nichols are, in large part, his own Dominican confrères. This makes his book too reminiscent of the inbred Thomism of the early nineteenth century.

Readers who have worked through Pasnau's book are likely to find Nichols' book superficial. By contrast, the Catholic readers to whom Nichols addresses himself will find a great deal of Pasnau's book very congenial. As he says, '[I]nasmuch as the Church's intellectual foundations lie in medieval philosophy, sympathy for his work naturally should translate into sympathy for Catholicism.'

But if we turn our attention back to Pasnau's book we quickly realise that Catholic readers will be brought up short by his fourth chapter, where he alleges that the Church has in recent years adopted a 'noxious social agenda' on the topics of homosexuality, contraception and abortion. The chapter is devoted to Aquinas' teaching on the question when human life begins.

Aquinas does not believe that human life begins at conception. The developing human fetus does not count as a human being until it possesses a human soul, and this does not occur, Pasnau says, until it has developed its brain and sensory systems to the point where it can support the distinctive intellectual capacities of a human being. The abortion of a fetus, prior to mid-term, is therefore not murder, even if it is immoral for other reasons. Aquinas' reasons for denying that human life begins at conception are, Pasnau believes, as valid in the twenty-first century as in the thirteenth.

Pasnau is right to draw attention to the discontinuity Aquinas sees in the development of the fetus. For him, the first substance independent of the mother is the embryo living a plant-like life with a vegetative soul. That substance disappears and is succeeded by a substance with an animal soul, capable of nutrition and sensation. Only at a later stage is the rational soul infused by God, changing this animate substance into a human being.

However, it is not clear what Pasnau means when he speaks of an organism capable of supporting 'the distinctive intellectual capacities of a human being'. Surely a child can only exercise these capacities after learning language. Does this mean that infanticide, no less than first-trimester abortion, can be absolved from the charge of murder?

Aquinas can reject this, Pasnau believes, only on the basis of a controversial empirical claim, namely that at some point around mid-gestation a fetus begins to engage in conceptual cognitive activity. I am very doubtful whether Aquinas ever made such a claim; but Pasnau is surely right to believe that it is a very implausible one.

He offers Aquinas a fall-back position. Perhaps what Aquinas is doing is simply, out of a cautious respect for human life, to place its beginning at the point where the fetus first conceivably has the potential for conceptualisation. 'His policy is like that of a union that protects all of its members, apprentice and skilled craftsman alike.' Our own respect for human life, Pasnau believes, should lead us to endorse something like Aquinas' account.

Few, I think, whether pro-life or tolerant of abortion, will find Pasnau's account here convincing. It is surely the potential for, not the actuality of, intellectual activity that makes the late-term fetus and the newborn entitled to the respect due to human life. It is possible to accept this while agreeing with Aquinas that there is not an unbroken continuity of substantial identity between the moment of conception and the full development of the fetus. On this issue perhaps Pasnau should have reflected more fully on the paradigmatically Thomist topic of the relationship between different levels of potentiality and actuality.

Times Literary Supplement, 5 October 2001

Brian Davies OP
Thomas Aquinas on God and Evil
Oxford University Press, 2011

For many people the undeniable existence of evil in the world presents an enormous objection to the belief that there is a good and almighty God. From Epicurus to Hume the questions echoed across the ages. 'Is God willing to prevent evil but not able? Then he is impotent. Is he able, but not willing? Then he is malevolent. Is he both able and willing? Whence then is evil?'

In recent times distinguished philosophers of religion have striven to offer solutions to the problem of evil. A popuar one is known as 'the free-will defence': it is presented in different forms by Alvin Plantinga and Richard Swinburne. It runs roughly thus. A world containing morally free agents is better than a world without them. But agents who are genuinely morally free must have the power to act badly. If they do act badly, that is not to be blamed on God. He created a world in which agents have the power of choice, which is a great good; it is the agents' misuse of that power which causes the evil.

I have long thought that the problem of evil is a strange kind of problem. At a time when it was fashionable to make a sharp distinction between statements of fact and statements of value, it seemed anomalous to draw a conclusion of fact (there is no God) from an evaluative premise (there is a lot of evil about). Philosophy students used to be taught in their first year that it was impossible to derive an 'ought' from an 'is'. But if that is so, then as a matter of simple logic it is impossible to derive an 'is not' from an 'ought not'. But a proponent of the problem of evil seeks to derive 'there is no God' from 'the world is not as it ought to be'. Surely, the fact–value barrier had to be a two-way barrier, or no barrier at all.

However, like most sensible people, I soon ceased to believe in any sharp distinction between statements of fact and statements of value. Nonetheless, a more serious difficulty remained. The traditional argument from evil does not lead to the conclusion that there is no God, if by 'God' we mean simply 'creator of the world'. The argument leads rather to the conclusion that any creator of the world is either less than omnipotent or less than morally good. But it is difficult to take seriously the idea of calling the creator of the world before the bar of human morality. Morality presupposes a moral community, and a moral community must be of beings with a common language, roughly equal powers and roughly similar needs, desires and interests. God can no more be part of a moral community with human beings than he can be part of a political community with them. It is surely absurd for frail and fallible creatures like ourselves to put ourselves in the position of telling God what he should or should not do.

This difficulty is expounded and expanded in dramatic fashion in Brian Davies' book *Thomas Aquinas on God and Evil*, in which he places it in the context of Aquinas' general metaphysical theory, to which he is an experienced and lucid guide. Davies shows that if the nature of God is conceived as it was by Aquinas, then the problem of evil is based on misconception. Equally, the premises of the free-will defence are undermined. For Aquinas there is no solution to the problem of evil because there is no problem to solve; and God needs no defence because there is no charge to answer.

According to Aquinas, God is not a moral agent at all. There are no moral demands upon him and he is under no obligations to anyone or anything. He is neither morally good nor morally bad. The idea of God as a moral agent, Davies believes, is an invention of twentieth-century philosophers, guilty of anthropomorphism. He mocks at philosophers like Plantinga and Swinburne for thinking of God as being 'the best-behaved person around'.

Davies goes so far as to say that Aquinas does not regard God as a person at all: 'By this I man that he does not take God to be what he takes human persons to be (animals with minds). He does not even take God to be a person in the sense of being an essentially nonmaterial individual able to think, remember, anticipate, or react.' The only sense in which God is personal is that he is 'an other to whom people can relate'.

But surely, a religious person would want to object, God is good and God loves us! Davies, agrees; but he insists that for Aquinas God's goodness is something totally different from human goodness. Humans are good by having good properties, such as talents and virtues; but God has no properties; he does not have goodness, but is goodness. When God loves a creature, he does not feel any emotion: he simply wills good to that creature.

All very well, we might say, but evils as well as goods fall within the lot of creatures, and nothing happens to creatures except by the will of God. Does that mean that God hates us all as well as loves us all? Not so, says Davies: for Aquinas evils are not realities in the way that goods are. Aquinas does not deny the existence of evils or treat them as illusions, but he claims that they are negative, not positive items in the world. Badness is not a form of being, but a lack of being. Hence, though God is the cause of all being, he is not the cause of badness.

To illustrate this Davies quotes Aquinas on sin:

> Sin can be called a being and an action only in the sense that something is missing. And this missing element comes from a created cause, that is, the freewill in its departure from order ... Accordingly this defect is not

ascribed to God as its cause, but to the freewill, just as the limping by people who are lame comes from a physical malfunction and not from their power to move, even though this power enables them to limp. (*ST* 1a, IIae 79.2)

Elsewhere Aquinas often reminds us that blindness is not a power in the way that sight is, but simply the lack of that power.

Such examples do not show, however, that all cases of evil are mere privations. Human vices are causally effective realities in just the same way as virtues are. And many cases of evils are the result of collision between positive powers of different functioning agents. Davies realises this, and he takes pains to consider the case of a person who is sick because of a virus of some kind. But he claims that such cases do not reflect upon God's goodness. 'Even a sick human being succeeds in being a human being and, in this sense, is good (in Aquinas's sense of "good"). And a virus able to make someone sick is also good considered as what it is. So where is the evil or badness in this scenario?'

Passages like this make one wonder what Aquinas' sense of 'good' really amounts to. If everyone who succeeds in being a human being is good, there seems no room left for a distinction between good and bad people. From time to time Davies reminds us that 'good', unlike, for example, the predicate 'blue', is an attributive adjective: there is no such thing as being just good or bad, there is only being a good or bad so-and-so. The qualities that make something a good bed are different from those that make a good doctor, and so on. So it is only to be expected that being a good God is something quite different from being a good human being.

The distinction between attributive and predicative adjectives is a sound one – but when Davies (and Aquinas) go on to say that God is pure goodness, they seem to have forgotten altogether that 'good' is an adjective at all. The notion of pure goodness was introduced into philosophy by Plato, who places the Idea of Good at the summit of the metaphysics of his *Republic*. The notion was severely criticised by Aristotle, and it is odd to find it surviving in the predominantly Aristotelian context of Aquinas' system.

But let us waive this, and ask whether Davies' treatment of illness really exempts God from responsibility for it. Let us accept that, for Aquinas, God loves viruses in just the same sense as he loves human beings, that is to say, that it is his will that confers on each their specific roles. But is God not responsible for the fact that the good of one is the evil of the other? Davies faces up to this question and his answer is clear: 'Aquinas's view is that God cannot make lions and lambs without the lambs having something to worry about.'

One must ask here whether Davies has not fallen into the error for which he blames the proponents of the free-will defence – that is, of regarding items in the world as being independent of God. No doubt he would say that a conflict of interest is neither a substance nor an accident, and therefore does not have being. And, to be sure, coincidences and collisions need not have any secondary causes within the world. But if the universe is created and controlled by an all-powerful and all-seeing creator, then from the point of view of the First Cause nothing is a mere coincidence. As Aquinas says on many occasions, God is active in every agent.

At this point I was reminded of the version of the free-will defence put forward by Descartes in a letter to Princess Elizabeth of Bohemia. He supposed that a certain king had forbidden duels, and knew with certainty that two gentlemen of his kingdom were so hostile to each other that if they met nothing would prevent them fighting. If this king ordered the two of them to go to the same place at the same time, Descartes argued, his knowledge that they would fight would not prevent him justly punishing them. The king's relationship to his two subjects, he claimed, was paralleled by God's relationship to the free actions of all men. I find Davies' attempt to exempt God from responsibility for physical evil no more convincing than Descartes' attempt to exempt him for responsibility for moral evil.

Davies says rightly that no consideration of Aquinas' views on God and evil can be complete without a consideration of his treatment of the doctrine of the incarnation, and he devotes a chapter to the Trinity and Christ. There is no space here to consider these strictly theological portions of the work, other than to make a single remark. Davies frequently reminds us that Aquinas sets strict limits to God's omnipotence, and says that God cannot do what is logically impossible. Aquinas takes it for granted, he says, 'that there cannot, for example, be people who are also iguanas, or dogs who are also cats'. This leaves one wondering whether there is any greater logical incompatibility between being human and being an iguana than between being human and also being God. But that no doubt is a topic for a different book.

Times Literary Supplement, 25 May 2012

Terence Irwin
The Development of Ethics. Volume 1: From Socrates to the Reformation
Oxford University Press, 2009

Terence Irwin's massive history of ethics is no common-or-garden doorstopper. When the first of three promised volumes by itself uses up some half a million words, the completed work will be grand enough to keep open the Great Gate of Kiev. It is the kind of book to make a reviewer wish that he was remunerated for billable hours.

The labour of reading does, however, bring its rewards, for *The Development of Ethics* is a remarkable work of scholarship. Very few philosophers could produce a work of such scale and such erudition. Professor Irwin has studied his chosen authors with minute precision, and has read exhaustively in the secondary literature. Sources are conscientiously recorded and ample quotations provided in footnotes. The treatment of controversial issues is always balanced, and the eventual verdicts are always judicious.

Despite its irenic temper and level tone, this volume contains some surprises. The greatest of these is evident already in the list of contents. The volume contains 29 chapters (each mercifully divided into short digestible gobbets, 422 in all). Among these chapters one is allotted to Plato, four to Aristotle and no less than nine to Aquinas. Aquinas receives twice as many pages as Aristotle and emerges as the hero of the entire volume. This is the more unexpected as Irwin is the Oxford professor not of medieval but of ancient philosophy. Clearly there have been some changes in that university since the days of A. J. Ayer, J. L. Austin and Irwin's predecessor G. E. L. Owen.

In an introductory chapter, Irwin explains the structure of the volume. He has focused, he tells us, on the philosophers who follow the Socratic pattern of moral argument, and among their teachings he gives pride of place to what he calls 'Aristotelian naturalism'. This is the tradition that identifies the ultimate end of action as happiness, and identifies happiness as a life that fulfils the capacities of rational human nature. Aquinas, Irwin believes, offers the best statement of the Aristotelian approach to moral philosophy and of the Aristotelian tradition of naturalism. The best way to study this naturalism, therefore, is to concentrate on Aquinas' presentation of the system rather than Aristotle's.

Following a stubborn scholarly tradition, Irwin bases his account of Aristotle on the *Nicomachean Ethics*, even though he accepts that the central books of that treatise were originally written for a context in the *Eudemian Ethics*. The key concept of Aristotelian ethics is *eudaimonia* or happiness; and according to Irwin the Nicomachean concept of happiness is a comprehensive one, including all non-instrumental goods, not just intellectual contemplation. *Eudaimonia* includes in addition the exercise of the moral virtues. This is because the distinctively human function, for Aristotle, consists not merely in the use of reason, and not merely in the use of reason to select one action over another, but also in the use of reason in *praxis*, in action chosen for its own sake.

Some familiar passages in Aristotle – in particular the treatment of incontinence – suggest that virtue cannot be identified with control by reason, since both the virtuous and the vicious person follow their concept of the good life. Nonetheless, Irwin presents and defends vigorously a rationalist interpretation of Aristotle. If reason is to be genuinely in control of action, there must be an acceptance of a distinctive set of ends grasped by practical reason. Prudence is not merely an apt choice of means to an end determined elsewhere: it involves a correct estimate of the nature of human fulfilment. Only the virtuous person has prudence, and the correct end is not perceived by anyone else.

The relationship between virtue and prudence entails as a consequence the reciprocity of virtue: individual virtues cannot stand alone but must all be present or all be absent together. Aristotle argues thus: each virtue requires prudence; if we have prudence we have all the virtues; and hence if we have one virtue we have all the virtues.

Irwin offers an illuminating discussion of the relation in the *Nicomachean Ethics* between morality and friendship. He defends Aristotle against the charge that his eudaimonism is too self-centred to count, by modern standards, as a morality at all. An Aristotelian rational agent, he explains, has reason to value virtuous action for its own sake, because it is fine, and because it is an expression of general justice. In all these ways the exercise of virtue contributes to the agent's own happiness, which includes the happiness of his family, friends and fellow citizens. Thus Aristotle's conception of morality is not inaccessibly remote from ours, and his explanation of morality may very well advance our own understanding of it.

The section on Aquinas is not only the longest but also the best portion of this first volume of *The Development of Ethics*. Irwin's interpretations of Aristotle are frequently ingenious and always well argued, but they are often controversial, and sometimes only barely defensible in the face of the texts. His detailed exegesis of Aquinas, on the other hand, is in general difficult to fault, and this is not only because Aquinas' writing is much less ambiguous than Aristotle's.

Irwin emulates Aquinas' practice of placing opposing positions in the fairest possible light, stating clearly and persuasively the theses he is about to attack. At its best his writing shares the lucidity, if not the conciseness, of the *Summa Theologiae*. He is more generous than Aquinas in providing concrete examples to illustrate philosophical points, and the illustrations are often both original and illuminating.

The account Irwin gives of Aquinas' system can be summed up as follows. Aquinas believes we are free to be either virtuous or vicious and are responsible for being one or the other. In his view, freedom belongs to the will in so far as it is capable of acting on the results of deliberation about alternatives. This deliberation about alternatives cannot be applied to the ultimate end itself, since we are not free to accept or reject it. This is not a real restriction: it specifies the conditions for being a rational agent, which are also the conditions for being free.

Human freedom consists in the exercise of will in rational choice. That we all pursue an ultimate end is not a baseless assumption of Aristotle's, nor a merely contingent feature of human beings, but a necessary feature of rational agency. The influence of the ultimate end extends beyond actions that are the result of deliberation. We can consent to an action without deliberation, for example by failing to dissent from it.

Irwin considers at great length whether Aquinas, as an ethicist, is an intellectualist or a voluntarist, and whether he is a rationalist or an anti-rationalist. He gives content to these two questions thus:

> (1) Is the will determined by the greater good as presented by reason? To answer Yes is to be an intellectualist. To answer No is to be a voluntarist. (2) Is the will determined by the strongest passion, as an animal's choice is determined? To answer No is to be a rationalist. To answer Yes is to be an anti-rationalist.

The two questions are answered at considerable length: Aquinas is both an intellectualist and a rationalist. This means that he is not committed to indeterminism, as a voluntarist may be, and that he implicitly accepts the compatibilist position that determinism can be reconciled with freedom, when that is interpreted as the expression of rational choice.

Irwin identifies many places where Aquinas improves on Aristotle's account: in the treatment of incontinence, for instance, and of the reciprocity of the virtues. Likewise, Aquinas is superior when he discusses the positive contribution to morality of the passions, and he fills a gap in Aristotle's system by his treatment of the role of conscience.

Irwin expounds sympathetically Aquinas' dovetailing of Aristotelian ethics with Christian doctrines of law, sin and grace. Sin, he explains, is in theological terms a violation of divine law, while being definable philosophically as an error contrary to reason. He insists correctly that virtue, not law, is foremost in Aquinas' ethical system. Aquinas' doctrine of natural law does not conflict with his eudaimonism about virtues. Aquinas is not a natural law moralist because he does not try to explain morality from some prior conception of law. The natural law in us is simply our disposition to deliberate with reference to our own ultimate end. Actions are right in themselves because they promote the end of human life, and that is why God commands them.

Irwin brings out well the gulf which separates Aquinas' system from that expounded by Duns Scotus just a few decades later. Scotus rejects eudaimonism: instead of seeking happiness in all their actions human beings are guided by two primary and irreducible affections, one for what is advantageous and one for what is just. Moreover, rejecting Aquinas' intellectualism, Scotus is voluntarist and indeterminist.

Irwin exhibits the vast difference between the two great scholastics' concept of freedom. Aquinas is an intellectualist and a compatibilist, Scotus is a voluntarist and an indeterminist. From the voluntarist point of view, Aquinas' conditions for freedom are inadequate, because they imply that the will is determined by our natural desire for happiness and our beliefs about what promotes it. Scotus believes that the will is not free unless it is free in relation to our natural desires. From Aquinas' point of view, however, the voluntarist conception of freedom is self-defeating, since it rejects determination by reason and hence prevents the will from being free in relation to non-rational desires.

The differences between Aquinas and Scotus extend to the divine as well as to the human domain. Scotus limits the extent of the natural law: while God cannot command us not to love and worship him, those commands of the Decalogue that concern human beings are a matter of contingent, positive, divine law. Murder, for instance, is wrong only because it violates a command of God. Accordingly, God can dispense from the prohibition on murder, as he did when he commanded Abraham to sacrifice Isaac.

By highlighting the distinction between Aquinas and Scotus (and his followers Ockham and Biel) Irwin brings out that Reformation objections to scholasticism are not necessarily objections to Aquinas. On the issue of free will, Luther's primary dispute was with Scotus and Ockham, and controversialists on all sides in the Reformation debate, whether Erasmus, the Reformers, or the Jesuit Molinists, rejected the compatibilist position that Aquinas had ably defended. The Reformers had good reason for rejecting the views of voluntarist scholastics, but not those of Thomist intellectualists.

On a number of issues Irwin is able to show that Aquinas' own position is compatible both with the Council of Trent and with the Anglican Thirty-Nine Articles. This thesis, it must be said, was already argued convincingly more than fifty years ago by Louis Bouyer in his *Spirit and Forms of Protestantism* – one of the very few relevant works not to appear in Irwin's copious bibliography.

In this volume we are never allowed to forget that it is only the first of a trilogy. From time to time Irwin introduces later philosophers, such as Butler, Kant and Sidgwick, to cast a backward light on the ancient and medieval philosophers that are his major concern. The earlier moralists, also, often allow us to re-evaluate their later and more familiar successor. Hume's dictum that reason is and ought to be the slave of the passions is not so shocking and innovative when we learn that in the thirteenth century Henry of Ghent maintained that reason directed the will only in the way in which a servant carrying a lantern guides his master how to go.

Irwin tells us that he did not design his book as a whole as an extended argument in favour of Aristotelian naturalism. However, that is how the present volume appears. Non-Aristotelian ancient philosophers – the Cyrenaics, the Cynics, the Sceptics, the Epicureans and the Stoics – are treated at appropriate length. But once we reach the Christian era, everything seems subservient to the exposition and defence of Aquinas. St Augustine is there to set the stage for St Thomas. The Blessed Duns Scotus figures only as the leader of the opposition. The arguments between Aquinas and Scotus are spelt out at great length, as if they were two Wimbledon competitors entering their fifteenth set. We watch the ball going over the net from side to side: at appropriate moments Irwin cries 'Advantage Aquinas' or 'Advantage Scotus'. But it is always Aquinas who ends as the triumphant champion

Times Literary Supplement, 17 October 2008

Richard Cross
Duns Scotus on God
Ashgate, 2005

The Franciscan friar John Duns Scotus lectured at Oxford during the last years of the thirteenth century. It is arguable that he is the cleverest philosopher ever to have been an Oxford lecturer, and he was accorded the sobriquet 'Doctor Subtilis', the subtle doctor. As time passed it became clear that he was *too* clever for Oxford, and less bright Oxonians took their revenge on him by using his name as a synonym for 'dimwit'. William Tyndale, in controversy with Thomas More, took occasion to denounce 'the old barking curs, Dunce's disciples and like trash called Scotists, the children of darkness'. Thomas Hobbes linked Duns with the scholastic bishop Peter Lombard, as 'two of the most egregious blockheads in the world, so obscure and senseless are their writings.'

King Henry VIII's commissioners, when they visited Oxford in 1535 to modernise the university curriculum, were gratified to see torn pages of the folios of Duns blowing around the quadrangle of New College. For centuries to come, no Oxford philosopher or theologian took any serious interest in the writings of Scotus. It is only in the last few years that this situation has changed, and this is due almost entirely to the energy and industry of Richard Cross of Oriel College.

In 1998 Cross wrote a book on Scotus' physics, and followed this up in the year after with a more general and popular book in the series 'Great Medieval Thinkers'. In 2002 he devoted a large part of his book *The Metaphysics of the Incarnation* to the teaching of Scotus, and in the present book he places the learned world even further in his debt. He invites us to follow him in close readings of some of the most difficult passages in Scotus' works: his proof of the existence of God as first cause, and his arguments to the effect that this God must be a Trinity of persons.

Cross writes as a theologian, but he is philosophically well informed and acute, and he rightly describes Scotus as the most philosophical of theologians. Of all the great schoolmen, he says, Scotus is 'the least likely to appeal to mystery and the most likely to try to solve a problem by intellectual gymnastics'. Scotus' theology rarely engages at all closely with Scripture: citations of Aristotle in his published works are ten times more frequent than biblical texts.

Accordingly, much of Scotus' theology may well be more interesting to contemporary philosophers than it is to contemporary theologians. Cross points out that a number of Scotus' theses – about the principle of individuation, about the nature of contingency and about liberty of indifference, for instance – have been topics of philosophical debate from his own time to our own. However, a philosopher with no interest in theology will find it a demanding task to follow Cross in his heroically painstaking analysis of such issues as whether it is in virtue of his essence or his personal properties that a member of the Trinity is produced in being.

During Oxford's centuries-long neglect of Scotus there was one outstanding exception to the general boycott: the Victorian Jesuit poet Gerard Manley Hopkins. The best known of his Oxford poems, beginning 'Towery city and branchy between towers', is a paean of praise to Duns. Hopkins rated him as a metaphysician superior to Aristotle and Aquinas, saluting him as 'Of realty the rarest-veined unraveller; / a not Rivalled insight, be rival Italy or Greece'.

At first blush it is surprising that one of the most sensuous of British poets should be so entranced with the most highly intellectual of British philosophers. The reasons, however, are not hard to discover. On the one hand, Hopkins welcomed Scotus' thesis that within each substance there is a unique individuating principle, the haecceity: this was, in the poet's terms, 'the being indoors each one dwells' which it deals out in selving, spelling out itself. Again, though Scotus' methods are austerely intellectual, the theological conclusions that separated him from other scholastics are ones that fuel the more emotional aspects of Catholic piety, for instance the doctrines that Mary was conceived immaculate, and that even before the fall of man she was predestined to be the mother of God. Finally, as Cross points out, Scotus' Latin syntax is dense and convoluted to a degree: it is therefore unsurprising that his taut and difficult writing should have been a congenial challenge to a poet who tested to the limit the syntactical possibilities of the English language.

Times Literary Supplement, 28 October 2005

PART THREE

RENAISSANCE AND REFORMATION

Introduction

Lovers of beauty have reason to be grateful to the Renaissance popes and their families. The Piccolomini in Siena, the Medici in Florence and the Borgias in Rome sponsored works of art which people still travel from all parts of the world to see and admire. But this beautification of Italy came at a price, much of which was paid by those subject to papal taxes in the countries of Northern Europe. Dubious methods of fund-raising triggered an explosion which would eventually divide Christendom into two warring halves. In 1517 Martin Luther, a German Augustinian monk, issued, in the University of Wittenberg, a public denunciation of abuses of papal authority, in particular of a scandalously promoted offer of an indulgence (remission of punishment due to sin) in return for contributions to the building of the great new Church of St Peter's in Rome.

Luther had made a close study of St Paul's Epistle to the Romans. This had made him question fundamentally the ethos of Renaissance Catholicism. He went on to denounce large parts of the Catholic sacramental system and to teach that the one thing needful for salvation is faith, or trust in the merits of Christ. In 1520 Pope Leo X condemned 41 articles taken from Luther's teaching and followed this up with an excommunication after Luther had burnt the bull of condemnation. In support of the Pope, King Henry VIII of England published an *Assertion of the Seven Sacraments*, which earned him the papal title 'Defender of the Faith'.

Both Renaissance and Reformation were the sixteenth-century consequences of the humanist movement which had grown up in Italy in the previous century. 'Humanism' meant not the replacement of religious with secular ideals, but simply an admiration for the literature and art of the ancient world. Scholarship, so humanists believed, if applied to pagan texts, would restore to Europe long-neglected arts and sciences, and if applied to the Bible would help towards a more authentic understanding of Christian truths.

One of the foremost humanists was the Dutchman Desiderius Erasmus who in 1516 produced the first printed version of the Greek New Testament alongside a novel Latin version. The Greek text he published was the foundation for the great vernacular testaments of the sixteenth century, beginning with the monumental German version published in 1522 by Martin Luther, followed shortly after by the English version of William Tyndale. One of Erasmus' closest friends was Sir Thomas More, humanist author of *Utopia* and briefly Chancellor of England.

Erasmus and More shared Luther's concern about the corruption of many of the higher clergy: they had both denounced it in print, Erasmus pungently in a satire on Pope Julius II, More with ironic circumspection in *Utopia*. But both were alienated when Luther threw off papal authority and rejected much of traditional Catholic teaching along with the philosophical subtleties of the schoolmen. Luther, of course, appealed to an older tradition: that presented by the books of the Bible, which retained for him unimpeachable authority. The content of the Bible was no longer to be subjected, as it had been in the Middle Ages, to professional scrutiny by philosophically trained theologians. Every Christian, Luther said, had the power of discerning and judging what was right or wrong in matters of faith. Tyndale boasted that his translation would make a boy driving the plough understand the Bible better than the most learned divine. Pessimism about the moral capacity of the trained intellect unaided by grace went hand in hand with optimism about the intellectual ability of the untrained mind illumined by faith.

The problem for Luther was that individual consciences, unconstrained by universal authority and unwilling to submit faith to rational arbitrament, began to produce a great diversity of beliefs. French and Swiss Reformers, such as Jean Calvin and Ulrich Zwingli, agreed with Luther in rejecting papal authority but differed from him in their understanding of the presence of Christ in the Eucharist and of the decrees through which God chose the elect. Calvin, like Luther, placed the ultimate criterion of religious truth within the individual soul: every faithful Christian experienced within himself a marvellous conviction of heavenly revelation which was more reassuring than any reasoning could ever be. But how could one tell who were faithful Christians? If one counted only the reformed, then Calvin's criterion was question-begging; on the other hand, if one counted all those who had been baptised, it led to an anarchy of belief.

The questions at issue in Europe at the Reformation were in the end settled neither by rational argument nor by interior enlightenment. In country after country conflicting answers were imposed by force of arms or by penal legislation. In England Henry VIII, irked by Vatican refusal to free him from a tedious marriage, broke with Rome and executed More for his loyalty to the Pope. The country then lurched from his schismatic version of Catholicism to Calvinism under his son Edward VI, to Counter-Reformation Catholicism under his daughter Mary, and finally to an Anglican compromise under her sister Elizabeth. This chequered history produced hundreds of martyrs, both Protestant and Catholic; but England was spared the sanguinary wars of religion which in continental Europe raged for many decades.

By the mid sixteenth century doctrinal positions had hardened into a form that they were to retain for some four hundred years. Luther's lieutenant Melancthon formulated at Augsburg in 1530 a confession of faith to provide the test of orthodoxy. A concordat agreed in the same city in 1555 provided that the ruler of each state within the Holy Roman Empire could decide whether his subjects were to be Lutheran or Catholic: the principle later known as *cuius regio, eius religio*. Calvin's *Institutes of the Christian Religion* (1536) provided the standard for Protestants in Switzerland, France, and later in Scotland. In Rome Pope Paul III (1534–39) promoted a Counter-Reformation, instituting a new religious order of Jesuits, and convening a Council at Trent to reform church discipline. The Council condemned the Lutheran doctrine of justification by faith alone and the Calvinist doctrine that God predestined the wicked to hell prior to any sin. Free will, it insisted, had not been extinguished by Adam's fall. It reaffirmed the doctrine of transubstantiation and the traditional seven sacraments. By the time the Council had finished its work, in 1563, Luther was dead and Calvin was dying.

The division of Christendom was an unnecessary tragedy. The theological issues which separated Luther and Calvin from their Catholic opponents had been debated many times in the Middle Ages without leading to sectarian warfare. Few twentieth-century Catholics and Protestants, if not professionally trained in theology, are aware of the real nature of the differences between the contrasting theories of the Eucharist, of grace and of predestination, which in the sixteenth century led to anathema and bloodshed.

Questions of authority, of course, are easier to understand and more difficult to arbitrate than questions of doctrine. But the unity of Christendom could have been maintained under a constitutional papacy subject to general councils, such as had been the practice in the fifteenth century, and such as even Thomas More, for the greater part of his life, believed to be the divine design for the Church.

John Bossy
Christianity in the West, 1400–1700
Oxford University Press, 1983

John Bossy's book is gripping to read. It arrived with the morning mail. I began to leaf through it, before putting it on the pile to take its turn. An hour later, I put it down reluctantly, shamed by the rest of the unopened post. I had got as far as the remarkable tale of St Guinefort, dog and martyr, venerated in the Lyonnais in the thirteenth century.

> Hero of a widely appreciated story, he had defended his master's baby from a venomous snake, and himself been killed by the father, who coming back to find a blood-boltered dog and an unturned cradle had assumed that he had killed the baby. God would certainly canonise him, people thought, even if the Pope would not, and mothers brought weak babies to his burial place to be cured.

Christianity in the West is indeed an interesting and unusual book. To see how unusual, you need look no further than the copyright page. The details which appear under 'British Cataloguing in Publication Data' do not normally provide much excitement to the reviewer. But this book has a double entry: it straddles the demarcation lines of the most up-to-date cataloguers, and has to be listed both under 'Church History – Middle Ages, 60–1500' and under 'Church History – Modern Period, 1500–'.

It is indeed, an intriguing idea: instead of writing a history of the Reformation to appear in the popular Oxford OPUS series, why not simply write a comparison between Christianity as it was before the Reformation began and Christianity as it was after Reformation and Counter-Reformation had done their worst or best? By 'Christianity', Bossy tells us, he does not mean the Church as an institution, but the beliefs, superstitions and way of life of Christian people.

So we are given first an account of the scenario of salvation accepted by the fifteenth-century Church, and a lively description of the sacraments and ritual of pre-Reformation Catholicism and its social framework. We are taken through the cycle of sin, carnival and penance. We follow the details of the eucharistic ritual of the Mass, and we have explained to us the social ramifications of the ceremonies associated with it. From the perspective of medieval Christianity we are given a glimpse of those beyond the pale: the usurers, the witches and the heretics.

In the second part of the book we look at the changes that had come over this Christian world by the seventeenth century. We learn of the altered view of God's Word when a printed vernacular Bible replaces the collective existence represented by sacraments, saints and the unwritten traditions of the Church. We are made acquainted with the claims of small groups, ever more eccentric and radical, to speak with the authentic voice of the Holy Spirit. We are told of the impact of the Reformation on charity, in the sense of social munificence; and we are offered an analysis of Richard Baxter's *Christian Directory* as a statement of what had happened to Western Christianity as a social regime during the sixteenth and seventeenth centuries.

Bossy has a keen eye for the telling detail, a lively gift for the illuminating epigram. Thus he observes, apropos of fifteenth-century ghosts: 'Unlike the modern ghost, the traditional ghost was personal not real: he haunted people not places.' He tells us how the Venetian inquisition in 1573 condemned Veronese's *Last Supper* on the grounds that it portrayed an apostle eating his meal with a fork. He sums up in a nutshell the difference between Anselm's theory of the atonement and Luther's: for Anselm the redemption was a transaction in the law of tort, for Luther it was a matter of the criminal or penal code.

But though Bossy writes vividly and insightfully, the reviewer cannot help asking whether his book can really achieve its task. Is it possible to make a non-expert reader understand the nature of the change wrought in Christianity between 1400 and 1700 without telling him anything about either the history or the theology of the Reformation? Yet that is what Bossy tries to do.

Bossy's book is lively and fascinating. But in reading it one is reminded of those television presentations of symphony concerts in which one is so captivated by the camera's panning to the double bass scratching his ear during a rest, or the second horn overturning his instrument to empty the spittle, that one actually ceases to hear the music being played.

The Listener, 8 August 1985

Nicholas of Cusa
Writings on Church and Reform
trans. Thomas M. Izbicki
The I Tatti Renaissance Library, Harvard University
Press, 2008

Desiderius Erasmus
Praise of Folly and *Pope Julius Barred from
Heaven*
trans. Roger Clarke
Oneworld Classics, 2008

To the ecclesiastical historian the century immediately
preceding the Reformation (1417–1517) is one of the most
fascinating and also the most tragic in the history of the
Church. In 1417 the Council of Constance elected Pope Martin
V, putting an end to decades of schism in which there had been
two, and eventually three, rival claimants to the papacy. In 1517
Martin Luther launched the Protestant Reformation with his 95
Wittenberg theses. In the hundred years in between, Christian
Europe was a cauldron of seething conflicts: between Greek and
Latin, between papalists and conciliarists, between scholastics
and humanists, and between kingdoms and principalities large
and small. The century was a tragedy of lost opportunities: the
division among the political powers caused the loss to the Turks
of Constantinople and much of Eastern Europe; the failure of
every attempt to reform the Catholic Church from within led
to the break-up of Christendom into separate and warring

confessions. Two figures stand out who, nobly but vainly, tried in different ways to arrest the descent into the abyss: Nicholas of Cusa at the beginning of the century and Desiderius Erasmus at the end.

The Council of Constance had deposed the schismatic pope who convened it, and defined the conciliarist thesis that a general council was the supreme body in the Church, which popes must obey. It also called for councils to be regularly held to oversee papal activity. The first such council was convened at Basle in 1431, with Nicholas of Cusa (then a young university canonist) as one of its prominent members. On behalf of the Council he negotiated with the Hussite heretics in Bohemia, urging them to rejoin the Church which they had left because of its refusal of the chalice to the laity. In 1433 he wrote his major work on church government *The Catholic Concordance*, an eloquent manifesto of conciliarism.

In the abstract, there was much to be said for the notion of a constitutional papacy subject to the authority of a council representative of the different parts of Christendom. Unfortunately, the Council of Basle proceeded to bring the idea into rapid disrepute. The reforms it proposed got no further than the diversion of church taxes from Rome to local prelates and princes, and when the current pope, Eugenius IV, complained of its activities, it declared him deposed. In 1439, when the last thing the Church needed was another schism, it elected an antipope, Felix V. But by this time Nicholas had lost patience with his Basle colleagues and had gone over to Eugenius.

In 1437 Nicholas was sent by the Pope on a diplomatic mission to Constantinople to invite the Byzantine Emperor and the Patriarch of Constantinople to join an attempt to end the schism between the Greek and Latin Churches. Outmanoeuvring the assembly at Basle, which was also negotiating with the Greeks, Eugenius held a council in Italy, which at Florence in

1439 proclaimed the reunion of the two Churches. The Pope smuggled into the decree a statement of papal supremacy.

The Latins hoped that as a result of the Council the Greek Church would accept a number of disputed doctrines. The Greeks hoped that the Western nations would come to their aid against the Turks. The hopes of both sides were dashed. The doctrinal concessions of the Emperor and Patriarch in Florence were disowned by their co-religionists in the East, and in the absence of effective European aid Constantinople fell in 1453.

The division between Basle and Rome continued after the Council of Florence. The German princes of the Holy Roman Empire in 1439 declared themselves neutral between the two. Nicholas of Cusa laboured as papal legate to bring them over to the Roman side, notably at the Diet of Frankfurt in 1442. These efforts were crowned when in 1449 the antipope Felix resigned, the Basle council dissolved itself, and the German Emperor accepted the authority of Eugenius. On the other hand, Nicholas failed in the task of reconciling the Hussites to the papacy's repudiation of a compromise they had been offered by the divines of Basle. Within the Catholic domain he instituted a zealous programme of reform of corrupt religious orders, restoring discipline among friars, monks and nuns. But the reforms he introduced did not long survive his death.

The handsomely produced volume in the I Tatti series presents, with an *en face* translation, the Latin text of a number of Nicholas' lesser-known works related to these diplomatic and reforming endeavours. We are given three pamphlets from the conciliar phase, supplementary to *The Catholic Concordance*. There follow six works after the change of allegiance, notably the speech at the Diet of Frankfurt, which earned Nicholas the title of 'The Hercules of the Eugenians'. Several sermons about St Peter give a moderately papalist explanation of the text 'Thou art Peter, and upon this rock I shall build my church'. The final section of the volume ends with a bull Nicholas drafted for Pope

Pius II (Aeneas Sylvius Piccolomini, a fellow ex-conciliarist) on reform of the Church in its head and members. It provides for a trio of eminent independent assessors to evaluate and amend, against precise standards, the performance of Pope, Cardinals and Curia. Sadly, Pius, preoccupied with a crusade against the Turks, never put the programme into effect.

This final paper is the most impressive among a collection of texts which, it must be said, are of very uneven interest. It must also be added that the texts have been very inadequately translated.

During his busy life Nicholas wrote a number of significant mathematical and philosophical works, the best known of which is *On Informed Ignorance* of 1440. Human knowledge, he there argues, is so limited that rational attempts to reach the ultimate truth are like a polygon inscribed in a circle: however many sides we add to the polygon, it will never coincide with the circumference.

In philosophy Nicholas stands on the cusp between medieval and modern ways of thought. By the time of his death in 1464 the dominant intellectual current was humanism. In the fifteenth century 'humanism' did not mean the replacement of religious values with secular ones. Rather, it denoted a belief in the educational value of the 'humane letters' of Greek and Latin classics. Humanists turned away from the technical logical and philosophical studies of scholasticism, and placed new emphasis on the study of grammar and rhetoric. They believed that their scholarship, when applied to the ancient texts, would restore to Europe forgotten arts and sciences, and, when applied to the Bible and the Church Fathers, would help Christendom to a purer and more authentic understanding of Christian truth.

Five years after Cusa's death there was born in Rotterdam the man who came to be regarded as the prince of the humanists, Desiderius Erasmus. Educated in the devout community of the Brethren of the Common Life, Erasmus became an Augustinian monk and was ordained priest in 1492. However, the monastic life did not suit him and he became an independent scholar, studying and teaching in Paris, Oxford, Cambridge and Louvain. In 1499, on his first visit to England, he met Thomas More, eight years his junior, and was introduced by him to the 8-year-old prince who was to become Henry VIII.

Erasmus and More remained lifelong friends. They shared an enthusiasm for humanism and a distaste for scholasticism: Erasmus had been unhappy at the Sorbonne and More mocked the logic he had been taught at Oxford. The two of them collaborated in a translation into Latin of the works of the Greek satirist Lucian. Erasmus was a frequent visitor to the More household during Thomas' first marriage to Jane (an ideal intellectual companion, he thought) and also during his second marriage to Dame Alice ('neither a pearl nor a girl').

In 1511 Erasmus dedicated to More a light-hearted Latin work with the punning title *Encomium Moriae*, which translates as *Praise of Folly*. According to his own account, this was composed on a long horseback journey from Italy to England, and written down during a brief illness in More's house. It is this work which is now offered in a paperback English edition by Oneworld Classics. The Latin text is not printed *en face*, but an appendix includes a portion of it sufficient to convince the reader that Roger Clarke's translation, while idiomatic and sometimes racy, is quite faithful to the original.

No one today is going to read *Praise of Folly* for laughs. By the time the reader has deciphered the classical allusions by referring to Clarke's generally excellent notes, the jokes have worn rather thin. Folly speaks in the first person throughout, claiming credit for most human institutions. Were it not for folly, who would ever get married? It is their foolishness that makes women and babies attractive, and only folly keeps families together ('What divorces, or worse, would take place everywhere, were it not for the support and nourishment that the domestic companionship of man and wife draws from flattery, from teasing, from permissiveness, deceit, dissimulation!'). Riches, reputation and learning bring far less happiness than folly does, and all human activity is full of folly, performed by fools to an audience of fools.

Through the mouth of Folly, Erasmus presents himself as the court jester of the Renaissance, mocking all the professions: physicians, alchemists, lawyers, theologians, even grammarians like himself. He shows the futility of the pomp of secular and ecclesiastical courts; he aims some of his fiercest barbs at superstitious practices encouraged by rapacious priests. He jeers at the chauvinism whereby each nation prides itself about its own special gifts. (Britons, we are told rather surprisingly, claim as their speciality good looks, music and fine meals.)

The book moves from mockery of the follies that surface in every age of human history to denunciation of the ills peculiar to the dissolute courts of the Renaissance and the corrupt institutions of the unreformed Church. This second prong of the attack is given a sharp point in the second text included in the Oneworld volume, *Pope Julius barred from Heaven*, a witty dialogue in which St Peter, the keeper of the keys of heaven, refuses to admit, or to recognise as his successor, Julius II, the warlike pope who died in 1513. The dialogue was published anonymously, and Erasmus himself always denied that he was its author. Some modern scholars accept his denial, but most readers, then and now, have assumed that it is his work.

From the time of Pius II the popes had devoted the greater part of their energies to building and defending a mid-Italian princedom. In pursuit of this they used both temporal and spiritual weapons, creating their own armies and excommunicating their enemies; they were involved in an ever-changing network of alliances and hostilities with other Italian states and larger kingdoms abroad. Julius II was the most warlike of all the popes, tramping through Italy at the head of his armies, clad in silver armour, thwacking any cardinal who fell behind in the march. He was an abomination to Erasmus, who hated war as the worst of human crimes.

In 1512 Julius, battered in conflict and ailing in health, called a council to meet at the Lateran to emend a Church now universally agreed to be corrupt. This was the last chance to reform Catholicism from within along conciliarist lines. The opportunity was not taken. Shortly after it was convened Julius died and was succeeded by the Medici Pope Leo X, who effectively tore up the reform agenda. Only five years later the issues were brought back by Luther to haunt the papacy for ever. When at last a reforming council was convened, at Trent in 1545, it represented only a portion of Christendom. One of its results was the placing of *Praise of Folly* on an Index of Forbidden Books.

Times Literary Supplement, 6 March 2009

Richard Marius
Martin Luther: The Christian between God and Death
Harvard University Press, 1999

Fifteen years ago Richard Marius wrote a biography of Sir Thomas More which attracted considerable attention. Now he has drawn on his capacious knowledge of the sixteenth century to produce a vivid narrative of the life of More's great adversary, Martin Luther.

For the biographer, Luther is a more difficult subject than More. The modest shelf containing the Yale edition of More's works (to which Marius was a distinguished contributor) provides a corpus more manageable by far than the 67 volumes of the Weimar *Gesamtausgabe* of Luther. It is true that More's family biographers do not let us get as intimate a glimpse as do the recorders of Luther's table-talk. On the other hand, the main outlines of More's character and beliefs are easier to discern than Luther's. More's biographers may find it difficult to reconcile the tolerance of *Utopia* with the hounding of Tyndale. But Luther's expositors have a greater struggle to get a coherent grasp on the billowing clouds of inconsistency with which Luther delighted to surround himself. Most of all, More's life, unlike Luther's, offers the biographer a powerful dramatic structure. A principled martyrdom borne with dignity and wit rounds off a life far better than an irritable and crapulous old age brought to an end by a stroke.

Marius' earlier book was an essay in psychobiography, aiming to show that the darker side of More's character was the result of sexual repression and tension. This new book is less given to psychological speculation. This is surprising, given that Luther's *nachlass* provides so ample a mass of data to tempt to posthumous psychoanalysis; but it is welcome nonetheless.

The first part of the book tells the story of Luther's years in the monastery, analyses his lectures on the Psalms and on the Epistles, and gives a lively account of the controversy about indulgences and the break with Rome. Marius is not always accurate in detail – he believes, for instance, that all Catholic clergy took vows of poverty, chastity and obedience, and he confuses Luther's adversary Cajetan with the saint of the same name – but in general the historical parts of these early chapters present a fascinating story well told.

The narrative of Luther's life is accompanied less by Freudian commentary than by theological reflection. Much Reformation theology clusters around a set of doctrines that are crystallised in a single verse of St Paul (Romans 8:30):

> Those whom He predestined, He also called
> Those whom He called, He also justified
> Those whom He justified, He also glorified.

Marius does not move comfortably within this thicket of concepts – predestination, vocation, justification, glorification. His explanations of Luther's theological innovations fail to throw a clear light on the issues at stake.

This is not surprising, for two reasons. In the first place, Luther's own rhetoric raised a great dust around concepts that had been patiently analysed by generations of scholastics. In the second place, the Christian doctrines in question are unlikely to be taken very seriously by twentieth-century readers. It is very rare, Marius observes, to hear a Lutheran sermon on predestination; and Catholics, we may add, are often astonished to learn that their Church teaches that no one is saved who is not predestined.

In one respect Marius' life of Luther resembles his life of More. In the earlier work, a great deal of weight was placed on an unfounded, and implausible, hypothesis: namely, that the marriage with Dame Alice was never consummated. Here, too, much is made to hang on an unlikely theory which is even less supported by evidence. Marius maintains that Luther did not believe in hell.

When, as very often, Luther expresses fear of death, what he is afraid of, Marius suggests, is annihilation, not perpetual damnation: there is no such thing as everlasting punishment of the wicked. This flies in the face of the prefaces in the September testament, and Luther's assertion, in conflict with the Anabaptists, that unbelievers will be punished in the eternal fires of hell. Marius honourably quotes these texts, but his attempts to explain them away are unconvincing.

As he takes us through Luther's life Marius strives to enter into his subject's mentality and to present his motivation as sympathetically as possible. As we progress from the breach with Rome into the controversies with Reformers such as Karlstadt, Muntzer and Zwingli the task becomes ever more difficult. Every so often, while doing his best for Luther, Marius is brought up short by some hate-filled and hateful paragraph. Even the most sympathetic biographer must find it hard to defend Luther's incitements to massacre during the Peasants' Revolt or his lifelong paranoia about Jews. Marius does not attempt to palliate such horrors.

It is, however, when he reached Luther's controversy with Erasmus over free will that Marius finally loses patience with his subject. Having described that controversy, and leaving the reader in no doubt where his sympathies lie, he brings his book to an abrupt end. A single brief paragraph mentions Melanchthon's Augsburg Confession of 1530 – a proposal for reconciliation worth detailed study in our ecumenical age. We are told only that this 'is a convenient place to leave Luther'. Marius acknowledges that a biographer, having told of Luther's early life and break with Rome, has 'a duty to the older man'. 'But here', he says, 'I will beg off.'

In a perceptive epilogue, Marius draws attention to two paradoxes. First, Luther's emphasis on the priesthood of all believers and the necessity of preaching has led to an enhancement, not a diminution, of the role of the clergy. Catholics will enter a church to worship the sacrament whether or not there is a priest about; for an evangelical, there is little reason to be in church if the minister is not present to preach. Again, Luther's preoccupation with Scripture and the close study of its text led ultimately to the desacralisation of the testaments by German higher critics in the nineteenth century.

Luther was a writer of remarkable power, and his translation of the Bible had a great influence not only on the devotion of believers but also on the history of the German language. Marius lays comparatively little emphasis on this, which in the eyes of many people is the Reformer's greatest positive contribution.

Many writers, whether Protestant or secular, while admitting Luther's enormous faults of character and judgement, believe that he placed the human race in his debt by breaking the tyrannical hold of a corrupt hierarchy upon the minds and hearts of ordinary Christians. Marius, in the end, seems unwilling to give his subject even this credit. For all we know, he muses, if Luther had never been born, 'Erasmus might have been the harbinger of a benign kind of reform and piety that would have brought the Catholic Church along slowly into the tolerance and charity practiced by legions of Catholics today.' What we do know is that 'for more than a century after Luther's death Europe was strewn with the slaughtered corpses of people who would have lived normal lives if Luther had never lived'.

Times Literary Supplement, 18 April 1999

Peter Ackroyd
The Life of Thomas More
Chatto & Windus, 1997

It is not easy to write a good life of Thomas More, because he was a saint. In one sense, a saint is a person who displays heroic virtue, as More did by voluntarily accepting imprisonment and death rather than commit perjury. His saintliness is indeed one reason for telling and retelling his story. But a saint is also someone who is held up as a model and standard-bearer by his co-religionists – in More's case Roman Catholics – and that is what makes his story difficult to tell. A saint, by definition, attracts hagiography; and hagiography can be the enemy of biography.

The problem is clearly seen in the case of the Gospels, which set the pattern for Christian hagiography. Different Gospels present Jesus in different perspectives; but for us who come after there is no getting behind them. If the life of Jesus was not, in broad terms, what the Gospels say it was, then we simply do not know what it was like. We cannot second-guess the evangelists and claim to tell a quite different story which is truer than the one they told. For this reason there are almost no good biographies of Jesus. Lives of Christ are commonly either works of devotion, academic essays in source criticism, or empty speculations by intellectual buccaneers.

The case is not quite the same, of course, with More. The story of his saintly life was written, in the decades after his death, by members of his family and Catholic admirers. But we can reach behind these early lives and check them by more primitive evidence. To make the gospel situation parallel we would have to imagine that Jesus had left behind a number of authentic letters to Peter, Judas, Pontius Pilate and the three Marys; some more literary works also, such as an early political satire in the style of Seneca, or a number of coarse polemical tracts against the Pharisees. We would have to suppose too that we possessed the complete state papers of the tetrarchy of Galilee and the procuratorship of Judaea.

But some of the difficulties that face a biographer of Christ also obstruct a biographer of More. All the early lives of him were written after the divisions between Catholics and Protestants had hardened, just as the Gospels were written after Christians and Jews had become sharply distinct religious groups. The earliest and best of them, the life by More's son-in-law William Roper, is a work of art as well as a work of piety. Indeed, the witty sayings with which More has charmed admirers through the ages come less often from his own writings than from the pages of Roper, just as Samuel Johnson comes more alive in Boswell's *Life* than in his own published works. As a biography of a Catholic martyr, the life gains weight from being written by one who had been himself a Lutheran: it is as if we possessed an authentic gospel by Doubting Thomas. Roper's portrayal of his hero, however, is not the whole story, any more than Foxe's depiction of More as villain in his book of Protestant martyrs.

In modern times many biographers have done their best, by research in early Tudor archives, to find the truth in the middle between the partisan exaggerations of the posthumous portraits. Most recently attempts have also been made to get behind not only the earliest biographers, but also the contemporary documents, with the aid of psychological theory. The results have not been impressive: psychobiography, no less than hagiography, impoverishes the story of a life by forcing it into a framework determined in advance of its actual course.

In this new biography Peter Ackroyd has no difficulty in avoiding the opposite pitfalls of hagiography and psychobiography. He follows the story of More's life where it leads, and he places it in the context of history, not of theory. He has gathered a rich harvest of biographical data from More's own writings and correspondence, and he has amassed a store of information about contemporary concerns and practices. He displays a superb skill in recreating the physical and institutional surroundings of the events he chronicles; in writing the life of this great Londoner he brings to bear an uncannily detailed knowledge of the city's history. The heraldic sacramental pageantry of the pre-Reformation world is recreated in brilliant colour, vivid sound and authentic odour. Whether More is visiting the Corpus Christi play in Coventry or negotiating with ambassadors from Antwerp in the Mercer's Hall, Ackroyd will be able to tell us what he wore and what he saw and heard.

Ackroyd is familiar not only with the Tudor sources, but with the writings of recent biographers, good and bad, though he wastes no time in his text agreeing with them or arguing with them. Most often, he gets on with the story and leaves his readers to form their own moral or psychological judgements. The character of More is delineated with sympathy and sensitivity: the picture presented is more like Roper's than Foxe's. Ackroyd sees no real conflict between More's austere spirituality and his worldly ambition: in his view the hair shirt fits easily under the Chancellor's velvet robe. He has kind words to say about More's wife Dame Alice, and he believes that despite their public teasing, husband and wife were very happy with each other.

Even admirers of More will find some of Ackroyd's judgements surprisingly favourable. He regards More as one of the most significant of early Tudor poets, and is prepared to describe him as 'the greatest administrator of his generation'. He explains away the virulent *History of Richard III* as 'a lesson in the arts of disputation and rhetorical debate'. He is even willing to praise the style of More's *Confutation of Tyndale's Answer*.

Ackroyd shrugs off, a little too easily, More's first speech as Chancellor, in which he described his fallen predecessor Wolsey – with whom, until a few weeks earlier, he had worked closely, and whose policies he had diligently carried out – as a 'great wether' who had 'craftily and scabbedly juggled' with that good shepherd Henry VIII. In the 1990s, readers of More's speech on Wolsey may be reminded of Geoffrey Howe's denunciation of Margaret Thatcher. But the advantage is with Lord Howe. More never resigned from Wolsey's service, and his speech was delivered after, not before, his chief's fall from power.

On the other hand, there are important issues on which, I believe, Ackroyd is unfair to More. In 1516 a canonry in Tournai which had been offered to Erasmus was conferred elsewhere by Wolsey. More drafted a letter designed to secure his friend a benefice of at least equal value. Ackroyd considers the terms of this proposal mendacious, and quotes More as writing, in his covering letter, a defence of *mendaciola* or white lies. In fact, More's proposed letter contains no falsehood, though it does conceal the fact that Erasmus had lost interest in acquiring the original canonry. The white lies that he jokingly defends (but does not actually tell) are the conventional excuses of a tardy correspondent, not a set of untruths designed to secure the financial advantages of a benefice.

Again, when More as Chancellor had the distasteful duty of introducing to the House of Lords the matter of Henry VIII's annulment, he said that Queen Catherine 'was both wedded and bedded with his brother Prince Arthur.' Ackroyd comments: 'More clearly spoke against his own belief here, since he was himself convinced of Catherine's virginity.' But there is no contradiction between More's words and his belief. Catherine undoubtedly shared the bed of the 15-year-old Arthur, even though it is more probable than not that she was a virgin at his death.

It is important for a biographer to decide whether More was willing to lie on issues of substance, since on so many matters we have to decide between taking More's word and another's. On such matters as whether More tortured heretics, or spoke treason when a prisoner in the Tower, Ackroyd is prepared to take More's word rather than that of William Tyndale or Richard Rich. In this he is surely right – but would he be right if More sat as loosely to the truth as he suggests elsewhere?

Rarely, Ackroyd descends into psychobabble. He quotes one of More's politically incorrect jokes about women and then suggests 'he feared or distrusted his own sensuality and therefore felt the need to caricature the women who ministered to it'. Of course More distrusted his own sensuality: what Christian, in any age, has not done so? But nothing follows about his attitude to women. Asked whether he preferred short or tall women, More answered, 'Short ones: they are the lesser of two evils.' If in our own age we ask 'What kind of person makes that kind of joke?' we know the answer, and we do not like that kind of person. But the answer to the question in More's age was 'Everyman', and we can draw no conclusion from the joke about the joker. What we do know about More, and what Ackroyd elsewhere stresses, is that he regarded women as the intellectual equal of men, and made his daughter the most learned woman of her generation.

Ackroyd, as I have said, is marvellously at home in the physical and social environment in which More lived. His grip is less sure on the intellectual environment; but it would be ungracious to allow his occasional errors there to affect one's gratitude for one of the most readable and most judicious biographies of More to appear for many a year.

The Tablet, 14 March 1998

Brian Moynahan
If God Spare My Life: William Tyndale, the English Bible and Sir Thomas More – A Story of Martyrdom and Betrayal
Little, Brown, 2002

William Tyndale deserves the gratitude of every literate user of English. His splendid translation of the New Testament, published in 1525 and revised in 1534, provided more than four-fifths of the text of the Authorised Version. Where King James' revisers made changes, they were, as often as not, changes for the worse. Those who prefer other Bible translations, or who do not read the Bible at all, still benefit from the influence that Tyndale's language has exercised on the greatest writers of English ever since his martyrdom in 1536.

A long-time Lutheran, and later a Zwinglian, Tyndale was assigned a star role in the *Book of Martyrs* of the Elizabethan Protestant John Foxe. In modern times, however, he has been neglected. While his enemy and persecutor, Sir Thomas More, has been the subject of many a laudatory book, drama and film, only two full-length serious biographies of Tyndale appeared in the whole of the twentieth century, that of J. F. Mozley in 1987 and that of David Daniell in 1994.

Brian Moynahan's book is in the tradition of Foxe, Mozley and Daniell, but it is greatly inferior to Daniell as a work of scholarship. While Daniell is meticulous in giving evidence for his statements and sources for his information, Moynahan frequently quotes in direct speech utterances for which no reference is provided. Often he is happy to take Foxe's unsupported word for what happened, and he reproduces passages in Foxe as if they were verbatim utterances of Foxe's protagonists. This produces a particularly comic effect in the introductory chapter on Wyclif, giving the impression that Wyclif spoke the English of the later Tudors.

Readers with a serious interest in Tyndale's biography will learn little from Moynahan that they would not learn better from Daniell, who is so much more at home in sixteenth-century England. On one important issue, however, Moynahan offers a fascinating new hypothesis that is not to be found in Daniell. This concerns the ultimate responsibility for Tyndale's arrest and execution in Belgium in 1535.

Tyndale had left England in 1525 and had worked abroad in a number of German cities, and later in Antwerp. In England his writings and translations had been banned by bishops, copies of his books had been burnt, and their importers had been savagely persecuted. Henry VIII, still Catholic in faith, had asked the Emperor Charles V for his extradition in 1531, and when refused had tried in vain to have him kidnapped. Eventually, Tyndale was betrayed to imperial officers in Antwerp by an English agent, Henry Phillips, and was imprisoned in the nearby castle of Vilvorde, where he was burnt as a heretic in 1536.

No one knows on whose behalf Phillips was acting. It is unlikely that he was commissioned by Henry VIII's government, since Henry was now married to the pro-Lutheran Anne Boleyn, and his minister Cromwell later tried to secure Tyndale's release. The chief suspect as Phillips' principal, named as such by Mozley and Daniell, is Bishop Stokesley of London, still an avid heresy-hunter despite Henry's breach with Rome. Moynahan, however, believes that Phillips' paymaster, and therefore the villain of Tyndale's tragedy, was Thomas More.

Moynahan states candidly that no hard evidence has ever emerged to link Phillips with a paymaster. However, the careerist Bishop Stokesley, he thinks, was unlikely to have risked the wrath of Cromwell by paying for Tyndale's betrayal. But More, he believes, was just the man to have the motive and the opportunity to employ Phillips. He was a viciously cruel persecutor of heresy; he feared and loathed Tyndale personally, and he was experienced in the use of spies and *agents provocateurs*. Even though, at the time of Tyndale's arrest, he had been a prisoner in the Tower of London for more than a year, he had, Moynahan believes, both the means and the opportunity to have masterminded the operation.

Moynahan's arguments do not carry conviction. More, as Lord Chancellor, was indeed a rigorous prosecutor of heretics, and boasted of the fact in his epitaph. But the allegations of personal cruelty are mythical. J. A. Guy, no apologist for More, wrote in his magisterial *The Public Career of Sir Thomas More*, 'Serious analysis precludes the repetition of the protestant stories that Sir Thomas flogged heretics against a tree in his garden at Chelsea. It must exclude, too, the allegations of illegal imprisonment made against More by John Field and Thomas Phillips' – all of which are repeated by Moynahan.

Undoubtedly, More hated Tyndale himself. His *Dialogue against Heresies* of 1529 is hard-hitting controversy, but for the most part it is reasonably fair, witty and urbane. But when Tyndale replied with a counter-treatise in 1530, More responded with half a million words of *Confutation*, which go far to bear out Moyhanan's claim that he had become obsessive. Crabbed, repetitive, scatologically abusive, they are an embarrassment to any admirer of More. They certainly convince any reader that if More, in the Tower, learnt of Tyndale's arrest, he must have rejoiced at the news.

Such conjectural *Schadenfreude* is a different matter from involvement in the plotting and execution of the arrest. Once he had ceased to be Lord Chancellor, More had no longer any obligation to pursue heresy by force. Moreover, he lost any power to control intelligence networks for the preservation of a religious system that was becoming hateful to the King. It is difficult to take seriously the idea that once shut up in the Tower he could still finance and direct an overseas heresy hunt. More's surviving writings from the period suggest that his mind was elsewhere, concerned with preparation for his own death rather than the procurement of others'.

Despite their hatred for each other, More and Tyndale resembled each other in many ways. Both were sincerely, passionately, religious men, austere in life, willing to suffer with fortitude. Both, in religious matters, were bigoted and unfair, gross and abusive in polemic. Both were courageous, and in different ways unworldly: each of the two rebuked Henry VIII for divorcing his wife Catherine of Aragon, Tyndale more bluntly than More. And when called to do so, both died bravely for their religious beliefs.

From this distance of time, what united them seems more important than what divided them. Sixteenth-century vilification, Moynahan aptly remarks, penetrates the modern mind 'with the shrill inconsequence of a faulty burglar alarm'. The doctrine of justification by faith alone is no longer a major matter of controversy between Protestant and Catholic. On the translation of crucial biblical terms – a key issue in the controversy – the Roman Catholic *New Jerusalem Bible* sides with Tyndale more often than it sides with More. The half-secularised Christianity of the present age would be greeted with equal horror by both Tudor apologists.

Even after half a millennium it seems difficult for biographers to be even handed between the two. Tyndale's admirers perpetuate myths of More's cruelty; More's defenders avert their eyes from the squalor of his polemics. Perhaps C. S. Lewis has been fairer to both than most; but he was writing as a critic of their writings rather than telling the story of their lives. It would be wonderful to have an even-handed comparative biography of the two martyrs, Catholic and Protestant. For with all their faults, they were two of the most admirable men of their age.

The Tablet, 14 March 1998

Louis L. Martz
*Thomas More: The Search for the
Inner Man*
Yale University Press, 1990

Richard Rex
The Theology of John Fisher
Cambridge University Press, 1991

There have been periods of history when Sir Thomas More was everybody's darling. The biography written by his devoted son-in-law, William Roper, has endeared him to many generations of readers. Roman Catholics have revered him as a martyr and saint especially since his canonisation by Pope Pius XI. The literary public was fascinated by the affectionate and witty humanist, the upright lawyer and politician portrayed by R. W. Chambers in his classic biography. Playgoers and filmgoers followed with admiration the career of the adamantine prisoner of conscience presented by Robert Bolt in *A Man for All Seasons*.

In recent years some historians have been scouring this glossy image and seeking to restore a less flattering portrait of More: the picture of a warped and vindictive persecutor, first painted in Foxe's *Book of Martyrs*. Sir Geoffrey Elton has been one of the most influential in urging that the real More was a far less genial figure than the More of Roper and Chambers. The most substantial product of this revisionist school is the massive 1985 biography by Richard Marius, which argues that More persecuted heretics with a hysterical frenzy generated by sexual repression. *The New York Times* tells us that this new interpretation has even begun to affect productions of Bolt's play.

Louis Martz's book is intended as a modest contribution to the case for the defence in this continuing debate. Like Marius, Martz has worked on the Yale edition of More's collected works; he appears to have come away from the experience with rather fewer scars. The book opens with a revised version of an R. W. Chambers Memorial Lecture of 1987, and then continues with three chapters, each devoted to an analysis of one of More's later writings.

In the Chambers lecture, Martz urges us to look on the gentle and relaxed features of More in the Holbein family group at Basle, rather than the stern and formidable face in the portrait in the Frick collection. He cannot deny that in controversy with Luther, More exhibited an extraordinary degree of vituperative violence. However, he argues, this should be seen as what John Milton, in another context, called 'a sanctified bitterness against the enemies of truth'. To say that the controversial fury represents More's inner personality would be as wrong, Martz maintains, as if we were to say that Milton's prose propaganda represents the real Milton, the inner man, rather than *Paradise Lost*.

As More's equivalent of *Paradise Lost*, Martz presents us with the *Dialogue of Comfort*, the treatise on the Passion, the *De Tristitia Christi* and the last letters from the Tower of London. But he is willing also to try to persuade us that the three volumes of the *Confutation of Tyndale's Answer* deserve to be brought out from under the dust that has gathered on even the most recent edition. The repetition and digression that has wearied many a would-be reader, he claims, has a rhetorical value which will reward those who persevere.

More's letters from the Tower to his family are undoubtedly among the treasures of English literature. Martz's special contribution is to show how More, knowing that these letters were likely to be intercepted by his enemies, wrote with an artful regard for the presence of more than one audience. He also brings out, as others have done, the close links that bind these letters to the simultaneous composition of *A Dialogue of Comfort*. In studying the *De Tristitia* Martz makes use of the Valencia autograph with its minute revisions which enable us, he claims, 'to understand in a way never before possible, the humanistic mind of More at work upon the creation of a Latin masterpiece'.

Richard Rex's book is something quite different from Martz's slender volume. It is packed with meticulous and original research, and in important respects places its subject in a new and surprising light. John Fisher has always stood in the shadow of Thomas More, close to whom he was martyred and with whom he was canonised. In these days when More's halo has been shining less brightly, the features of Fisher may be discerned more clearly. Rex's book vindicates beyond doubt the claim made in his introduction that the theological works of Fisher were 'more solid, enduring, original and influential than those of More'.

The book is not a biography but it describes in often vivid detail the biographical context of Fisher's writings. Two of the most interesting items are the account of the Cambridge curriculum during Fisher's student days of the 1480s, and the reconstruction of the library confiscated from him by royal commissioners in the year of his martyrdom.

Rex is particularly illuminating about Fisher's relationship to Christian humanism. We may understand humanism as involving four elements: (1) the pursuit of accurate editions and versions of original classical and canonical texts; (2) the admiration and imitation of the style of classical authors; (3) a contempt for the philosophical and theological methods of the schoolmen; (4) a rejection of the teaching authority of the medieval hierarchy. In the history of any individual thinker the adoption of each of these elements might lead on to the next, there was no necessity in the nature of things why this should be so. Many people were humanists in one of these senses and not in others.

Thus Fisher, while prepared to die for the authority of the papacy, was one of the most enthusiastic devotees of the study of ancient texts. He brought Erasmus to Cambridge to teach Greek, becoming himself one of the great man's pupils. He endowed a lectureship in Greek at his new college of St John's. The statutes of St John's also included provision for the study of Arabic and Hebrew, and it was a fellow appointed by Fisher who became Cambridge's first university lecturer in Hebrew. Fisher's enthusiasm for the language, we are told rather surprisingly, was due to fascination with the Cabbala.

Some humanists disliked what they regarded as the logic-chopping of the medieval scholastics. Fisher was quite free of this disdain. While he was not quite at ease with the later scholastics of the *via moderna*, he admired Thomas Aquinas, and admired Duns Scotus even more, prescribing at St John's the study of his writings. And in his own writings he made free use of the syllogism.

However, Fisher was not by any means a systematic philosopher or theologian. If it is true, as Rex claims, that he was the foremost intellectual of his age in England, then there had been a sad fall in English academic standards since the times of Scotus, Ockham and Wyclif. But unlike these schoolmen Fisher was not a university teacher but a busy bishop, and the works he has left behind are sermons and controversial tracts. Though they cannot be described as pamphlets – even a single one of his eight books on Henry VIII's divorce ran to 60,000 words – his theological works are all directed to a particular debate in a particular context, whether academic or forensic.

Fisher's first dispute was with the humanist Lefèvre d'Étaples concerning the identity of St Mary Magdalen. In the Gospels we read of (i) a woman who was a sinner, who anointed Jesus in the house of a Pharisee in Galilee (Luke 7:36), (ii) Mary, the sister of Martha and Lazarus, who anointed Jesus at Bethany shortly before his death (Matthew 26:6), (iii) Mary of Magdala who was the first to encounter the risen Jesus (John 20:11). Medieval hagiographers, unwilling to multiply Marys beyond necessity, treated these three incidents as episodes in the life of a single saint, who was venerated throughout Europe as St Mary Magdalen. Lefèvre wrote a tract pointing out – what is now a commonplace among exegetes – that there is no reason to conflate these three evangelical figures. But Fisher sprang to the defence of the single Magdalen. He regarded the tract, as Rex says, as a threat to the cult of the saints. The controversy could be seen as a dry run for the Reformation debates over Scripture, tradition and ecclesiastical authority.

It is of course Fisher's anti-Lutheran writings that form the most important part of his *oeuvre*. A modern reader is likely to find them tedious compendia of commonplaces of Counter-Reformation controversy. Rex, however, brings out brilliantly that many of the arguments that became commonplaces were first devised by Fisher and borrowed gratefully from him by other controversialists before, during and after the Council of Trent. Moreover, strongly conservative as he was, Fisher showed greater insight into his opponents' position than many of his contemporaries. For instance, if Rex is right, it was Fisher who first realised the fundamental significance in Luther's system of the doctrine of justification by faith – a doctrine that is not even mentioned in the 41 articles condemned by Leo X in the bull *Exsurge Domine*. Rex shows that in a number of respects – in his attitude to St Augustine's anti-Pelagian writings, in his emphasis on fiduciary faith, in his sympathy with the demand that the justified sinner should be certain of his own justification – Fisher was closer to Luther than were many of his own orthodox followers.

Rex's discussion of his author's eucharistic theology is less interesting than his treatment of his views on the inspiration and interpretation of Scripture. Surprisingly for a humanist and Hebraist, Fisher believed in the inspiration of the Greek Septuagint translation of the Old Testament, and entered into a lively debate on this topic with his friend Richard Pace, the Dean of St Paul's. This debate, as Rex observes, shows that English humanism on the eve of the Reformation was far from being ideologically homogeneous. After centuries of Protestant polemic, it may come as a surprise to learn that in principle Fisher was in favour of vernacular versions of the Bible, and that his chaplain owned English copies of the New Testament and of the whole Bible.

In his later years Fisher's polemical energies became wholly taken up in the controversy that would eventually lead to his own death: the question of the validity of Henry VIII's marriage to Catherine of Aragon while she was the widow of his wife's brother. There are arid tracts of disputation about the limits of the Pope's dispensing power. Rex tries to make the journey through them as painless as possible, and he does likewise with the relative merits of Leviticus 18:16 ('Thou shalt not uncover the nakedness of thy brother's wife') and Deuteronomy 25:5 (when a man leaves a widow without issue 'her husband's brother shall go in unto her, and take her to him to wife').

Rex's book is not always easy reading, but it is impressively documented, full of novel and interesting information, and makes a good case for redressing the balance of judgement between Fisher and Luther as well as between Fisher and More. There is also one other imbalance Rex is keen to redress: that between Oxford and Cambridge. It is wrong, he argues, to regard Oxford as the centre of humanism in England: during

the first part of the fifteenth century Cambridge had every right
to regard itself as Oxford's academic equal.

Journal of Ecclesiastical History 43:4, October 1992

The Poems of Saint John of the Cross, a
bilingual edition with English versions and
introduction by Willis Barnstone
Indiana University Press, 1967

St John of the Cross was both mystic and theologian. He was a
better theologian than most mystics, and a greater mystic than
most theologians. Today he is most widely read neither as a
mystic nor as a theologian, but as a poet. His poems, Professor
Barnstone tells us, are 'unsurpassed in the Spanish language'
and bear comparison with Sappho and Li Po, Emily Dickinson
and Cavafy.

St John's life work was to aid St Teresa of Avila in the
Counter-Reformation reform of the Carmelite order in Spain.
He incurred the enmity of the unreformed Carmelites who
in 1577 kidnapped and imprisoned him in Toledo. While in
prison he wrote a number of verses of which the most famous
are the *Cantico Spiritual* and the *Noche Oscura*. Someone who
approached these verses ignorant of their background might
take them as straightforward expression of a woman's love: he
would be reminded, in different ways, of Sappho and of Sidney.
But the frequent reminiscences of the *Song of Songs* betray the
allegorical intent; and the *Noche Oscura* has a subtitle, 'Songs of
the soul in rapture at having arrived at the height of perfection,
which is union with God by the road of spiritual negation'.

The poems were circulated, as devotional works, among the
friars and nuns of the Carmelite reform. St John was pressed to
write commentaries on them, and it was thus that his mystical
treatises came into being. He left four main prose works, all

written as commentaries on his poems: the *Spiritual Canticle*
and *The Living Flame of Love*, commentaries on the poems
of the same names; and the *Ascent of Mount Carmel* and the
Dark Night of the Soul, which are not really separate works, but
two incomplete parts of a single projected commentary on the
poem *Noche Oscura*.

St John's commentaries are classics of mystical theology, but
they do not help a modern reader to appreciate his poems. They
allegorise in the heavy-handed manner once dear to biblical
commentators. Two verses of the *Cantico* read thus:

> Buscando mis amores
> Iré por esos montes y riberas
> Ni cogeré las flores
> Ni temeré las fieras
> Y pasaré los fuertes y fronteras
>
> !Oh bosques y espesuras
> Plantados por la mano del Amado
> Oh prado de verduras,
> De flores esmaltado,
> Decid si por vosotros ha pasado.

In his commentary, St John explains this noun by noun. The
mountains are virtues, the banks are mortifications, the beasts,
the mighty and the frontiers are the world, the devil and the
flesh respectively. For 'woods' read 'earth, air, fire and water'; for
'thickets' read 'living creatures'; the meadow means heaven, and
the flowers are the angels and saints. The final line is decoded,
'Say what excellences He has created in you.'

St John's stanzas are so limpid and so musical that the
translator can perhaps best help the reader who lacks Spanish
by translating them literally and leaving him to figure out the
correspondences for himself. Professor Barnstone has chosen

to translate them into verse, but in the *Cantico* he has not attempted to preserve the rhyme scheme. The two stanzas quoted above are translated thus:

> To find my love I'll go
> Along the riverbanks and mountains
> I shall not pick the flowers
> Nor fear the prowling beasts
> I'll pass by fortress and frontier
>
> O open woods and thickets
> Seeded by the lover's hand
> O meadow of green plants
> Enamelled in bright flowers
> Tell me if he has come your way.

This is closer to the Spanish than Roy Campbell's well-known rhymed translation, which preserves the ABAAB pattern of the original

> My loves to search for there
> Amongst these mountains and ravines I'll stay
> Nor pluck flowers, nor for fear
> Of prowling beasts delay,
> But pass through forts and frontiers on my way
>
> O thickets, densely-tramelled,
> Which my love's hand has sown along the height
> O field of green, enamelled
> With blossoms, tell me right
> If he has passed across you in his flight.

In the *Noche Oscura*, however, Professor Barnstone has attempted to preserve something of the rhyme, and in this he is not so successful. Here is the second stanza with his translation.

> A oscuras, y segura,
> Por la secreta escala disfrazada
> Oh dichosa ventura!
> A oscuras, y en celada,
> Estando ya mi casa sosegada.

> Blackly free from light
> Disguised and down a secret way
> O lucky turn and flight!
> In darkness I escaped,
> My house at last was calm and safe.

Campbell's version of the same stanza seems to me superior in fidelity, musicality and naturalness.

> In safety, in disguise
> In darkness up the secret stair I crept
> (O happy enterprise!)
> Concealed from other eyes
> When all my house at length in silence slept.

Notes and Queries, 1968

PART FOUR

THE NINETEENTH CENTURY

Introduction

In the seventeenth and eighteenth centuries the division between Catholic and Protestant Christianity stabilised, after a period of ferocious religious warfare brought to an end by the Peace of Westphalia in 1648. Controversy over the relation between divine grace and human freedom continued, but developed in parallel lines on both sides of the religious divide. Among Catholics, Jesuits emphasised the freedom of the will, Dominicans emphasised the power of grace: the controversy between them was silenced, but not resolved, by Pope Clement VIII in 1605. In the Protestant camp a divine named Arminius propounded views close to those of the Jesuits: they were declared incompatible with Calvinist orthodoxy by the Synod of Dort in 1619.

Again and again, the same issues led to conflict and division. In the seventeenth century the Dutch bishop Jansenius defended a pessimistic and rigorist version of Catholicism, stressing the weakness of human nature in a world in which sin was unavoidable and grace was irresistible. His work led to a controversy which lasted until the Jansenists were finally condemned by Pope Clement XI in the Bull *Unigenitus* of 1713. A century after Jansenius, when the Methodist movement had broken with what it regarded as an excessively worldly Church of England, it split into two branches, one headed by John Wesley and the other by George Whitefield: the debate between the two about predestination was a replay of the earlier one between Arminians and Calvinists.

The innovative intellectual movements of the eighteenth century took place outside the Churches. Throughout the

Europe of the eighteenth century members of the intelligentsia saw themselves as bringing the light of reason into regions darkened by ignorance and superstition. Adam Smith and Thomas Reid were two ornaments of what came to be known as the Scottish Enlightenment, but it was France which was seen by itself and others as the home of the Enlightenment par excellence. The high point of the French Enlightenment was the publication in the 1750s and 1760s of the 17 volumes of the *Encyclopédie, ou Dictionnaire raisonné des arts et des metiers* edited by Denis Diderot and Jean d'Alembert.

While the Enlightenment philosophers were all anti-clerical, they were not all atheists. Voltaire, for instance, thought that the world as explained by Newton manifested the existence of God just as much as a watch shows the existence of a watchmaker. If God did not exist, Voltaire famously said, it would be necessary to invent him – otherwise the moral law would carry no weight. But he did not himself believe in a God who had freely created the world.

Jean-Jacques Rousseau, though himself an encyclopaedist, is often taken as the founding father of a movement at the opposite pole from the Enlightenment – romanticism. Rather than putting his faith in scientific and social progress, Rousseau exalted the 'noble savage' whose simple goodness put civilised man to shame. Humanity, for Rousseau, was naturally good, and its corruption was due to social institutions.

In the nineteenth century, Christians tried, in different ways and in different degrees, to come to terms with both romanticism and the Enlightenment. Protestant thinkers, especially in Germany, allied themselves with the Enlightenment and sought to introduce scientific methods into the study of Christianity's foundation texts. Among Catholics there was more sympathy for the Romantics: while Pope Pius IX denounced the errors of the heirs of the Enlightenment, a European-wide Gothic revival placed an emphasis on the non-rational, aesthetic and emotional aspects of religion.

One nineteenth-century thinker who faced up to both challenges was John Henry Newman. At one time a leader of what might be called the Gothic wing of the Church of England, he was later one of the most enlightened of Roman Catholic thinkers. He was one of the first theologians to accommodate Darwinism, and he insisted that if we are to believe articles of religion that are unprovable by reason, we are obliged to show that such faith is itself a reasonable attitude. He made a heroic attempt to establish this in his classic *Grammar of Assent*.

In the nineteenth century many who had been brought up Christians gave up their faith under the pressures of the Enlightenment and became either Unitarians or atheists. But many hankered for the more romantic aspects of religion, and established secular quasi-churches, offering ritual without belief. A number of these survive today, even though in the meantime many mainstream Churches have ceased to demand adherence to the doctrines against which the early Unitarians protested.

John Cornwell
Newman's Unquiet Grave: The Reluctant Saint
Continuum, 2010

To be canonised as a saint by the Roman Catholic Church a person should be proved to have exercised, during their life on earth, a level of virtue described as 'heroic'. No doubt, once Pope Benedict XVI has beatified John Henry Newman much energy will be devoted, in the literary weeklies no less than in the church courts, to debating whether his virtues did or did not reach that high standard. What is already certain is anyone who wishes to write a successful life of Newman must himself be possessed of academic virtues of a heroic kind.

In the first place, the biographer must be prepared to read a prodigious amount of material. Newman's own published works filled 36 volumes in the edition that he brought out in his own lifetime, and a further dozen volumes appeared after his death. He sent letters at the rate at which we fire off emails, and since 1961 32 copiously annotated volumes of correspondence and diaries have appeared, the best of them monuments of formidable scholarship in themselves.

Secondly, a writer today has to digest without regurgitating the work of a series of gifted biographers, beginning with Newman himself, whose *Apologia pro Vita Sua* has long been recognised as a classic of spiritual autobiography. The earliest and still one of the best posthumous biographies was that of Wilfrid Ward, the son of Newman's Anglican colleague and Catholic sparring partner W. G. Ward. In the last century distinguished scholars devoted their talents to writing lives of Newman, whether, like Ian Ker, in a massive and magisterial tome or, like Owen Chadwick, in a short but shrewd pamphlet.

Thirdly, Newman's own character is full of paradox. Here is a man who spent the first half of his life trying to persuade the Church of England to be more like the Church of Rome, and the second half of his life wishing that Roman Catholics were more like Anglicans. Beyond other theologians, he exalted the episcopal office; yet he spent much of his life annoying the bishops of both his Churches. A Catholic of liberal bent, he repeatedly denounced liberalism as one of the greatest evils. Even his most obvious virtues provide obstacles for his biographer. Anyone who writes about him quickly discovers that he is such a gifted writer, and his style is so bewitching, and so superior to one's own, that one hardly dares to paraphrase his thought, and ends up overloading one's text with verbatim quotations.

Undeterred by these challenges, John Cornwell has taken on the task of writing a biography of Newman to make his life intelligible to the largely secular public which in a few weeks will watch on television the ceremony of his beatification. He has followed a *via media* between the hagiography of Meriol Trevor and the mockery of Lytton Strachey, and he has produced a life which is readable, sympathetic and judicious. His quotations from Newman's writings are always aptly chosen and are never too long. Altogether, he has succeeded in building up a vivid picture of Newman's personality.

The title of the book alludes to the attempt made in October 2008 to translate Newman's mortal remains from his Worcestershire grave to a place where they could be publicly venerated. The excavation recovered fragments of a coffin and an inscribed brass plate, but no trace of any bodily remains either of Newman himself or of the close friend he had been buried beside, Fr Ambrose St John. The upshot of the attempted exhumation was not to provide a shrine for a relic, but to trigger a media debate about whether Newman was gay.

The question is anachronistic. Nineteenth-century Anglicans and Catholics did not classify themselves in accordance with forms of sexual orientation. According to the Christian moral code, sexual activity, whether solitary, homosexual or heterosexual, was sinful except in marriage. For men, therefore, who had given up matrimony and obliged themselves to celibacy, sexual activity with either male or female was forbidden, and sexual attraction whether to male or female could be nothing but a temptation. No doubt different people would find themselves beset by different kinds of temptation, but they did not see these temptations as in any way defining their personality.

I do not know whether those who wish to set up Newman as a gay icon believe that he was homosexually active, but the suggestion is absurd. A man so devout and conscientious would have recoiled from what his Church condemned as one of the worst of sins. Well into the twentieth century, the Catholic Catechism listed 'the sin of Sodom' – along with wilful murder and defrauding the poor of their wages – as a 'sin crying out to heaven for vengeance'.

Partly because of this rigorous prohibition of homosexual activity, Victorian Christians felt free to express to members of the same sex affection in language which in our very different climate would appear ambiguous. Cornwell deals sensitively and temperately with this issue, comparing Newman's attachments with the earlier literary intimacies between Wordsworth, Coleridge and Southey. He goes on to show, by listing parallels, that the burial of friends side by side need have no erotic significance. He might have added to his list the recent case of the philosopher Elizabeth Anscombe, who at her request was buried beside the grave of Ludwig Wittgenstein.

While bringing out many aspects of Newman's character and personal relationships, Cornwell wisely chooses to focus on his literary output. 'Newman's claim to eminence', he writes, 'consists not in his status as a prelate, not in claims for conventional piety, but his genius for creating new ways of imagining and writing about religion.' And not only, we might add, about religion – as Cornwell's own treatment brings out.

By common consent, and in the considered judgement of Gerard Manley Hopkins and James Joyce, Newman was the greatest Victorian master of English prose. His extraordinary gifts first appeared in the sermons he gave in the University Church of St Mary in Oxford in the 1820s and 1830s. They held his congregation spellbound and still strike a reader with great force. These parochial and plain sermons are in general superior to the more famous set pieces of later days, such as the *Second Spring* sermon of 1850, which celebrated the restoration of the English Catholic hierarchy.

Newman's first published book was *The Arians of the Fourth Century*, the fruit of his deep reading in the Church Fathers. From his patristic learning he drew parallels from this period to rebuke the Anglican bishops for kowtowing to heretical governments, and, later, to rebuke the Catholic authorities for failing to consult the faithful in matters of doctrine.

Of the Anglican writings, the one to which Cornwell devotes most attention is *The Development of Doctrine*, written while Newman was thinking his way out of the Church of England into the Church of Rome. The Christian revelation was held, by Protestant and Catholic alike, to have ceased with the death of the last apostle; and the Christian faith was proclaimed to be unchanging. How can that be reconciled with the manifest variation in the theological beliefs recorded during the long history of the Church? That was the problem that Newman hoped to solve by presenting a theory of the development of doctrine and offering a set of criteria for distinguishing healthy from unhealthy growth.

Cornwell exaggerates the merits of *The Development*, apparently endorsing the astonishing claim that it is as important a work as Darwin's *Origin of Species*. Newman's book gives an interesting conspectus of the history of dogma, and it is full of powerful metaphors carefully worked out: doctrine is a plant growing from a seed, or a stream broadening to a river and becoming ever purer and truer to itself. But the metaphorical criteria offered will not enable anyone to settle objectively whether the *Filioque* was a legitimate addition to the creed, or whether Jean Calvin or Ignatius Loyola has a greater claim to be an authentic successor to St Augustine.

Before bringing *The Development* to a conclusion Newman had entered the Catholic Church. Cornwell often reminds us that Newman maintained that religious conviction was not just a matter of logic, but of imagination and emotion. Nonetheless, Newman's conversion was a remarkable example of a thinker following an argument wherever it leads. At the time of his conversion, Newman had no friends among English Catholics, found Italian Catholics dirty and superstitious, and disliked Catholic music and architecture. His tastes and emotions were bound up with the language of the English Bible and the traditions of Oxford. Yet he left the Church of England with hardly a backward glance, simply because his studies of church history had convinced him that, unlike the Roman Catholic Church, it was not continuous with the Church of the apostles and the Fathers.

After his conversion, Newman's next important work was *The Idea of a University*. Asked to found a Catholic University in Dublin, Newman gave a set of lectures to lay down the notion of a university 'viewed in itself and apart from the Catholic Church'. It is worth taking time to contrast Newman's ideal with the typical university of today.

Whereas today all the leading world universities see themselves as research centres no less than teaching institutions, Newman thinks that research is not part of the function of a university and should be left to academies. Whereas modern universities encompass within themselves law schools, medical schools, business schools and sometimes agricultural and engineering schools, Newman insists that a university must be quite distinct from a professional school. Its function is not to prepare students for the exercise of a profession of any kind, but rather to lay a foundation upon which professional training may build. 'That philosophical or liberal education, as I have called it, which is the proper function of a University, if it refuses the foremost place to professional interests, does but postpone them to the formation of the citizen.'

The purpose of a university, for Newman, was to ensure that those educated there had 'a cultivated intellect, a delicate taste, a candid, equitable, dispassionate mind'. This, surely, is still the central aim of pre-professional undergraduate education. Whatever discipline an undergraduate pursues, or majors in, it is not so much the acquisition of that particular body of knowledge that is important, but the acquiring, through that discipline, of a sense of the aims and methods of science and scholarship. It is the function of liberal education to make one aware of the boundaries of the domains of the sciences, and a grasp of which questions can be settled by science and which cannot. However, even those dons most impressed by Newman's ideal are likely to disagree with his insistence on the separation of teaching from research. Many would claim that an academic who engages in research will make a better teacher, and that an academic who has pupils will make a better researcher.

The Idea of a University remains a classic; as Cornwell puts it, it has become 'a master-class on the ideals of university education across many cultural and political divides'. But the book that established Newman's reputation as a writer in his lifetime was *Apologia pro Vita Sua*, an autobiography written in response to charges brought against his integrity by the novelist Charles Kingsley.

It is to that work that Cornwell devotes his best chapter. He compares it, appropriately, with the *Confessions* of St Augustine. The spiritual autobiography of the greatest intellectual convert of the modern world does indeed resemble in many ways the spiritual autobiography of the greatest intellectual convert of the ancient world. Both conversions, as Gerard Manley Hopkins stressed, were slow, lingering processes, quite unlike anything on the Damascus road. Each writer uses a variety of artifices – and in the case of Newman, documentation – to recreate the mentality of former selves long left behind.

Newman resembled Augustine in other respects also. Both men re-edited, late in life, their early works; both were enormously concerned that their *Nachlass* should be passed on in the appropriate condition. Newman, indeed, went to great lengths to ensure that one kind of *Nachlass* would *not* survive: he gave orders that compost be sprinkled in his grave to ensure the rapid dissolution of his body.

Newman's last major work was his *Essay in Aid of a Grammar of Assent*, published in 1870, but drawing upon ideas already to be found in his early university sermons. This book centres upon a question of primary importance in the philosophy of religion: how can religious belief be justified, given that the evidence for its conclusions seems so inadequate to the degree of its commitment? Newman quotes Locke as giving, as the unerring mark of the love of truth, the not entertaining any proposition with greater assurance than the proofs it is built on will warrant. 'Whoever goes beyond this measure of assent, it is plain, receives not truth in the love of it, loves not truth for truth-sake, but for some other by-end.'

Newman demolishes this doctrine of Locke's by showing that there are many beliefs reasonably held which do not depend on evidence or proof. His favourite example of a firm belief on flimsy evidence is our conviction that Great Britain is an island. But there are many others.

> We laugh to scorn the idea that we had no parents though we have no memory of our birth; that we shall never depart this life, though we can have no experience of the future; that we are able to live without food, though we have never tried; that a world of men did not live before our time, or that that world has no history.

Newman's treatment of the nature of belief makes *The Grammar of Assent* a classic of epistemology, unmatched in subtlety until Wittgenstein's posthumous *On Certainty*. But the book is not adequate as a justification of religious faith in a secular age, since it is addressed only to those who already believe in God and in a final judgement. Faith can only be justified, it argues, from a basis of antecedent probability. Newman, who is often at his best when stating a position against which he intends to argue, states the difficulty candidly:

> Antecedent probabilities may be equally available for what is true and what pretends to be true, for a revelation and its counterfeit, for Paganism, or Mahometanism, or Christianity. They seem to supply no intelligible rule what is to be believed and what not; or how a man is to pass from a false belief to a true. If a claim of miracles is to be acknowledged because it happens to be advanced, why not for the miracles of India as well as for those of Palestine? If the abstract probability of a Revelation be the measure of genuineness in a given case, why not in the case of Mahomet as well as of the Apostles?

But this means that there is not the parallel which Newman drew between the belief that Great Britain is an island and the religious faith of a Christian believer. For faith to be faith and not mere belief it has to be belief on the word of God. If that is so, then the fact of revelation has to be better known than the content of revelation. But this Newman does not even attempt to prove.

When the First Vatican Council proclaimed papal infallibility in 1870 Newman was distressed. The definition, he thought, was unfortunate and ill-advised, and the dogma had been imposed 'very cruelly, tyrannically, and deceitfully'. In a *Letter to the Duke of Norfolk* he put the best face he could on the Council's proceedings, concluding, 'If I am obliged to bring religion into after-dinner toasts (which indeed does not seem quite the thing) I shall drink – to the Pope, if you please – still, to conscience first and to the Pope afterwards.' In recent years this famous remark has been quoted countless times by Catholics who wished to disobey the Pope without leaving the Roman Church.

Looking back on his life during the last years of Pio Nono's reign, Newman may well have felt that his life had been futile: all his projects, small and large, had ended in failure. He had tried and failed to reform the Oxford tutorial system, and he had not succeeded in bringing the Church of England into conformity with its Catholic past. He had not been able to instil a spirit of brotherly love between the two Oratorian communities of priests that he had founded – indeed, what Cornwell calls the 'acidulous piety' of his correspondence with the head of London Oratory would provide ample ammunition to a devil's advocate, if such an officer still existed. The University in Dublin fell far short of incarnating the ideals he had spelt out in *The Idea of a University*. He had become editor of a liberal Catholic journal, the *Rambler*, but he had been forced to resign. And he had been helpless to stem the tide of ultramontane fervour that had triumphed at the Vatican Council. It was no wonder that he suffered from bouts of depression, which devout biographers have christened 'a dark night of the soul'.

However, the depression turned out not to be permanent. In 1877, Trinity, Newman's old college, made him its first honorary fellow and he returned to his beloved Oxford in triumph. A year later, the new Pope, Leo XIII, made him a cardinal. His last years were passed in the warmth of personal contentment and the glow of national and international regard. Edward Elgar's 1900 setting of his great poem on death, *The Dream of Gerontius*, was a fitting final tribute to a great man.

Posthumously, Newman's earlier disappointments were at least in part reversed. The colleges of Oxford adopted his model for the tutorial system and observe it to this day. In its obituary, the *Guardian* described him as 'the founder, we might almost say, of the Church of England as we see it', citing the changes resulting from the Oxford Movement. Within the Roman Catholic Church the theologians who steered the Second Vatican Council were all under his influence, so that Pope Paul VI could describe it as 'Newman's Council'. His writings have remained continuously in print and for many years now there has been a campaign to have him canonised.

John Cornwell does not decide for the reader whether Newman was or was not a saint. He stresses Newman's devoutness and austerity, but he also lays emphasis on the touchy and egotistical element in his make-up. 'My overarching purpose', he says, 'is to show that Newman's unrelenting literary obsession was the story of his own life: he was the ultimate, self-absorbed autobiographer.'

Newnman's Unquiet Grave is a substantial achievement. One could wish that the author had had more time at his disposal because the text is that rare thing, a book that the reader wishes had gone on longer.

In an epilogue to the book Cornwell tells the story of the Boston deacon Jack Sullivan, whose recovery from excruciating spinal deformities was accepted by the Vatican as a miracle, attributable to Newman, inexplicable by natural causes. Cornwell sets out the facts fairly, but his conclusion is that it is arguable that the relief of pain was a placebo effect, and that it was surgery, rather than prayer, that cured the underlying problem.

If Newman is to be canonised, a further miracle is required. If there is any problem about this, Pope Benedict could appeal to an august precedent for downgrading the importance of miracles in the canonisation of a holy scholar. The process of canonisation of St Thomas Aquinas lasted from 1316 to 1323, in the pontificate of Pope John XXII. Though there was no shortage of miracles attributed to him after his death, the devil's advocate insisted that there were no convincing miracles attributed to him in his lifetime. One story, however, was attested by several eye-witnesses. When Thomas lay dying in the Abbey of Fossanova, they said, he had been unable to eat for days, when suddenly he expressed a wish for herrings. Herrings, his family explained, might be easy to come by in Paris, but were not to be found in the Italian seas. But to everyone's surprise, the next consignment of sardines from the local fishmonger was found to contain a consignment of herrings. The judges in the canonisation process seem to have been sceptical whether their untravelled witnesses would be able to tell a herring when they saw one. But the Pope overruled the devil's advocate. 'There are as many miracles as there are articles in the *Summa*', he is reputed to have said; and he declared Thomas a saint.

Times Literary Supplement, 30 July 2010

*The Letters and Diaries of John Henry
Newman Volume X: The Final Step, 1
November 1843 – 6 October 1845*
ed. Francis J. McGrath FMS
Oxford University Press, 2006

The year 1845 was the turning point in the life of John Henry
Newman, the year when he left the Church of England in
which he had lived for 44 years, and joined the Roman Catholic
Church in which he was to spend the remaining 45 years of
his life. The years covered by the letters in this volume and its
predecessor are the hinge years of his conversion.

Newman had been a Fellow of Oriel College since 1822, and
since 1828 Vicar of the Oxford University Church of St Mary's.
With John Keble and E. B. Pusey he was one of the founders of
the Anglo-Catholic movement, which aimed to foster within
the Church of England an emphasis on the mystical power
of sacramental rites and symbols. The movement was called
'Tractarian' because of the *Tracts for the Times* in which it
propagated its tenets.

In the 1830s Newman had propounded the thesis that
the Church of England offered a middle position between
the opposite excesses of Roman superstition and Protestant
Puritanism. This was the famous *via media*. But his thought
began to tilt more and more in favour of the Roman position
and against the Protestant one. This Romeward movement
reached its climax when in 1841 he published the ninetieth, and
last, of the Tracts for the Times. In that Tract he maintained

that the Thirty-Nine Articles – the Anglican formula which the authorities of the University imposed upon its members – could be conscientiously accepted (with the exception of the article on the Pope) by a member of the Roman Church.

Tract 90 caused an uproar in Oxford. The University's governing body, the Hebdomadal Board, resolved that the principles of interpretation it proposed were inconsistent with the statutes of the University. The Bishop of Oxford pronounced the Tract dangerous in its tendencies. William George Ward, on the other hand, a Fellow and Tutor of Balliol, wrote two pamphlets in its defence. He admitted that the natural meaning of some of the Articles was Protestant, but he recommended subscribing to them in a 'non-natural sense'. Ward's pamphlets cost him his Balliol tutorship, and Newman was forced to terminate the series of Tracts.

While retaining his Oriel fellowship, Newman now retired to Littlemore, a village parish attached to the living of St Mary's. He was living there during the entire period covered by this volume. In his absence, no clear leader emerged for the Tractarians. Pusey headed the Anglo-Catholic mainstream, while Ward was the most prominent of the Romeward faction. Each of the two fell foul of the University authorities. In June 1843 Pusey was condemned for a Catholicising sermon on the Eucharist. One year later Ward tested the authorities' patience to the utmost, with his book *The Ideal of a Christian Church*, which argued that the Church of England fell far short of the Christian ideal of holiness and should be reformed to bring it in line with the Church of Rome. Newman, living in his quasi-monastic community at Littlemore, wanted only to be left in peace and was distressed that the fires of controversy had been rekindled by the impetuous Ward.

In the following December the University authorities announced three propositions to be voted on by the convocation of all the Oxford MAs. The first condemned specific passages in the *Ideal*, the second deprived Ward of his degrees, and the third imposed a general test by which all who signed the Articles must be accepted in the sense in which they were interpreted by the University. The third proposal was dropped because liberals made common cause with the Tractarians in objecting to its intolerance. But in its place a proposal was made to condemn Tract 90 and thus associate Newman with the degradation of Ward.

On a bitter February day fifteen hundred Masters of Arts travelled to the Sheldonian Theatre to vote. The passages from the *Ideal* were censured by a vote of 777 to 391 and Ward was deprived of his degrees by 569 to 511. Then came the proposal to condemn Tract 90. Above the shouts of 'placet' and 'non placet' from the throng was heard the voice of the Senior Proctor: *'Nobis Procuratoribus non placet'*. It was the last time the Proctor's veto was used in Convocation.

No sooner had Ward been condemned than he made public that during the previous December he had become secretly engaged to be married. Many in Oxford thought it was hypocritical for a priest who had written in favour of clerical celibacy to choose matrimony for himself, and the town was full of sneers against 'Hildebrand the married man'. 'This will do more', wrote one of his friends, 'to quiet the storm of his Romanizing doctrine than half a dozen votes of the Oxford convocation.'

Newman, meanwhile, was engaged in writing a theological treatise, *The Development of Christian Doctrine*, in vindication of his now overwhelming conviction of the validity of Roman claims. After he had sent it to the printer, he was in October 1845 received into the Church of Rome at Littlemore by a visiting Italian missionary. He had been preceded in his submission, one month earlier, by W. G. Ward and his new wife.

Newman was a spectator rather than an actor in the events of this period, which marked the effective end in Oxford of the movement to which it had given its name. Nonetheless, the letters and diaries of the period are of extreme interest not only theologically but also from an epistemological and psychological point of view.

During the period of this volume Newman, as he later put it, was on his deathbed as regards the Anglican Church. King Charles II, when on his actual deathbed, apologised to his courtiers for 'being an unconscionable time a-dying'. It is impossible not to feel that Newman took an extraordinarily long time to take his leave of a Church which he had believed, ever since 1839, to be in schism.

Charles Kingsley was later to accuse Newman of dishonesty during these years. While holding a cure of souls in the Church of England, he maintained, Newman was secretly encouraging people to join the Church of Rome. The charge was literally false, as these letters show. Never does Newman urge anyone to become a Roman Catholic; often he tries to dissuade others from doing so and he is distressed if they reject his advice. He makes his own position painfully clear to his friends, but he always insists that no one else is obliged to take the same line. These letters, and especially a series to Mrs William Froude, read like a dossier of defence prepared in advance against Kingsley's future libel. This dossier was to form the backbone of Newman's classic autobiography, Apologia pro Vita Sua.

It was surely from the Catholic viewpoint rather than from Kingsley's that Newman was open to criticism. Convinced as he was that there was no salvation outside the Church of Rome, how could he remain in a schismatic institution? To be sure he no longer held office within it, having resigned as Vicar of St Mary's in 1843. But was it not his duty as a believing Christian to submit himself to the one true Church? He himself admitted, in more than one of these letters, that while he felt justified in continuing to live as an Anglican, he did not feel he could die as one. This made him frightened of going to hell whenever he was in any life-threatening situation.

His position was, indeed, theologically untenable. He continued to believe in the validity of Anglican orders, and the effectiveness of the Anglican Eucharist, which he continued to celebrate himself. However, he also held that within a schismatic Church the sacraments conveyed no grace to their recipients. It followed that the members of his congregation should kneel in worship to the host he consecrated, but that actually taking communion would, short of some special divine intervention, do them no good at all.

Many times in these letters Newman justifies his remaining in the Church of England on the grounds that his present belief that it is in schism may be a delusion: he has changed his mind before, and he may do so again. One might think that if such an argument is ever valid, it must always be valid, so that we could never act on any certainty. And could not that very argument have prevented him from ever going over to Rome, however convinced he was of her claims?

Years later Newman was to write a treatise of epistemology, the *Grammar of Assent*, in which he spelt out the general relationships between certainty, belief and knowledge. As an example for discussion he imagined himself, while walking among trees in the moonlight, confidently mistaking a shadow for a man.

> I come quite close to him and put out my arm. Then I find for certain that what I took for a man is but a singular shadow, formed by the falling of the moonlight on the interstices of some branches or their foliage. Am I not to indulge my second certitude because I was wrong in the first?

The sense of certitude, Newman tells us, is as it were the bell of the intellect and sometimes it strikes when it should not. But we do not dispense with clocks because on occasions they tell the wrong time.

The *Grammar of Assent* presents to a general public, concerned with general philosophical issues, the reflections which Newman's individual predicament had forced upon him in these earlier years. The letters in this volume contain the germ of what was to become a unique epistemological classic. But what the argument of the *Grammar* justifies is Newman's eventual Roman certainty, not his earlier Anglican procrastination.

But if Newman's position between 1840 and 1845 is difficult to vindicate either theologically or logically, it is surely psychologically easily comprehensible. He was drawn to the Roman Church not by any ambition or by any affection for its rituals or adherents. His letters make clear that his conversion was based entirely on religious and intellectual grounds. But in the lives of many besides Newman, the intellectual conviction of a duty to say farewell to the ambitions, affections and familiarities of a lifetime has often taken periods of years to take effect. In the life of St Augustine, for instance, five years elapsed between his disillusionment with Manicheism and his baptism as a Christian.

Such a time lag between conviction and action occurs not only in converts to Catholicism. At the same time as Newman was moving Romewards, his Oriel colleague Arthur Hugh Clough was moving away from Anglicanism in the opposite direction. Each of them had begun to doubt the official interpretation of the Thirty-Nine Articles long before they took the step of resigning their college fellowship. In Clough's case the interval was five years, very little shorter than Newman's delay. To take a secular example from the next century, Roy Jenkins lost his faith in the Labour Party in 1975; it was not until 1981 that he founded the SDP. Indeed, anyone who has resigned from office, changed profession or decided on divorce is familiar with that painful period between a life-altering decision and its execution. What makes Newman remarkable is simply the honesty and the eloquence with which the pain and the procrastination is expressed in these letters.

Times Literary Supplement, 15 December 2006

The Letters and Diaries of John Henry Newman, Volume XXXII (Supplement), edited at the Birmingham Oratory with Notes and an Introduction by Francis J. McGrath

Oxford University Press, 2008

The publication of Newman's letters and diaries was begun in 1961 by the late C. S. Dessain who brought out a collection of letters that had been written immediately after Newman's conversion from Anglicanism to Roman Catholicism in 1845. He numbered this as Volume XI, and proceeded to publish 20 further volumes relating to the Catholic period of Newman's life. Having completed Volume XXXI Dessain went back to Newman's earliest days and published Volume I. Publishing the remaining papers of the Anglican period has been the work of four editors. Ian Ker and Thomas Gornall were responsible for Volumes II–V, taking the story up to 1836, while Gerard Tracey produced Volumes VI–VIII. Volumes IX and X, which complete the chronological series, were edited by Francis J. McGrath FMS in 2006. We are now offered a supplementary volume containing letters and papers which came to light too late to be included in the original sequence. We are promised a final volume containing an index of all 32 of its predecessors. This will complete a magnificent series which in its extent and scholarship will stand comparison with any edition of the correspondence of any other great English writer.

No one will wish to acquire this supplementary volume who does not already have access to the chronological series: the footnotes, naturally enough, are full of cross-references to earlier volumes. Nonetheless, the volume is far from being the ragbag which might have been expected from the miscellaneous provenance of its contents. There are substantial clusters of letters focusing on important periods of Newman's life: his rectorship of the Catholic University of Ireland, his foundation of the Oratory School in Birmingham, and his elevation to the cardinalate. There are individual letters of interest written on the margins of some of his most famous works, such as the *Apologia pro Vita Sua*, the *Grammar of Assent*, and the *Letter to the Duke of Norfolk*. Every letter that Newman wrote is beautifully written, even if it is only a thank-you note for a brace of pheasants, or a warning to a correspondent to beware of the damp sheets in a friend's house.

All but a handful of these new letters belong to Newman's Catholic career. This is no doubt the consequence of the policy that dictated the order of publication of the earlier volumes. Since the letters of the Anglican period are those most recently published, there has been a much shorter time for the discovery of overlooked correspondence.

The most interesting body of new material concerns the rectorship of the Catholic University. We are given a hitherto unpublished journal which Newman kept throughout the first 29 months of his time in Dublin. This reveals Newman as a surprisingly energetic and resourceful administrator, who achieved a great deal during his brief tenure as chief executive, despite the autocratic procrastination of his chairman, Archbishop Cullen. The letters and papers that Newman submitted to his episcopal governing body also provide a supplement to the lectures which became the classic *Idea of a University*. But his heart was not in the enterprise: rather, it remained always with his brethren at the Birmingham Oratory, to which he decamped in 1857.

A subsequent body of letters concerns the boys' school which Newman attached to the Oratory. Though Newman was not the headmaster of the school, he took it on himself to write many a letter in response to parents' concerns. Thus, he assures one parent that there is no fagging at the school and that corporal punishment is very rare; to another he explains the excessive expense that would be incurred by homeopathic medicine. He reports to Prince Pamphili that his son eats too many sweets, and he responds to the complaint of the Countess of Kenmare that the school beef is underdone. In a response of 1879 to an address from the Oratory School Society he declares that 'no other department of the pastoral office requires such sustained attention and such unwearied service' as that of a master in a boarding school.

A correspondent who straddles the worlds of Dublin and Birmingham is Thomas Arnold Jnr, son of Newman's ancient adversary Dr Arnold of Rugby, and younger brother of Matthew Arnold. Thomas had been a schools inspector in Tasmania, where he became a Roman Catholic, to the fury of his wife who threw a brick through the window of the cathedral where he was baptised. Anti-Catholic prejudice forced Arnold to give up his job, and he returned to the British Isles. In 1856 Newman appointed him Professor of English Literature in Dublin, but two years later poached him to teach classics at the Oratory School. In 1865 Arnold gave up this job, and left the Church because he could not stomach the doctrine of infallibility.

Newman wrote, in response to the news:

> A man must follow his own convictions, and it is not I who am his judge. While I say this I must ask your indulgence also to say, what in honesty I cannot keep from saying, that I think such a step as you have taken a sin, that I shall

ever pray you may one day reverse it, and that I believe you will. Meanwhile, having said this once I don't see why I should say it again.

Newman was proved right, and in October 1876 Arnold visited him and was reconciled by him to the Church. This second conversion was just in time to prevent him – so his family believed – from being appointed to the chair of Anglo-Saxon in Oxford. Arnold's wife wrote to Newman a letter which began, 'You have now for the second time been the cause of my husband's becoming a member of the Church of Rome and from the bottom of my heart I curse you for it. You know well how very weak and unstable he is, and you also know that he has a wife and eight children.'

Only a small proportion of the present volume consists of letters actually written by Newman. His last letter appears on page 488, when there are still nearly 250 pages to come. Copious appendices include 94 obituary notices, including those from *The Vegetarian* and from *Rod and Gun*. Even in the earlier pages, the large print of Newman's own letters is often a small island amid a sea of annotation, often superfluous. For instance, a brief note by Newman commending a friend's book to Macmillan's is accompanied by notes three times longer than the letter, which includes the information that Harold Macmillan died at the age of 92 years and 322 days. And any person who has ever heard of Newman surely does not need a footnote to explain that Martin Luther was a German Reformer.

We hear much talk nowadays of the possibility of Newman's canonisation. Candidates for sainthood do well to leave behind them very little in the way of correspondence. It is not that Newman's correspondence exhibits any scandals to delight a devil's advocate. The problem is rather that it does not provide evidence for a superabundance of those natural virtues that are no less necessary for sainthood than are the theological virtues. Newman comes across in his letters as too distant and too touchy. He was, of course, capable of great affection; but the general tone of his letters is one of chill courtesy rather than of human warmth. It is interesting to compare his correspondence with that of Matthew Arnold, contemporaneous and for periods almost as copious. From each of Arnold's letters one can form a lively impression of the person he was writing to: not so from Newman's.

If Newman was not good enough for canonisation, we may ask whether canonisation is good enough for Newman. In the words of an obituary from the *Freethinker*, printed in this volume, 'Here is one who is more than a Catholic, more than a theologian, one who has lived an intense inner life, who understands the human heart as few have understood it, who follows the subtlest workings of the human mind.' Newman had one of the keenest intellects of the nineteenth century, and was one of the finest English stylists of all time. If he does not belong in the first rank of British philosophers with Locke and Hume, he can certainly claim a place in the second echelon with Berkeley and Mill. Given the claims that Newman's genius has on the world outside his two Churches, and given the grade inflation introduced by Pope John Paul II into the canonisation process, it may well seem that petitions for him to be made a saint are no more appropriate than would be a proposal for the award of a posthumous CH to Charles Darwin.

Times Literary Supplement, 12 June 2009

Timothy Larsen
Crisis of Doubt: Honest Faith in Nineteenth-Century England
Oxford University Press, 2007

It has long been a commonplace to speak of the Victorian age as a period of religious doubt. The arch-Victorian Alfred Tennyson famously intoned, 'There lives more faith in honest doubt,/ Believe me than in half the creeds.' A. N. Wilson's recent *God's Funeral* proclaims on its dust jacket, 'By the end of the nineteenth century, almost all the great writers, artists, and intellectuals had abandoned Christianity.'

Timothy Larsen, Professor of Theology at Wheaton College, Illinois, sets out to show that this view is one-sided. In nineteenth-century England there was, he claims, as much honest faith as honest doubt, and it was of equal significance for its religious history. In order to substantiate his claim he does not attempt to present an array of intellectuals who retained their faith throughout their lives. Instead, he focuses on a very particular group: men who, having lost their faith and then been active in propagating secularism, later reconverted to one or other form of Christianity. All of them were self-taught plebeians, and most of them were political radicals.

The book presents chapter-length biographies of seven such men: William Hone, Frederic Rowland Young, Thomas Cooper, John Henry Gordon, Joseph Barker, John Bagnall Bebbington and George Sexton. In each case Larsen documents the early secularism and the eventual reconversion. He stresses the intellectual nature of the reconversions and defends each reconvert from imputations of unworthy motives or emotional instability. The dramatis personae do not include many household names, but as an illustration of the kind of man we are dealing with we may take the one who appears the most remarkable of the group: the chartist Thomas Cooper (1805–92).

The son of a poor widow of Leicester, Cooper learnt to read at an early age and read voraciously as a child. Converted to Methodism, he was apprenticed as a shoemaker, but at the age of 23 set up a school in Gainsborough with the aim of teaching Latin to the working classes. This was not a success, and he went to London to work as a journalist. Returning to the Midlands to write for a Leicester newspaper, he was appalled by the poverty he encountered, and joined the Chartist movement, editing a number of their publications. A fiery speech he made to striking workers in Hanley led to arson and criminal damage, and he was convicted of seditious conspiracy and imprisoned for two years from 1843 to 1845.

Extensive reading in prison turned him into a religious sceptic, and on his release he earned his living for several years as a highly popular secularist lecturer, describing himself as an 'unfettered thinker and plain speaker for Truth, Freedom, and Progress'. He lectured on an enormous number of topics, exhibiting an enviable acquaintance with contemporary learning. But soon he became as disillusioned with secularism as he had been with Christianity, and in 1865 he astonished a London audience who had expected a lecture on Sweden with a homily on 'the existence of a divine moral governor'. He became a Baptist and devoted the rest of his life to Christian apologetics, delivering 4,292 lectures, preaching 2,568 sermons and publishing several best-selling books on Christian evidences. 'I cannot live in a world of cold negations,' he wrote shortly before his death in a passage quoted by Larsen. 'It is a wonder to me that other men can live in such a world. But I do not condemn them for it. I only wish that they felt the satisfaction, the happiness, the thankfulness that I feel in receiving Christianity.'

The erudition that Cooper displayed, whether as freethinker or apologist, is astonishing when one realises that it was all self-administered. But this fits into a pattern which Larsen weaves skilfully throughout his book. Sceptical ideas, he maintains, influenced working-class radicals long before they began to infect the academical elite. Several of these men had imbibed materialism from d'Holbach's *System of Nature*. Tom Paine's *The Age of Reason* had made them familiar with the arguments later used by biblical critics to show the inconsistencies and absurdities in the Old Testament. The atheistic journal *The Oracle of Reason* had been propounding a doctrine of evolution for nearly twenty years before Darwin wrote *The Origin of Species*. One of the first English readers to master the contents of George Eliot's translation of Strauss's critical *Life of Jesus* was none other than the chartist Cooper.

By contrast, the middle-class intellectuals who became famous for their loss of faith had in their youth been protected in domestic and academic shelters from serious contact with radical political and religious ideas.

The picture that emerges from Larsen's biographies is one of religious doubt as a phenomenon of adolescence in cultures as well as individuals. The plebeian radicals caught the disease at an early stage: a striking number of them recovered after a longer or shorter illness and ended their lives as champions of Christianity. Members of the social elite, on the other hand, were infected at a later stage with a more virulent form of Victorian doubt, and never grew out of it in their lifetimes. The literary class as a whole had to wait until the twentieth century to return to a healthful zest for religion.

Larsen's thesis is intriguing, and is presented with a wealth of erudite supporting evidence. There is indeed something attractive in the idea that the reconverted should be given equal time with the apostates, even though, as Larsen candidly admits, the fact that A and B were believers while Y and Z were atheists is simply an item of history which cannot be used to argue in favour either of religion or irreligion. But considered simply from the historical point of view, can it seriously be claimed that those Victorians who lost faith in their doubts are as significant as those who continued to doubt their faith? None of the personnel of *Crisis of Doubt* have left writings that are read today by anyone except historians of religion. But many people today, with no specialist interest in history and no religious or anti-religious axe to grind, still read with pleasure and profit the works of George Eliot, Arthur Hugh Clough, Matthew Arnold, Henry Sidgwick and Leslie Stephen.

Times Literary Supplement, 1 June 2007

Mary Midgley
The Solitary Self: Darwin and the Selfish Gene
Acumen, 2010

In this book Mary Midgley attacks neo-Darwinians at several levels. According to her, they misrepresent the process of evolution, they espouse an obnoxious social ideology and they are unfaithful to the teachings of Charles Darwin.

Neo-Darwinians, she claims, exaggerate the role of natural selection in evolution. Natural selection is a destructive factor, a filter that removes unsuccessful biological systems. But a filter can never be the sole cause of the stuff that flows out of it. To explain that stuff you need also to understand the input. Strainers strain out coffee grounds; they do not create coffee.

Midgley's opponents might respond that of course they study the material that is subjected to natural selection. The most popular neo-Darwinian treatise, Richard Dawkins' *The Selfish Gene*, is devoted precisely to this study and offers a characterisation of the predominant quality of genes. In a highly competitive world, he argues, if a gene is to survive it must be endowed with ruthless selfishness.

Here again, Midgley argues, we meet with misrepresentation. She quotes a famous passage from Dawkins' book:

> [Genes] swarm in huge colonies, safe inside gigantic lumbering robots, sealed off from the outside world, communicating with it by tortuous indirect routes, manipulating it by remote control. They are in you and me;

they created us, body and mind; and their preservation is the ultimate rationale for our existence.

This, she claims, is no more than a piece of rhetoric: with different imagery the same facts have a directly opposite meaning. In case the reader should think that a mere philosopher is in no position to second guess a biologist, she quotes the parody of this passage by the Oxford physiologist Denis Noble in his book *The Music of Life*:

> [Genes] are trapped in huge colonies, locked inside highly intelligent beings, moulded by the outside world, communicating with it by complex processes, through which, blindly, as if by magic, function emerges. They are in you and me; we are the systems that allow their code to be read, and their preservation is totally dependent on the joy that we experience in reproducing ourselves. We are the ultimate rationale for their existence.

Neo-Darwinian theorising, Midgley claims, is vitiated by a fundamental error which we can call 'methodological atomism'. This is the belief that physical and biological phenomena are to be understood by focusing on the smallest identifiable individual items involved in the natural processes in question. This leads, in the case of evolution, to a dogmatic emphasis on individual selection as the dominant explanatory factor, in spite of mounting evidence of a significant role for group selection.

The methodological preference, Midgley claims, takes its rise not from an impartial survey of the phenomena to be studied, but rather from an ideological stance that is to be traced back not to any scientific inquirers, but to the philosophers Hobbes and Nietzsche. It was Hobbes who invented the ego that thinks it exists quite on its own, and who believed that a state of pure nature would be a war of every individual against every other individual. It was Nietzsche who exalted solitude and self-assertion as the guiding principle of life.

Not only, Midgley claims, do neo-Darwinians derive their template of evolutionary progress from a philosophy of egoistic individualism; some of them make use of their account of evolution to promote a political agenda of social atomism. They reduce all human motivation to self-interest, and hold out as the only recipe for social co-operation the intellectual enlightenment of that self-interest. In political and economic thinking they insist on tournaments between individuals as central to human life. They may even go so far as to say that there is no such thing as society.

All this, Midgley claims, is very distant from the teaching of Darwin himself, particularly in *The Descent of Man*. Darwin observed that of all the differences between man and the lower animals, the moral sense or conscience is by far the most important. This, for him, is not simply the product of intellect: the central peculiarity of humans is their wider perspective: they have a longer view backwards and forwards in life. He illustrates this in a touching passage about the habit of parent swallows of deserting their young, because their parental instinct is overwhelmed by the urge to migrate. Suppose, he says, they had a human overview of their lives.

> When arrived at the end of her journey, and the migratory instinct ceases to act, what an agony of remorse each bird would feel, if, from being endowed with great mental activity, she could not prevent the image continually passing before her mind of her young ones perishing in the north from cold and hunger.

As in her earlier books, Midgley emphasises the kinship and continuity between human and animal life. In this context she can call in aid Darwin's insistence that *Homo sapiens* is a

social species, with motives that are close to those that make
sociability possible in other species. Other mammals display
parental affection, and our evolutionary cousins, the great apes,
are well known for their rich variety of social interaction. The
human species did not arise as an isolated miracle but as just
one in a wide spectrum of other social creatures.

Darwin, in a passage highlighted by Midgley, explicitly
denounced the Hobbesian tradition:

> Philosophers of the derivative school of morals formerly
> assumed that the foundation of morals lay in a form of
> Selfishness ... [but] [a]ccording to the view given above,
> the moral sense is fundamentally identical with the social
> instincts, and in the case of the lower animals it would
> be absurd to speak of those instincts as having been
> developed from selfishness.

Today's neo-Darwinians are commonly atheists, often of a
particularly pugnacious kind. Midgley has no difficulty in
showing that here too they have come some distance from
Darwin's own position. As he told several correspondents, 'I
have never been an atheist in the sense of denying the existence
of God.' In his autobiography he spoke of the impossibility of
conceiving the universe as the result of blind chance or necessity:
'When thus reflecting I feel compelled to look to a First Cause
having an intelligent mind in some degree analogous to that of
man, and I deserve to be called a theist.' A little later, in the same
work, he said, more cautiously, 'the mystery of the beginning of
all things is insoluble, and I for one must be content to remain
an Agnostic'.

Mary Midgley's bracing polemic is highly readable, and
rhetorically persuasive. The writers she targets can, and no
doubt will, object that the argument is sometimes a little too
brisk. In particular they may complain that neo-Darwinists

of various kinds are lumped together in a way that imputes guilt by association. But she presents them all with a serious challenge, and one must hope that it will be met with argument rather than with abuse.

The Tablet, 15 January 2011

Ian MacKillop
The British Ethical Societies
Cambridge University Press, 1985

'Ethics' in Victorian England meant morality without religion; perhaps, more precisely, moral sentiment and moral uplift without religion. Intellectuals who lost their faith and could no longer accept Christianity in any literal sense were often reluctant to embrace atheism or secular agnosticism. A famous lay sermon given by the philosopher T. H. Green in a Balliol lecture room in 1883 on the text 'By faith, not by sight' offered an Idealist alternative to agnosticism. The sermon was immortalised in Mrs Humphry Ward's novel *Robert Elsmere*; it influenced many of Green's pupils and admirers, including J. H. Muirhead who founded the London Ethical Society. This was the first of a number of societies that catered for serious-minded people who craved religious sentiment without religious dogma. These societies are the subject of Dr MacKillop's book.

The most interesting of these was the work not of a British Idealist but of an American ex-Spiritualist: the Ethical Church of Stanton Coit. Coit, the son of abolitionist parents, celebrated the end of the Civil War, in 1865, at the age of 8, by burning his hand flinging a hot stone at the burning effigy of Jefferson Davis in Columbus, Ohio. At Amherst in the 1870s he fell under the influence of R. W. Emerson, who had preached that there should be

> A new church founded on moral science: at first cold and naked, a babe in the manger again, the algebra and

mathematics of ethical law, the church of men to come, without shawms, or psaltery, or sackbut; but it will have heaven and earth for its beams and rafters; science for symbol and illustration; it will fast enough gather beauty, music, picture, poetry.

After an apprenticeship in New York in Felix Adler's Society for Ethical Culture, and a doctorate at Berlin on *Die innere Sanktion als der Endzweck des moralischen Handelns*, Coit came to London to put Emerson's precepts into practice. From 1887 to 1891 he was minister at the sub-Unitarian chapel of South Place, which he renamed an Ethical Society, giving 50 Sunday ethical addresses a year and devoting his weekdays to social work in Kentish Town. In the late eighties and nineties he founded a West London Ethical Society, an East London Ethical Society, a South London Ethical Society and a St Pancras Ethical Society: four bodies which in 1896 federated a Union of Ethical Societies, the progenitor of the British Humanist Association.

In 1898 Coit founded the Society of Ethical Propagandists, recruited from 'young men, who for conscience sake, cannot take holy orders, but who still desire to become teachers of social righteousness'. The propagandists helped with his journal *The Ethical World* and wrote books with titles like *Onward and Upward: A Book for Boys and Girls*. One of his propagandists, Ramsay MacDonald, went on to become the first Labour Prime Minister. Coit himself twice ran for Parliament in Wakefield, but he was unsuccessful and he returned to London to turn one of his ethical societies into the Bayswater Ethical Church.

Services at Bayswater catered for homesick ex-Anglicans. The service began with an introit, sung from *Ethical Hymns*. There followed opening sentences, perhaps from Emerson. Next followed a Canticle: 'Woe unto him that buildeth his house by unrighteousness, and his chambers by wrong.' No creed was said, of course, but there was a Declaration of Ethical

Principles, followed by a silence. The sermon or discourse was flanked by hymns and anthems, which might be poems of Shelley or Clough set to the music of Palestrina or Bach. After the announcements, the final hymn and the collection, the 'Dismissory Sentences' might be taken from William Blake.

All this took place in a semi-circular church, with two galleries, from the upper of which the choir sang, invisible. A sculptured Buddha and a sculptured Christ stood on fluted wooden plinths on each side of the pulpit. Above the pulpit was a large painting, 'The Torch bearers', depicting seven naked figures running across the top of a globe, set in a blue firmament, passing flaming torches from hand to hand. Stained-glass windows showed Elizabeth Fry, Bernard Shaw and St Joan. A white marble column in front of the lectern was inscribed 'An altar to the Ideal, the True, the Beautiful and the Good'.

The Ethical Church survived until 1953; but Coit, in his seventies, retired in 1933. He devoted his last days as Minister to the translation of Nicolai von Hartmann's *Ethik*, which had been brought to his attention by the American philosopher Sidney Hook. It was not until 1944 that he died, after a long, hale and placid old age.

Like Coit, many of the ethicists described by Dr MacKillop cannot help but appear comic to modern readers. But the reasons for this may well throw more credit on them than on the present age: the last laugh may well be on us. If few people nowadays would find an ethical church inviting, it is partly because the doubts and disbeliefs of the ethicists are now so widespread that no one need fashion a conventicle in which to confess them. Agnostics who would have been turned out of doors by a Victorian parson are now welcomed with open arms if they are willing to attend church at all. From a religious point of view, ethicists have withered away as victims of their own success. From a moral point of view, can we be so sure that our casual permissiveness is superior to their scrupulous solemnity?

The Listener, 12 March 1986

PART FIVE

THE TWENTIETH CENTURY

Introduction

The twentieth century saw two opposite movements in the history of Christianity. Within Protestantism the official Churches became more flexible and tolerant of doctrinal diversity; the Catholic Church, on the contrary, became more centralised and authoritarian. Neither strategy prevented church members, in large numbers, from lapsing into secularism or decamping to ephemeral fringe congregations.

After the papacy lost its temporal dominions in 1870 it sought to increase its international spiritual authority. In the same year the Vatican Council proclaimed the dogma of papal infallibility. Aided by the accelerating speed of international communication, the successors of Pius IX strengthened papal control over the appointment of bishops and the details of teaching in schools and seminaries worldwide. A biblical commission laid down strict rules for the interpretation of particular controversial passages of Scripture. In 1917 a Code of Canon Law set up a uniform international regimen of church government and practice. Concordats between the Vatican and the governments of individual countries were drawn up over the heads of the local hierarchies. A climax of papal triumphalism came when in 1950 Pope Pius XII in the exercise of his infallible authority proclaimed as a doctrine of the Christian faith the Assumption into Heaven of the Blessed Virgin Mary.

Meanwhile, the mainstream Protestant Churches were shedding rather than adding dogmas. To take the Church of England as an example, the Thirty-Nine Articles, which had been a stumbling block for many liberal clergy in the nineteenth century, began to be reinterpreted or sidelined in ways that would have astonished the divines who drew them up. (This process, ironically, had been begun by the Romanising members of the Oxford Movement in the nineteenth century.) In matters of sexual morality, the Church of England gradually adopted more permissive attitudes to divorce and contraception. A landmark in this process was the Lambeth Conference of 1930.

When, in 1959, Pope John XXIII convened the Second Vatican Council, it looked for a while as if the Catholic drive to centralisation had been reversed. The authority of the episcopate was affirmed alongside that of the papacy, vernacular liturgies replaced the uniform Latin of the Mass, the role of the laity was recognised in the formulation of belief and practice. Significantly, the Council instituted a new alignment in the Catholic attitude to other Christian Churches. While it did not authorise full communion with Protestant and Orthodox believers, the Council inaugurated a new era of co-operation and collaboration with them. Joint commissions to study doctrinal issues identified many points of congruence between Catholics, Lutherans and Anglicans in the understanding of the nature of grace, sacraments and the nature of the Church itself.

However, the period of rapprochement proved short-lived. Pope Paul VI and still more his successors John Paul II and Benedict XVI strove to reinforce those elements in Catholicism that in the twentieth century marked it off from other Christian denominations. Against the advice of his own expert commission, Paul VI reaffirmed the traditional condemnation of contraception. John Paul II marginalised the organisations by which the fathers of Vatican II had sought to balance the power of the papacy with the influence of the episcopate. Benedict XVI opened the door for a reintroduction of the once universal Latin liturgy.

At the present time the matters that obstruct the reunification of Christian Churches are as much matters of discipline as of dogma. The most important such issue is that of the ordination of women as priests and bishops. Conservative Catholics try to present this as a matter of doctrine, but only by the argument that since all the apostles were male, only males can be priests. This is no more convincing than would be an argument that since St Peter was married, only married men can be popes.

John Cornwell
Hitler's Pope: The Secret History of Pius XII
Viking, 1999

Pius XII, pope during the Second World War, has long been condemned for his reluctance to condemn Nazi Germany and to protest against the massacre of Jews in the Holocaust. In 1943 Sir D'Arcy Osborne, the British envoy to the Holy See, told Pius that 'a policy of silence in regard to such offences against the conscience of the world must necessarily involve an abdication of moral leadership'. From that day to this, many writers, including some Catholics, have claimed that by his reticence in the face of unparalleled atrocity, Pius shamefully disgraced his high office. Others, including some Jews, have vigorously defended his wartime role, and today in the Vatican the legal processes are well advanced towards his proclamation as a saint.

Traditionally, in every such canonisation, an official (the Promotor Fidei, popularly called 'The Devil's Advocate') was charged with making as strong a case as possible *against* the candidate for sainthood. Today, the adversarial pattern of proceedings has given way to a more investigative process; but in this book John Cornwell, himself a Catholic and once a partisan of Pius, offers a devastating devil's advocate's brief. Unlike some other authors, he does not restrict his criticisms to the Pope's conduct during the war. Many of his most damning accusations are made against the young Eugenio Pacelli as he rose through the Vatican civil service for 38 years before reaching its summit in 1939. In preparing his case, he had access to the evidence provided by witnesses in the procedures leading to canonisation, and to the archives of the Vatican secretariat of state.

Cornwell's principal charges against Pacelli are these:

1. In 1914 he was responsible for a treaty ('concordat') between Serbia and the Holy See that was a cause of the outbreak of the First World War.

2. He was the principal author of the Code of Canon Law of 1917, which centralised the Catholic Church and gave the papacy the unprecedented powers that he was himself later to abuse.

3. As the Pope's nuncio or ambassador in Germany in the 1920s he drew up concordats with Bavaria and Prussia that reduced the powers of the local, anti-Nazi bishops.

4. As Cardinal Secretary of State from 1930 he forced the German Catholic Centre party to vote in favour of giving Adolf Hitler dictatorial powers and eventually to disband itself.

5. By the time of the 1933 Reich concordat, which he secured by these means, he cut the ground from under the Catholic opposition to Nazism and secured Hitler in power.

6. Once he became Pope, in 1939, he softened the anti-Nazi stance that had been belatedly adopted by his predecessor Pius XI.

7. In 1941 and 1942 he turned a blind eye to the persecution of the Serbs and Jews in Croatia.

8. He was deaf to all appeals to condemn the Holocaust, of whose horrors he was kept fully informed.

9. During the German occupation of Rome, he was indifferent to the deportation of Jews to death camps, and was concerned only with the autonomy of the Vatican and the preservation of the Holy City.

10. In the years after the war he used the Pope's absolute
power over Catholics to suppress theological debate
and to impose a repressive morality.

Not all of these charges are of equal gravity and not all are
convincingly substantiated. (Was the young Pacelli in charge of
the negotiations with Serbia, and did they really cause the First
World War? Was the Code of Canon Law so much more than
a codification of existing canons?) Cornwell's denunciations of
Pius when he did wrong would be more effective if they were
not accompanied by sneers when he was doing good (as when
relieving starvation in Germany in 1918, or striving to instil
ethical principles in the 1950s). But when all this has been
discounted, there remains a case for the prosecution that is very
substantial.

Some distinctions, however, need to be made. Was Pacelli,
as Cornwell maintains, anti-Semitic? In answering this
question we must distinguish between religious and racist
anti-Semitism. Religiously, Pacelli – like every other Catholic
of his age – was anti-Semitic in the sense that he believed that
the Jewish religion was inadequate for salvation, and that the
conversion of Jews to the Catholic faith was universally to be
desired. But he was no racist, as is shown precisely by the warm
welcome he gave to Jewish converts, such as the Chief Rabbi
in Rome, Israel Zolli, who took refuge from the Germans in
the Vatican and gratefully accepted baptism after the war. Of
course, to a Jew who finds Catholic proselytism offensive in
the first place, it merely adds insult to injury when Catholics
make a sharp distinction between the sufferings of converted
and unconverted Jews, as the German bishops did when they
protested against the Nuremberg laws. But it is quite unfair to
equate the attitude of Pius and the bishops with that of Hitler
and the Nazis who persecuted Jews because of their descent,
no matter what their current religious or political affiliation.

The stereotyping *obiter dicta* that Cornwell quotes to prove Pacelli a racist can, sadly, be paralleled in the correspondence or table talk of almost any member of the non-Jewish European intelligentsia in the first decades of the century.

Cornwell's Pacelli is not a coherent character. While nuncio and Secretary of State, he pursues consistently, skilfully and sometimes ruthlessly a single goal of Catholic advancement. But once he becomes Pope, he no longer seems to know his own mind. At one moment he takes every precaution to avoid offending the German government; at another he does his best to assist a generals' plot to oust the Führer. The euphemistic circumlocution of his criticism of Nazism contrasts sharply with the forthright eloquence of his denunciation of communism. The lowest point of the pontificate is reached on 16 October 1943, when Jews were deported from Rome. Pius spent the day in Hamlet-like indecision – when even Hitler's own ambassador was urging him to make a public protest.

Cornwell offers no very convincing explanation of the character he depicts. The reason is, perhaps, that he is too inclined to blame the Pope personally for policies and attitudes that flowed from his position as head of the Catholic Church. His anger might more properly be directed to the institution rather than to the man. Pius XII was not indifferent to the fate of the Jews: there is no reason to doubt that he was appalled and anguished by their fate. But their sufferings took second place to his concern for Catholics, and his decisions were guided, above all, by his judgement as to which actions and inactions would best promote the safety and welfare of Catholics. Communism and Nazism were both inconsistent with Catholic teaching, but communists attacked priests and religious as a matter of policy, whereas Nazis did not: that is what accounts for the difference in the Pope's attitude to the two malign ideologies.

There is nothing surprising or novel in such a papal attitude. It was normal Catholic teaching that whether you are a Catholic or not is of much greater importance, in the light of eternity, than what crimes you have committed. This was stated, with stark clarity, in the Pope's encyclical of 1943, *Mystici Corporis*, which Cornwell quotes. But it is wrong to suggest, as Cornwell does, that it was a novelty to emphasise the soul over the body and to attach supreme importance to the eternal life of which the Church has the key. Such had been papal teaching ever since there had been a papacy.

In one respect, Cornwell is perhaps too kind. He acquits Pius, on several occasions, of the charge of pusillanimity. It is hard to deny, however, that the Pope's loudest condemnations were of those who were furthest away, and that his support for the plot against Hitler came at a time when Italy was not yet a belligerent. (Even at home he never plucked up courage to fire his impossible and terrifying housekeeper, Mother Pasqualina.) On the fateful 16 October his dominant emotion was a worry that the Vatican would be invaded, whether by German storm troopers or communist partisans. The most obvious motive for his silence about the Holocaust was fear – fear that whatever he said would make matters worse. It is hard for us, and perhaps it was hard for him too, to determine how much was fear for himself and how much was fear on behalf of the Church; just as in his lifelong love of pomp, it is hard to know how much was reverence for the office he held and how much was, in Cornwell's phrase, 'self-incensing'.

Certainly, it ill becomes us, who have never had the Pope's awesome responsibilities or shared the pressures and dangers he underwent, to accuse him of cowardice. Cornwell seems willing to acquit him of that charge only because he has more grievous accusations to press. He succeeds, in my view, in showing that many of Pacelli's actions and omissions had catastrophic political consequences. He fails, however, to prove that Pacelli was a wicked man: bad political judgement, however disastrous, does not amount to wickedness. But to say that he was not a monster is not to say that he was a saint: there are possibilities in-between. A saint, according to Catholic teaching, is a person who practises heroic virtue, and the facts related in Cornwell's book show beyond doubt that whatever Pacelli's virtues may have been, they were not the virtues of a hero.

Weekend Post, Toronto, 6 November 1999

Garry Wills
Papal Sin: Structures of Deceit
Doubleday, 2000

In these days of ecumenism, if you come across a swingeing attack on the papacy, it is very likely written by a Catholic. So it is here. Garry Wills is a devout Mass-goer and the author of an engaging life of St Augustine; he sees himself as the heir of medieval writers and painters like Dante and Orcagna who were not afraid to place popes in the depths of hell. The book's theme is that the role of the papacy in the modern world has created a sustained bias towards dishonesty. The Vatican, Wills maintains, issues dictates and employs arguments which even its own priests cannot take seriously; the respect they have to pretend for them forces them into a life of deceit.

Wills' first attack is on the Church's relationship to the Jewish people. The present pope has been a good friend to Jews, but Wills believes that he is too eager to cover up the Church's anti-Semitic past, which is illustrated with the story of how Pope Pius IX kidnapped a 6-year-old Jewish boy, Edgardo Mortara, in order to bring him up as a Catholic. In 1998 John Paul II canonised Edith Stein, the converted Jewish nun who died at Auschwitz in 1942. To do so, Wills maintains, he had to misrepresent the motives of Stein's killers and to claim as a miracle a cure that medical experts regarded as normal. It is a distortion of history to see victims of the Holocaust as Catholic martyrs.

If some of the sins Wills castigates are attempts to distort and disown the past, most of his criticisms concern something quite different. The papacy is criticised for *not* being willing to disown its past, and for persisting in teachings which many of the faithful dislike and ignore.

In 1864 Pius IX drew up a Syllabus condemning a number of errors of the modern world. These 'errors' included liberty of conscience, the separation of Church and State, and freedom of worship. The final condemned proposition read, 'The Roman Pontiff can, and ought, to reconcile himself and come to terms with progress, liberalism, and modern civilization.'

Wills' book can be seen as a counterbalancing Syllabus of papal errors. Among the erroneous doctrines Wills condemns are the following: the use of contraceptives is sinful; women may not be ordained to the priesthood; celibacy should remain obligatory for priests; the Bible condemns homosexuality as unnatural; abortion is against the natural law.

Wills does not deny that all these doctrines have been taught by the Church for a very long time. His criticism is that the teaching continues even though the original reasons in support of it have been given up. What is deceitful is the substitution of new, and usually incredible, arguments to shore up conclusions detached from their original premises.

Wills makes a particularly strong case in connection with the ordination of women. Over the centuries two reasons were given for excluding women from the priesthood: that they were inferior beings unworthy to hold that dignity, and that they should not approach the altar because of their ritual impurity. Neither of these positions would be defended by the Church today, and thus bizarre symbolic reasons are dreamt up for restricting the priesthood to males. The primary reason for this is to avoid the loss of face in changing the rule.

Again, the prohibition on contraception, Wills claims, was historically linked to the erroneous view that the male semen alone contained the blueprint for developing a future human being. By 1965 a majority of the Vatican's own expert advisers had ceased to believe that contraception was against the natural law; but Paul VI reaffirmed the traditional teaching in his encyclical *Humanae Vitae*. If the Church reversed itself now, as one of his spokesmen put it, 'it would prove that the Holy Spirit had been with the Anglicans at Lambeth, not with the Pope in Rome'.

Not all of Wills' criticisms are well taken, and at times he lapses into the exaggerated rhetoric and selective Scripture quotation for which he castigates the popes. But *Papal Sins* is eloquently written and compulsively readable, and deserves to be taken seriously by defenders of the papacy. The book does, however, leave one wondering why Wills himself remains attached to an institution that he thinks has gone so badly astray.

Someone who thinks that the Pope is in such serious moral error should surely think twice about serving under his banner. There is no need to conclude, as some Protestants have done, that the Pope is Antichrist. Let us not question that he is fighting on the side of Christ. Yet a Catholic who shares Wills' views must surely regard him as a very untrustworthy leader. A pope who teaches his worldwide flock that contraception is a mortal sin, when it is in fact perfectly permissible, is like a general who sends millions of his soldiers into a pointless battle in which they will likely be killed. The Pope is, indeed, in worse case than the general because (in his own view of the matter) the death to which he is condemning his followers is an eternal one.

National Post, Toronto, 24 June 2000

Hans Küng
Disputed Truth: Memoirs, trans. John Bowden
Continuum, 2008

Of all Roman Catholic theologians Hans Küng must be one of the best known: for many years he was a darling of the media, he has lectured all over the world and his books have been translated into a multitude of languages. In fact, only one Catholic theologian can claim greater fame: Joseph Ratzinger, who in 1968, when this second volume of memoirs commences, was Küng's colleague in the theology faculty at Tübingen. The two men had been the youngest theologians summoned to the Second Vatican Council in 1962. Today Ratzinger is Pope Benedict XVI, while Küng now presents himself as a kind of unofficial antipope, the leader of His Holiness's loyal opposition.

Küng's disaffection with the official Church, as here narrated, went through three different, though overlapping, stages. Between the end of the Council in 1965 and 1970 he was primarily concerned to advocate reforms in current church discipline: a removal of the ban on artificial contraception, a more welcoming attitude to mixed marriages, a greater role for women in the Church, the relaxation of compulsory celibacy for the clergy, recognition of the sacramental life of non-Catholic Christians, and a democratisation of the election of bishops and the pope. From 1970 onwards he made a more frontal attack on the hierarchical Church by denying the key Roman doctrine that the pope, and the bishops as a collectivity, are infallible in their solemn teaching on matters of faith and morals. In the

third and final stage he set himself to reinterpret fundamental
Christian doctrines concerning the person and nature of Jesus
the Son of God. He did so in a way which appeared to many
to evacuate these doctrines of any substantial significance. This
third stage lasted from 1974 until 1979 when his licence to teach
Catholic theology was revoked on orders from the Vatican.

During the first of these phases Küng could reckon on wide
support within the Roman Catholic Church. Many observant
Catholics did, and do, long for precisely the reforms he was
advocating. They felt, and feel, that the prospect of democratic
renovation in the Church held out by Vatican II had proved
illusory, as conservative curial control was re-imposed from the
top. They would agree with Küng that the internationalisation
of the Church turned out to be only external, the collegialisation
only apparent, and the decentralisation only cosmetic.

In 1970, the year in which he was listed by *Time* as one of
the 100 most important people in the world, Küng published a
book with the title *Infallible?* The publication date was 18 July,
the centenary of the definition of papal infallibility at the First
Vatican Council. The book called in question the scriptural and
ecumenical foundation for papal infallibility and claimed that
the infallibility of the episcopate was a Counter-Reformation
invention of Robert Bellarmine. To be able to write such a
book, Küng tells us, 'one must be as expert in Roman theology
as in German exegesis and history of dogma. One must have a
degree of independence, say as a university professor, and at the
same time a rare steadfastness. One must have an appropriate
scholarly method and a precise and understandable style.'
This is a fair, if not unduly modest, description of Küng's own
qualifications.

An attack on church infallibility might seem to be of little
interest to anyone except Roman Catholics, since no one else
has ever believed the doctrine. Anyone who does not accept the
authority of the Roman Church must think that at least one of

its solemn doctrines is erroneous; and if any one such doctrine is wrong then infallibility must be a fiction. But in fact the issue of infallibility has a much wider significance: because if a church claims infallibility it rules out for itself the possibility of correcting its past mistakes. Indeed when the doctrine of papal infallibility was first mooted in the fourteenth century, the Pope of the day, John XXII, denounced it as a pestiferous doctrine, because it would prevent him from overruling decisions of his predecessors.

Those who dislike the First Vatican Council's definition of papal infallibility often comfort themselves with the thought that it was softened down at the Second Council. In fact the scope of infallibility was widened rather than narrowed when Vatican II defined, without discussion, that the ordinary magisterium of bishops was infallible. The wrongness of contraception has never – unlike, say, the Assumption of the Virgin Mary – been the subject of a solemn papal definition; but there is no doubt that for many decades the bishops have consistently taught it. Hence the difficulty the Church has felt in revising this teaching, and hence the global importance of the issue of infallibility.

Many non-Catholics welcomed Küng's attack on the doctrine. The Secretary of the World Council of Churches told him that if his ideas were accepted in Catholicism 'Protestantism will no longer have any serious reason for protesting'. Reaction among Roman Catholics was rather different. The German, French and Italian bishops condemned the book, and the revered Jesuit Karl Rahner enrolled 14 leading theologians to write a critical response. In July 1971 the Inquisition (now renamed the Council for the Doctrine of the Faith) began proceedings against the book, and its Prefect wrote to Küng in August asking him to show how his theses could be reconciled with Catholic doctrine. Küng, engaged on a world tour, did not reply for nearly six months. His response took the form of a series of procedural complaints: he had not been given access to his dossier, he had not been allowed a choice of defence counsel, he had been given too short notice for a reply, and no clear account had been given of the basis of complaint.

In July 1973 the Inquisition published a declaration on the Catholic Doctrine of the Church (*Mysterium Ecclesiae*). Though no names were mentioned, it was clearly aimed at Küng. The German cardinals, in a meeting in 1974, told him that if he accepted the declaration all proceedings against him would be dropped. He refused to do so, and consistently rejected summonses to wait on the Inquisition in Rome. Eventually, in February 1975, proceedings against *Infallible?* were terminated. The Roman authorities believed, rightly or wrongly, that Küng had agreed to keep silent thenceforth on the topic of infallibility.

Now, in the third stage of the quarrel, the focus shifted to a new book, *On Being a Christian* (1974). For centuries Christians, whether Catholic, Orthodox or Protestant, have believed that Jesus, in the words of the fifth-century Council of Chalcedon, is truly God and truly man, a single person sharing the divine nature of the Father and the human nature of mankind. In his book, without challenging head-on this historic definition, Küng offered to interpret it for present-day Christians in such a way as to liberate them from the Hellenistic terminology in which it was couched.

On publication the book became an international best-seller and simultaneously made its author a more than ever controversial figure. It was denounced in print by a group of well-known theologians led by the heavyweight Urs von Balthasar. Küng professes to be shocked and dismayed by the attacks on his Christology. To prove his orthodoxy, he quotes more than once in his memoir the following passage:

> [F]or believers, God himself as man's friend was present at work, speaking, acting, and definitively revealing himself

> in this Jesus who came among men as God's advocate and
> deputy, representative and delegate, and was confirmed by
> God as the Crucified raised to life.

The subjectivising introduction 'for believers' makes this a statement that could be accepted by an atheist. If this passage is the closest that the book comes to traditional orthodoxy, one can hardly be surprised that it was regarded as wholly insufficient by those who held the age-old Christian belief in the eternal pre-existence of Jesus as God's Word and Son.

In 1977 the German conference of bishops distributed a lengthy declaration denouncing _On Being a Christian_. Still no action was taken in Rome against the author in person. But in 1978 the timidly liberal Paul VI was succeeded by the hard-knuckled conservative John Paul II. In 1979 Küng took two provocative steps: he broke his silence on the topic of infallibility and he published worldwide a set of bitterly critical reflections on the new Pope's first year in office. Retribution was not slow in coming. In December the German bishops announced that Küng had violated the terms of the 1975 agreement and that his permission to teach in a Catholic theology faculty had been withdrawn by the Vatican. 'He no longer speaks in the name of the Church,' the statement ran; but 'he is not excluded from the Church and he remains a priest'.

The removal of the licence to teach did not end Küng's theological career. Initially the entire faculty of Catholic theology at Tubingen protested against the proceedings. The local bishop, who under the concordat between Germany and the Holy See had the responsibility for putting the Vatican decision into effect, was reluctant to do so and vainly endeavoured (with little co-operation from Küng, who went skiing) to get it withdrawn. But John Paul II was adamant, and by February a majority of the Tübingen Catholic theologians (seven out of twelve) accepted that Küng should be expelled from their faculty. He continued to refuse to recant or to answer any summons to Rome. In the end he secured a compromise whereby he remained a professor in his university on full salary, a member of no faculty but presiding over an ecumenical institute reporting directly to the Senate and President.

The story is a remarkable one, and its telling is full of drama. For a single theologian to stand up against the majesty and power of the hierarchical Church demanded quite unusual determination. One should not underestimate the courage required to reject repeated demands for recantation from ecclesiastical authorities when one has been brought up to believe that one's eternal fate depends on one's status in the eyes of those very authorities. It was a very considerable achievement for a Catholic priest to maintain an unorthodox stance over decades without being either unfrocked or excommunicated.

Küng believes that he was treated outrageously by the Church and by his colleagues. The Roman proceedings against him were clearly a shambles, but the eventual outcome surprises not by its brutality but by its leniency. A church, no less than a political party or a professional body, has the right to determine what can and cannot be said and done in its name. The proceedings against Küng appear stately and generous by contrast with, say, Edward Heath's instant dismissal of Enoch Powell after his 'rivers of blood' speech, or the Royal Society's swift reaction to the suggestion of one of its officers that intelligent design should be confronted in the science classroom.

Given the three stages of confrontation that we have identified, it is clear that it became harder and harder for Küng's friends and colleagues to continue to support him without renouncing their faith. But in his eyes the story is one of cowardice and betrayal. A band of brothers is broken up as one after the other succumbs to pressure and drops out, until at last only our Hans is in step. In the book, a Curse of Gnome attaches to those theologians who let its author down. Cardinal Danielou dies in the arms of a 24-year-old danseuse. Karl Rahner's reputation is dashed by the posthumous publication of a series of love letters. Urs von Balthasar dies in ambiguous circumstances the day before he is due to receive a cardinal's hat.

By 2007, Küng tells us on his first page, 'almost all my great comrades-in-arms in the fight for the renewal of theology and the church since the time of the Council are dead or inactive, with one exception, and he has become Pope'. At every point in the story the author compares his conduct and achievements with those of Ratzinger, and the comparison is always to his own advantage. Küng, we learn, was socially superior, wrote the better dissertations and was more courageous during the student revolution. It is he who was the better Scripture scholar and the more up-to-date theologian, and it was he who was the more honest in controversy and negotiation. This is one of the least attractive features of this book. Even if we let ourselves suppose that all these statements are true, Küng should not be the person making them.

No doubt a high valuation of one's self-worth provides great support when one has to stand alone against powerful and oppressive authority. But it is not essential. Nelson Mandela, for instance, stood up to much greater hardship in the service of a much solider cause; but his autobiography does not breathe any air of self-conceit.

Every reader will put down this book with one question: why does Küng remain a Catholic at all? His conception of the Church has long been much closer to Lutheranism than to post-Reformation Catholicism, and he has clearly no sentimental attachment to Catholic devotional practices, many of which he dismisses as medieval accretions. He himself offers no answer except that one does not migrate from one's fatherland; a slightly odd statement from a Swiss who has spent his working life in Germany.

Küng is fond of attributing base motives to colleagues who criticised him: this one acted out of pique, that one out of spite, a third because he wanted to be a bishop, a fourth because his books were not selling well enough. If we are to indulge in this unlovely practice, we might conjecture that Küng remained a Catholic because if he had left the Church he would have lost the celebrity status that he clearly relishes. He would have disappeared from sight like the late Father Charles Davis, the only English theologian mentioned in the book.

Against this, it must be said that if early in his life Küng had been willing to compromise his independence he would undoubtedly have enjoyed the glittering ecclesiastical career which awaited many of his more compliant theological colleagues. We may end with a joke that he tells against himself. The story went round that during a conclave the cardinals reached an impasse; it was decided, in order to break the deadlock, to inquire whether Küng would be willing to be drafted as pope. 'No way!' he told the Vatican emissaries, 'I don't want to give up being infallible.'

Times Literary Supplement, 12 December 2008

James Hagerty
Cardinal John Carmel Heenan: Priest of the People, Prince of the Church
Gracewing, 2012

None of the Cardinal Archbishops of Westminster has deserved a full-length biography more than John Carmel Heenan (1905–75). Not that he outshone in character or intellect his predecessors and successors: rather, his episcopal career straddled the most dramatic period in the history of English Catholicism since the restoration of the Hierarchy in 1850. Surprisingly, we have had to wait nearly forty years since his death for such a book. This is no accident. In his lifetime, Heenan refused permission for the preparation of a biography and himself published two pre-emptive memoirs.

Dr Hagerty takes us through the stages of a remarkable career. Born in Ilford, Essex, in 1905, John Carmel decided in 1913 that he had a vocation to the priesthood. He was educated by the Jesuits at Stamford Hill and in the junior seminary at Ushaw. A scholarship enabled him to proceed in 1924 to the English College in Rome to study philosophy and theology at the Pontifical Gregorian University.

The English College, then under the rectorship of the future Cardinal Hinsley, had two notable characteristics: loyalty to the Holy See, combined with English exceptionalism. Centuries of persecution, so the staff and students believed, gave the heirs of English recusants an insight into the essence of the Catholic Church unshared by Catholics in other countries. The attitude of the seminarists to their continental confrères at the

Gregorian University was not altogether unlike that of today's UKIP members to continental citizens of the EU. The ethos of the college marked Heenan for life, and his experience at the Gregorian gave him a lifelong distaste for theology.

Once ordained, Heenan returned to England to work in the Brentwood diocese. As a curate, his pastoral concern was exemplary, triumphing over obstacles placed by his parish priest and his bishop. At the then unusual age of 32 he became a parish priest himself. Of all the offices he held throughout his life this was the one in which he most revelled.

In 1947 Heenan became superior of the Catholic Missionary Society. In this role he travelled the country, encouraging individual parishes to improve their Catholic practice and discussing religious issues in public places with potentially hostile audiences. The debating practice obtained at this time stood him in good stead when he became, on radio and television, the national spokesman for Roman Catholics. A fluent writer, by the time he left the Society he had published 12 books of popular apologetics and pastoral piety, of which *The People's Priest* (1951) became the best known.

Promotion to the episcopacy became inevitable. From 1951 to 1957 Heenan was Bishop of Leeds. He decided that he needed to wake up a sleepy diocese, and he did so by moving priests from one parish to another at an unprecedented rate. This gave Leeds the nickname of 'the cruel see' and led to the canard that at his final Vatican audience as Bishop the Pope was left in tears, lamenting to his aides, 'He has moved me to Avignon.'

Promoted to be Archbishop of Liverpool (1957–63), Heenan was more circumspect in his relations with the clergy. But he took many significant decisions. Dedicated, like many of his colleagues, to the preservation of segregated Catholic education, he presided over the building of 49 schools. Saddled by his predecessors with plans for a gigantic cathedral which the archdiocese was never going to afford, he held a competition for the design of a more modest building. This resulted in 1967 in the opening of an imaginative, if controversial, building of modern design in modern materials, a crowned rotunda which has since been a notable feature of the Liverpool skyline.

The Vatican Council (1962–65), in the course of which Heenan was translated from Liverpool to Westminster, was a turning point in his life. Forever loyal to successive popes, he found uncongenial the direction in which many of the Council fathers wished to take the Church. His distaste for academic theology found expression in speeches attacking the experts, or *periti*, who came from monasteries, seminaries or universities: he saw them as ignorant of 'the real world'. For him theology consisted in an unquestioning acceptance of Vatican dictates, even if that meant (as in the case of the morality of contraception) a reversal of his own considered opinion on the topic. And for him the worst sin was 'giving scandal' – that meant doing anything that showed the Church in a bad light, even if it was a true light. This laid up trouble for his successors.

As Archbishop of Westminster, Heenan was uncomfortable in implementing the reforms initiated by the Council – the revision of the liturgy, the empowerment of the laity, the ecumenical approach to the separated Churches. His last years were saddened by the defection of so many of his priests, especially figures of the clerical intelligentsia – Charles Davis, Peter de Rosa, Hubert Richards and others.

Heenan was a classical tragic figure: a man of many virtues whose career was shattered by a single debilitating fault, which was well described by his assistant Bishop Butler:

He thinks (almost unconsciously) of the faithful as a crowd of uneducated East Londoners of the first decade of this century; and any lay person who shows more than

a purely passive acceptance of the penny catechism is,
for him, a tiresome person who does not understand his
proper position in the Church.

Hagerty writes soberly and fairly; he documents carefully and
he is not afraid to record episodes he considers disastrous
mistakes. Rather than being judgemental himself he prefers to
record criticisms voiced by others. His book presents a balanced
history of the Roman Catholic Church in England and Wales
as seen from Heenan's desk. It does not, however, place it in
the broader context of the universal Church: thus, he seems
to accept Heenan's view that Cardinal Bea and Monsignor
Willebrands, who engaged in constructive dialogue with
Anglican prelates, were interfering continental busybodies. On
the other hand Hagerty gives us no intimate picture of Heenan
as a man: his sources seem to be almost exclusively published
works and official correspondence. We look in vain for private
personal letters; maybe there were none.

However, I can testify that Heenan was not the heartless
apparatchik depicted by many of his critics. As Hagerty narrates,
when a young priest in the Liverpool archdiocese I fell into
disfavour because I several times attacked in print the British
Government's policy of nuclear deterrence. I failed to persuade
the Archbishop of the immorality of the policy and eventually
he forbade me to write in diocesan publications. During one
of our discussions I recall saying to him, 'Episcopacy corrupts,
and archiepiscopacy corrupts absolutely' (a remark of which, I
regret to say, I was at the time rather proud).

Later in life, as Master of an Oxford college during the years
of student revolt, I had my own experience of dealing with
bright and bumptious young men who were confident that they
were in possession of the moral high ground. I cannot recall
any of them ever being as rude to me as I had been to Heenan.

Yet he continued to exhibit a benevolent, and indeed generous, care for my welfare.

The Tablet, 2 March 2013

Karen Armstrong
The Battle for God
Alfred A. Knopf, 1999

Jim Wallis
Faith Works
Random House, 1999

Karen Armstrong, once a Roman Catholic nun and teacher, is now well known in the United Kingdom and the United States as a broadcaster and writer; she reached the best-seller lists with *A History of God*. This new work is not really one book, but two. The reader would do well to start with the second one, for it is very much better than the first and does not depend upon the first to be intelligible.

Part One tells the history of the sects of Christianity, Judaism and Islam from the fatal year 1492 in which the Muslims finally lost their grip on Western Europe, the Jews were driven out of Spain, and the Christians began their expansion into the New World. It moves at a breathless pace: it is simultaneously too erudite and too superficial. One after another, sects, reformers and prophets make a brief appearance and are swept off again, leaving the reader bewildered and confused.

Part Two is a history of four types of fundamentalism from 1870 to the present day. By 'fundamentalism' Armstrong means 'militant piety'. There are fundamentalist versions of many religions, but she selects for treatment Protestant fundamentalism in America, Jewish fundamentalism in Israel, and Muslim fundamentalism in Sunni Egypt and in Shiite Iran. These monotheistic traditions have in common that they are 'religions of the book' with privileged texts at their base: the Bible, the New Testament and the Quran. All these fundamentalists have in common a claim to be in exclusive possession of the authentic interpretation of their sacred books.

Armstrong sees the heyday of fundamentalism as being between 1960 and 1979, with the 1960s as years of mobilisation and 1974–79 as a period of offensive. She tells the story of the development of an Islamic liberation theology in Egypt, and the resistance to secular and westernising government initiatives that led to the assassination of Anwar Sadat in 1981, an act justified by Sunni fundamentalists as part of a war against the apostasy typified by the Camp David peace between Egypt and Israel. She shows how Camp David was seen as an abomination also by some in Israel, who regarded the territories won in the Six Day War of 1967 as irrevocably committed by God to Jewish settlement. In a detailed and gripping narrative she shows how in Iran the secularisation ruthlessly imposed by the Pahlavi monarchy, abetted by the 'Great Satan' of the United States, provoked the Islamic evolution that installed Ayatollah Khomeini in power and led to the lengthy imprisonment of American hostages in Tehran.

The year of the Islamic revolution, 1979, was also the year of the creation by Jerry Falwell of the Moral Majority, which turned fundamentalism into a political movement that helped bring Ronald Reagan to power in the USA. It was also the year that saw the election of Margaret Thatcher as Prime Minister in Britain. All the fundamentalisms we encounter in this book are in part protests against the permissive, relativist, materialist culture of Western democracies, seen as destructive of community values. The philosophy of Thatcher and Reagan, though it called itself 'conservative', can itself be regarded as a liberalist fundamentalism, a return to the original, unregulated, materialistic competitiveness of laissez-faire economics. 'There is no such thing as society,' Thatcher famously said, and Adam Smith's work was invoked as Thatcherism's defining charter.

Fundamentalists cling to the literal interpretation of their foundation texts, but as Armstrong observes they are selective in the portions they stress. Jim Wallis is no fundamentalist, although he was 'saved' when he was six years old by a fiery evangelist who told him, 'If Jesus came back tonight, your mommy and daddy would be taken to heaven, and you would be left all by yourself.' He too, however, is selective in the texts he emphasises. They are not the first verses of Genesis, but Isaiah's exhortations 'to share your bread with the hungry, and bring the homeless poor into your house'.

With a history of anti-war civil disobedience and political activism, Jim Wallis is the founder of the Sojourners community of Columbia Heights, a refuge for endangered children in a rundown portion of Washington DC. He is the convener of Call to Renewal, a federation of faith-based organisations that are trying to overcome poverty. He is a preacher, and his book is really a series of sermons. They are good sermons, whose appeal will be all the wider because they have little or no dogmatic content. He draws inspiration from many Christian traditions, and his heroes include Nelson Mandela as well as Martin Luther King, Dorothy Day and Cardinal Bernardin of Chicago.

Wallis does not conceal his dislike for the religious right in the USA, and his own version of Protestantism is clearly liberal rather than evangelical. But he aims to transcend the dichotomies of liberal and conservative, left and right. He writes:

> It's true enough that the conservative ideals like personal responsibility, hard work, strong families and moral values are absolutely essential for social change, as are the liberal ideals of social and racial justice, human rights,

and economic fairness. But the old solutions posed by conservatives and liberals have created false choices between these ideals.

The book is full of examples of individuals and groups who have tried to combine the best in both traditions in order to overcome social problems in US cities such as Boston, Los Angeles and Chicago.

'Religion', an atheist friend once said to me, 'makes good people better and bad people worse.' On this basis one could say that Armstrong's book is about the way in which religion makes bad people worse, and Wallis's book is about the way in which religion makes good people better. But there is an artificiality in the idea that people can be classified as good or bad in advance of their religious identity. There is good and bad in all of us, and what is true in my friend's remark is that, when a person is extraordinarily virtuous, or extraordinarily vicious, there is very often a religious motive at work. This is vividly illustrated in the stories of saints and fanatics that fill the pages of these two different, but equally instructive, books.

Weekend Post, Toronto, 22 May 2000

Arthur Kirsch
Auden and Christianity
Yale University Press, £18.95

W. H. Auden was born into a devout Anglo-Catholic family, and was confirmed at the age of 13. During the 1920s and 1930s he lost interest in religion, devoting his passion to social and political causes. In 1940, however, after his migration to America, he resumed religious practice and for the latter part of his life was a serious member of the Anglican Communion.

A volume Auden published in 1944 contained a poem entitled 'The Sea and the Mirror: A Commentary on Shakespeare's Tempest'. This, he told Ursula Niebuhr, was an attempt to work out a Christian theory of art. The religious message of the poem, however, has mainly to be read between the lines, and the other work that gives the 1944 volume its title, *For the Time Being*, is much more explicitly Christian in content – indeed it is subtitled 'A Christmas Oratorio'.

In the book under review Arthur Kirsch spends a substantial chapter on close readings of these works, bringing out allusions and explaining echoes that might escape a non-Christian reader. He devotes another chapter to similar treatment of 'Horae Canonicae', a sequence of poems completed in 1954, in which Auden presents an oblique narrative of the events of Good Friday in verses that correspond to the hours of the office from Prime up to the following day's Lauds.

There is no doubt that religion was very important to Auden in the later part of his life, but it must be said that in comparison, say, with T. S. Eliot his oeuvre provides a rather meagre harvest of explicitly Christian verse. Indeed Auden himself said that he was one of those 'who feel a Christian ought to write in prose, for poetry is magic'. Kirsch may be right to say that 'Christianity is the governing subject' of many of Auden's poems, but in order to substantiate this he has to interpret every reference to religion and every scriptural tag as evidence of an underlying Christian theme.

Kirsch supplements his close readings of poems with an informative chapter on Christian topics in Auden's criticism. He concentrates on his writings on Shakespeare, and especially on the proposal that Falstaff in the Henry IV plays is a 'comic symbol for the supernatural order of Charity' – a suggestion that enraged William Empson. In an essay on Christianity and art quoted by Kirsch, Auden wrote 'the only kind of literature which has gospel authority is the parable, and parables are secular stories with no overt religious reference'. These words may be the key to understanding the oblique way in which Auden incorporated the gospel message into his poems.

Kirsch's book is particularly interesting when it treats of the relationship between Auden's Christianity and his homosexuality. For most of the poet's lifetime, homosexual practice was not only an offence in criminal law, but condemned as sinful by mainstream Anglican teaching. Two remarks of Auden quoted by Kirsch are revelatory of the tensions resulting from his orientation. 'Few, if any, homosexuals', he wrote in 1969, 'can honestly boast that their sex-life has been happy.' 'Sexual fidelity', he told Alan Ansen in 1947, 'is more important in a homosexual relationship than in any other. In other relationships there are a variety of ties. But here, fidelity is the only bond.'

A major crisis in Auden's life was his discovery, in July 1941, that his much loved partner, Chester Kallman, had been unfaithful to him with another lover. This revelation, which tempted him to a murderous revenge, occurred just as he was beginning to resume religious practice, and in later life he described the shock he suffered as a major cause of his return to the Anglican Church. The most explicitly Christian poem quoted by Kirsch in this book is in fact a letter written to Kallman on Christmas Day 1941, in which Auden compares himself to Joseph, Herod and the Magi, and compares the two men's relationship to the paradox of the incarnation. This striking letter, as Kirsch remarks, 'is private and confessional, but it illuminates the less explicit mixture of Auden's homosexuality and his Christian faith in many of his poems'.

The publishers tell us that this is the first book-length study of the relationship between Auden's faith and his art. All admirers of Auden's poetry will be grateful to Professor Kirsch for his devoted and informative attention to the religious strand in his writings.

The Tablet, 26 November 2005

Herbert McCabe OP
God Still Matters, edited and introduced by Brian Davies OP
Continuum, 2008

Herbert McCabe, who died in 2001, was a very remarkable human being. To think of him brings to mind what Samuel Johnson said of Edmund Burke: 'If a man were to go by chance at the same time with Burke under a shed, to shun a shower, he would say – "this is an extraordinary man". If Burke should go into a stable to see his horse drest, the ostler would say – "we have had an extraordinary man here". Something similar could be said of McCabe, except that a chance encounter with him was more likely to take place in the public bar of a public house than in a shed or a stable.

Born to a Catholic family in Middlesbrough in 1926, and baptised John Ignatius, McCabe studied philosophy at Manchester in the 1940s. He was taught by Dorothy Emmet and was one of a group of student friends who went on to distinction in various fields – Robert Bolt as a dramatist, Frank Kennedy as a diplomat, Robert Markus as a historian, Alasdair MacIntyre as a philosopher. McCabe was a man of extremely sharp intelligence and there is no doubt that if he had chosen to pursue an academic career he could have become one of the most distinguished philosophers in the country. Instead, in 1949 he joined the Dominican Order of Preachers, taking, as a friar, the new name Herbert, by which he was known for the rest of his life.

It is hard, indeed, to imagine Herbert as a conventional faculty member, and had he not become a Dominican his career might well have been bohemian rather than academic. But he was not a conventional friar, either, even if to some of his friends he came to embody the ideal of what a twentieth-century Dominican should be. He always acknowledged a great debt to the Dominicans who taught him theology prior to his ordination in 1955, especially Victor White and Columba Ryan. From them he acquired a close familiarity with the works of Thomas Aquinas, a rare and precious thing in a period when most Catholic students of philosophy and theology were fed on second-hand manuals of Thomism.

Besides a love of Aquinas, membership of the Order of Preachers gave much to Herbert to which only his fellow Dominicans are in a position to testify. So loyal was he that he was willing to defend some of the less popular features of the Order's history. He once wrote that in the Europe of its time 'the Spanish Inquisition seems to have been a shining light of rationality, gentleness, and sanity' in respect of the use of torture.

Despite his lifelong passion for the thought of St Thomas, McCabe hated to be called a Thomist, and his own spoken and written presentations of the saint's teaching bore a highly personal mark. He only rarely provided textual documentation for the ideas that he credited to Aquinas, yet his exposition has a ring of authenticity often lacking in commentators of a more scholarly bent.

Apart from the Bible and Aquinas, the greatest influence on McCabe's thought was that of the later Wittgenstein. He sought to graft the insights of the twentieth-century thinker on to those of the thirteenth-century thinker not out of a desire to appear up to date – he showed no inclination to endorse any of the trendy intellectual fashions of the age – but because he recognised a genuine affinity between the two masters. Both share a conviction that it is through an unconstrained attention to the operation of language that we achieve philosophical understanding of human nature. The two philosophers present a vision of human beings as intelligent bodily agents that is far removed from the dualisms or physicalisms characteristic of the ages that separate them in time.

In 1987 McCabe published a collection of lectures, papers and sermons under the title *God Matters*. Abandoning the pun, his colleague Brian Davies has entitled this posthumous collection of papers *God Still Matters*. Like the earlier collection, this book is divided into four parts, three of which are essays treating in turn of God, sacraments and ethics, and the fourth of which consists of sermons.

The first paper in the section 'God' addresses the problem, 'How can God love us?' True love – as opposed to kindness – can only be between equals. But we are creatures, totally dependent on him for everything we are and everything we have. There is no way in which a creature can be loved by God in the full sense of adult love.

> God therefore seems confined to an infantile relationship of authority to his creatures, he is not capable of the self-abandonment that love involves, there is no one to whom he could abandon himself. In this sense surely we are more adult, more mature than God. And this is what Nietzsche saw and that is why, since Nietzsche, bourgeois Europe has been atheist.

But the God who is rejected by the modern atheist is, McCabe insists, pre-Christian. Jesus' message is that the Father is, after all, capable of love, and that he, Jesus, is the object of that love. So too are we: for though God cannot love us as creatures, in Christ we are taken up into the exchange of love between the Father and the incarnate Son of God. This is the grace that makes us free, that is to say, liberates us from a slave–master relationship to God. A number of the themes of this first essay recur in other papers in the volume, especially in one entitled 'Original Sin', which expounds how the crucifixion makes it possible for God to love the monstrous animal species that we have become.

McCabe's regular practice, when expounding a Catholic doctrine, is first to state it in a way that would seem familiar both to those who accept it and those who reject it, secondly to deny that the doctrine, stated in those familiar terms, is true, and thirdly to urge that such a denial is not only compatible with, but essential to, the underlying Christian tradition.

Take, for example, the thesis that the Trinity is the mystery of three persons in one God. In his essay 'Aquinas on the Trinity' McCabe maintains that, for Aquinas, the Trinity is hardly more mysterious than the plain existence of God. When we talk of God at all we do not know what we are talking about; we do not have even a rough idea what God is. Moreover, if we use 'person' in its modern English sense, we have no warrant for saying there are three persons in God; because in the Trinity there are not three distinct centres of consciousness. Instead of speaking of 'God the Father' we could as well speak of 'God the Parents': the plural 'parents' would be no more misleading than the sexual connotation of 'Father'.

Or consider the essay in which McCabe discusses petitionary prayer. 'Here is God just about to make it rain for the sake of the farmers and their crops in the fields around Clyst Honiton when he overhears the urgent prayer of the vicar who is running his garden party that afternoon and changes his mind.' Of course God cannot be manipulated in this way, so what is the point of asking for things in prayer? Aquinas' answer, McCabe says, is that we should not say, 'In accordance with my prayer, God wills that it should be a fine day', but rather, 'God wills: that it should be a fine day in accordance with my prayer.' God brings about my prayer just as much as he brings about the fine day. Prayer is not a means of getting anything done: it is, McCabe says, a real absolute waste of time. But that does not mean we should not pray.

Take, again, the Catholic doctrine of eucharistic change. Protestant critics of this doctrine, and many Catholics too, understand it as follows. In the course of the Mass, the bread and wine change into a different kind of substance, flesh and blood, in fact the flesh and blood of Christ; but this is disguised from us by the fact that to all appearances the bread and wine are unchanged. This, McCabe maintains, is a caricature of the doctrine. Transubstantiation is not a change at all, any more than creation is. When St Thomas teaches that the shape, size, colour etc. of bread and wine cease to be the appearances of bread and wine, this is not because they become the misleading appearances of something else. They cease to function as appearances at all, they have become sacramental signs.

McCabe's account of central Christian doctrines will seem surprising, perhaps even shocking, to some believers. At one point he makes ironic reference to the possible presence of heresy hunters in his audience. In fact, he always took great pains to avoid heresy (more so than is obvious on the surface). Whether or not these efforts were always successful I do not pretend to judge.

There is, however, something unsatisfactory in McCabe's procedure, illuminating though it is. His skill in demolishing the constructions he regards as caricatures is so great that it often obscures the nature of his own positive account. It is not that he sets up straw men to attack: on the contrary – like his masters Aquinas and Wittgenstein, and unlike, say, Descartes and Hume – he is commonly scrupulous to present fairly the positions he wishes to attack. The problem is that his forensic skill distracts the reader from examining the accuracy or plausibility of the assumptions on which his own substitute version of the doctrines depends.

Those who do not share McCabe's Christian commitment will no doubt find the most interesting part of the book the section labelled by the editors 'People and Morals'. An essay entitled 'Sense and Sensibility' gives a brilliant exposition of the enormous difference that language makes between humans and other animals. One on the role of tradition acknowledges a debt to Alasdair MacIntyre, who contributes a preface to the volume.

A paper called 'Aquinas on Good Sense', besides containing an interesting discussion of Jane Austen as a moralist, draws a contrast between prudence understood as the virtue of practical reasoning and conscience understood as a set of private rules for behaviour. A similar theme is followed in an essay on the teaching of morals, which attacks the idea that there can be textbooks of moral philosophy or a science of casuistry.

Some will see McCabe as being in the tradition of the Catholic writers of the early twentieth century. In his admiration for St Thomas, and in his constant employment of paradox, he resembled G. K. Chesterton, though his Aquinas was very different from G. K.'s. Just as Hilaire Belloc revelled in the celebration of wine, McCabe liked to evoke the beauty of Guinness and Irish whiskey. He always loved to point out that when, after Pentecost, the apostles were accused of being drunk, St Peter, instead of saying, 'We are teetotallers', said, 'Nonsense, it's only nine o'clock in the morning.' Like Belloc and Chesterton, McCabe's writing presents an optimistic version of Christianity; but in a post-Hiroshima age he is even more pessimistic about the social and political institutions of the world we live in. St John, he tells us, told us that the world here is past praying for: it can only be smashed.

McCabe also resembles, in a surprising way, that very un-Catholic writer Edward Gibbon. Of course, his brief urgent sentences are at a distant remove from the orotund periods of *The Decline and Fall*; but both authors made some of their most important points by throwaway lines of mockery. Gibbon is best read in small doses, being, like Christmas pudding, too rich to be consumed in large quantities. McCabe too is best read at essay length, though his richness is not one of rhetorical elaboration, but of the swift intellectual development of novel ideas.

Those who do not share McCabe's Christian beliefs would make a great mistake if they skipped the sermons that make up the final section of this book. If you went to a sermon by Herbert, you knew you were in no danger of falling asleep: his style as a preacher was at the furthest possible remove from that of the Revd J. C. Flannel. One of his favourite devices was to take some ecclesiastical commonplace – such as 'the church welcomes sinners' – and spell out what it meant, freed of cant. 'People who are really welcome to the Catholic Church are the murderers, rapists, torturers, sadistic child molesters, and even those who evict old people from their homes.' It was for such people, he said from the pulpit, that the Church existed: but he went on to admit, with a certain show of reluctance, that many of his congregation, perhaps even a majority, did not come into any of these categories.

A three-page sermon for Easter Sunday, included here, is a masterpiece, with much to tell the unbeliever as well as the believer about what it means to be a human being. It is excellent news that Fr Davies hopes to edit further volumes of unpublished sermons. Not only Herbert's friends, but all those who have read *God Still Matters*, will look forward to the publication with keen anticipation.

Times Literary Supplement, 17 October 2008

Alasdair MacIntyre
God, Philosophy, Universities: A Selective History of the Catholic Philosophical Tradition
Continuum, 2009

At the outset of his book Alasdair MacIntyre lists three problems that are inescapable for theism. The first is how to reconcile the goodness of God with the evil in the universe. The second is this: if God is the cause of every happening, it seems that finite agents have no real powers. The third is that it seems doubtful whether one can speak meaningfully in human language of a God who exceeds the grasp of human understanding. MacIntyre sets out the problems bluntly and fairly, but he does not set out to solve them. Instead he urges that the history of theism shows that a thinker can maintain faith in God while treating his existence and nature as philosophically problematic.

The first Christian philosophers discussed are Augustine, Boethius, pseudo-Dionysius and Anselm. These, however, are regarded only as prologues to the Catholic philosophical tradition. So too are the Muslims Ibn Sina and Ibn Rushd, and the Jew Moses ben Maimon, whose views are illuminatingly presented in one of the most valuable chapters of the book. For MacIntyre the Catholic tradition really begins with Aquinas, whose teachings on the knowledge of God and the life of practice are expounded in two central chapters. There follow treatments of Scotus and Ockham, Vitoria, Montaigne, Descartes, Pascal, Arnauld and Malebranche.

Between 1700 and 1850, we are told, Catholicism was effectively absent from philosophy. The history of the tradition resumes with Antonio Rosmini and John Henry Newman in the mid-nineteenth century, and with the launching of neo-scholasticism by Leo XIII in 1879. The story is rounded off with a consideration of John Paul II's encyclical *Fides et Ratio*.

Each of the historical chapters is clear and judicious, but a reader following the sequence begins to question the nature of the historical project as a whole. We seem to be offered a biographical dictionary of philosophers who were Catholics rather than a narrative of a coherent philosophical tradition. Is there really a Catholic philosophical tradition, in the same sense as there is a Catholic theological tradition, and as there are Platonic and Aristotelian traditions in philosophy?

Many of the authors treated by MacIntyre disagreed with each other on fundamental metaphysical and epistemological issues. Even in the heyday of scholasticism, Aquinas and Scotus were as far apart from each other as ever Plato and Aristotle were in classical Greece. In the early modern age, Catholic Cartesians were in the opposite corner from Catholic Aristotelians. And if MacIntyre's methodology makes strange philosophical bedfellows, it also separates from one another philosophers who were close kin. Malebranche, for instance, was much closer in thought to the Jewish Spinoza than to many of the Catholics in the roll call.

We are told that this book originated in an undergraduate course that MacIntyre has taught at Notre Dame since 2004. One cannot help wondering whether this was the *only* course in the history of philosophy that these students attended. If so, they will have carried away a rather hazy view of the subject's history, with Locke, Hume, Kant and Hegel left out of the picture.

On the other hand, MacIntyre's remarks on the nature of universities, scattered throughout the book, are always interesting and insightful. Unlike Newman, he believes that teaching and research belong with each other and should not be relegated to separate institutions. He writes:

> The schools that were the predecessors of universities had been primarily places of teaching and only secondarily, and on occasion, places of enquiry. But even in them it had been becoming clear that teaching, which is to succeed in making the resources of past learning available in the present, is inseparable from ongoing enquiry, from reformulating old questions, testing established beliefs, asking new questions, and so providing new resources for teaching. With the establishment of universities this relationship between teaching and enquiry becomes institutionalised.

MacIntyre agrees with Newman, however, that in a university it is important that there should be a discipline that integrates the various arts and sciences, and considers the contribution that each makes to the overall understanding of the nature and order of things. Newman assigned this task to philosophy, but MacIntyre laments that contemporary analytic philosophy has become fragmented and esoteric, with no pretensions to providing a framework for other disciplines. He casts an almost nostalgic glance at the communist universities of the past, where physics, history and economics were all taught in a way that made their mutual relevance clear, and Marxist philosophy was assigned that task of spelling this relevance out.

In the contemporary research university, philosophy has been marginalised in two ways. First, it is treated as no more than one discipline among all the others. Second, its practitioners seem concerned only to address colleagues who share a technical vocabulary and an acquaintance with professional literature.

Such philosophers, MacIntyre justly observes, inadvertently co-operate with a philosophically uneducated public in making philosophy appear not just difficult – which it is – but inaccessible – which it need not be.

On most philosophical topics there are commonly two or more rival and competing views. Professional practitioners argue for one or other of these views with great sophistication, but without apparently getting nearer any resolution of the disagreement. An outside observer, anxious to learn which of the contending views is true, is likely to conclude that it is something other than the arguments presented that determines why particular philosophers take one rather than another set of reasons to have compelling force.

MacIntyre himself has always been a splendid exception to the generalisation that philosophers have professionalised and trivialised their subject. He has always seen philosophy as a discipline crucial to human flourishing, one that concerns issues that are accessible to everybody. In his final chapter he sets out what he sees as the crucial task for Catholic philosophers: to give an account of what it is to be a human being, an account that would integrate what can be learnt from both physical and social sciences. Besides setting out our relationship to God as first and final cause, such a programme would deal with the limits of scientific explanation, the body–soul–mind relationship, the acquisition of self-knowledge and the overcoming of self-deception. It would, in addition, set out the social dimensions of human activity and inquiry.

Such a programme, MacIntyre admits, is highly ambitious, and he is not optimistic about the possibility of its realisation. The project could only be carried out within a university, but the structures of the contemporary research university (whether secular or Catholic) are deeply inimical to such concerns. The only comfort offered in the book's final line is 'in the life of the mind as elsewhere there is always more to hope for than we can reasonably expect'.

The Tablet, 9 January 2010

Lee Oser
The Return of Christian Humanism: Chesterton, Eliot, Tolkien, and the Romance of History
University of Missouri Press, 2007

Once upon a time, according to Professor Oser, there was a precious and glorious thing called Christian humanism. Founded by Erasmus, its leading characteristics were erudition, love of truth, and peacefulness. It almost succeeded in making the Reformation unnecessary. Through writers like Swift and Pope, it was handed on from generation to generation, until in the nineteenth century it suffered two terrible blows.

On the one hand, Schopenhauer introduced into the bloodstream of Western Christian culture the virus of Eastern fatalism, which, via Wagner, led to the anti-humanism of Nietzsche. On the other hand, in the universities science began to replace theology and intelligent people began to doubt the faith in which they had been brought up.

Matthew Arnold, despairing of a rational defence of dogma, promoted a liberal humanism which sought to replace religion with culture. In this endeavour he has had many distinguished followers, including Charles Eliot Norton, Irving Babbit, I. A. Richards, F. R. Leavis, Lionel Trilling and Walter Jackson Bate. But this, for Oser, is not Arnold's real significance. Rather, having himself come at the end of the tradition of Renaissance humanism, Arnold wrote the prologue to a new Christian version, which became incarnate in the first half of the twentieth century in the writing of G. K. Chesterton, 'the most gifted defender of Christian humanism since Erasmus'.

In the battle against the various forms of anti-humanism, there stood beside Chesterton a powerful ally: T. S. Eliot. The two writers – one from an Anglo-Catholic, the other from a Roman Catholic perspective – insisted that only religion makes the best life possible for human beings. The humanism they presented conserved the radical middle between materialism and superstition.

Sadly, this new religious humanism, like the old, was too good to last. In the last half of the twentieth century a dogmatically relativist type of modernism pushed it out of the academy. Among those who corrupted the Christian humanist paradise Oser singles out for disdain two particular serpents: Helen Vendler and Harold Bloom. In the 1970s these two challenged the authority of Eliot, Vendler portraying him as a complete fraud, a worthy successor to that Victorian bugbear Arnold, and Bloom claiming that all his works, both verse and prose, had been massively overrated.

Oser believes that the rejection of Eliot led literary academics into a critical desert. He responds to Vendler's and Bloom's shrill denunciations with some coloratura vituperation of his own. ('Venom poured like honey from the hollow of Vendler's pen.' 'Bloom piles mania on mania, like a crazed titan.') Most damningly he points out that in the decades since their critical onslaught the number of those enrolling as English majors in the USA has halved.

Oser's own remedy for what he sees as the cataclysmic state of English literary studies at the present time is a return to the vision of Chesterton and Eliot: 'We need to affirm a Christian poetics, an imaginative capacity for myth that is not hostile to reason and nature. We need to keep the tradition of humanistic scholarship alive, so that we may escape our current antirenaissance.' We must rediscover the romance of history, and this means, in a manner not made totally clear, refocusing our vision on Rome, perhaps especially the Rome of the popes.

Such is the narrative of Oser's book. What is the reader to make of it? That depends on what is meant by 'Christian humanism'. Eliot once remarked that 'Arnold had little gift for consistency or for definition'. The same, it has to be said, is true of Oser. In his book words like 'reason', 'nature', 'romance', 'gnosticism' and 'modernism' are thrown about, not without meaning, but with a wild variety of meanings. As for 'humanism' we are never given an explicit definition, but the definitions implicit in the word's different contexts are multiple and inconsistent. Though he gives us a guided tour of the relevant *OED* entry, Oser never identifies which sense of the word he is operating with at any given moment. He gives many a description of Christian humanism – it is in the middle between secularism and theocracy, for instance, or between classicism and romanticism – but never a definition.

In order to evaluate Oser's thesis, then, we need to start afresh. The first step is to identify different senses of 'humanism', the next is to work out which of them are compatible with Christianity, and finally we must inquire which, if any of these, are instantiated in Chesterton and Eliot.

Among relevant senses of 'humanism' we may begin by isolating three: Renaissance humanism, universalist humanism and secular humanism.

Renaissance humanism was not a Christian movement: on the contrary it was a turning away from Christian texts in order to focus on the Latin and Greek authors of pagan antiquity. Instead of reading Christian authors like Anselm and Bonaventure, the humanists studied Tacitus and Horace; to the Christianised Aristotelianism of Aquinas they preferred the metaphysics of Plato. They replaced the living Latin of Scotus and Ockham with the dead Latin of Cicero and Livy. To be sure, Erasmus sought to apply scholarly techniques to the Bible and ancient church writers as well as to classical pagan texts, and several humanists were orthodox and indeed devout Christians. But if orthodoxy is to be identified with tolerance (as Oser says on his first page) then the Renaissance humanists were far from orthodox. Thomas More, the most Christian of them all, boasted in his epitaph that he was a hammer of heretics.

Oser claims that Erasmian humanism almost rendered the Reformation superfluous. It did so only in the sense that it might well have gone on to eliminate Christianity altogether – as in a fantasy elaborated in Arthur Hugh Clough's *Amours de Voyage*:

> Luther, they say, was unwise; like a half-taught German he could not
> See that old follies were passing most tranquilly out of remembrance
> Leo the Tenth was employing all efforts to clear out abuses;
> Jupiter, Juno and Venus, Fine Arts, and Fine Letters, the Poets
> Scholars and Sculptors, and Painters, were quietly clearing away the
> Martyrs and Virgins and Saints, or at any rate Thomas Aquinas:
> He must forsooth make a fuss and distend his huge Wittenberg lungs and
> Bring back Theology once yet again in a flood upon Europe.

In reality, the effect of the Renaissance was to exacerbate, not to soften, the Reformation quarrel. Many of the matters at issue between Protestants and Catholics had been subjects of controversy among scholastic theologians for centuries, but the medieval debates had been conducted in a manner that if sometimes arid was generally sober and courteous. It was the Renaissance's elevation of rhetoric over philosophy, and its choice as literary models of attorneys like Cicero and of satirists like Juvenal, that led to the bitter polemics of the debate between Luther and More and that made the Reformation so divisive.

Whatever the merits and demerits of Renaissance humanism, it played little part in the world-view of either Chesterton or Eliot. Both men held the Greek and Latin classics in the esteem typical of educated gentlemen of their generation; but neither of them drew their main inspiration from them. For Eliot the relevant pinnacles of literature were occupied by Dante and Shakespeare. Chesterton held the erudition of the Renaissance humanists in something like contempt. Describing his education he writes:

> As for Greek accents I triumphantly succeeded, through a long series of school terms, in avoiding learning them at all; and I never had a higher moment of gratification than when I afterwards discovered that the Greeks never learnt them either. I felt, with a radiant pride, that I was as ignorant as Plato and Thucydides. At least they were unknown to the Greeks who wrote the prose and poetry that was thought worth studying; and were invented by grammarians, I believe, at the time of the Renaissance.

For Chesterton and Eliot, the philosophy of Thomas Aquinas was greatly to be preferred to the neo-Platonism of the Renaissance. And both writers, while skilled in the use of irony, parody and paradox, preferred the courtesy of the medievals to the invective of the Renaissance.

There is a humanism, different in kind from Renaissance humanism, which takes as its motto a tag from the Latin dramatist Terence: *homo sum, humani nihil a me alienum puto* (I am human, and I regard nothing that is human as being alien to me). This kind of humanism traces its origin back to Stoic rather than Christian sources. Its key doctrine is that every human being, regardless of race, religion or culture, is to be regarded as of equal significance.

Universalist humanism cannot be counted as Christian humanism any more than Renaissance humanism can. To be sure, Christianity, at least in its more benign forms, holds out the hope of salvation to every member of the human race – but only on condition of becoming a Christian. The Christian does, and must, regard other religions and cultures – Judaism, Islam, Hinduism, Buddhism and the rest – as being to a greater or less degree alien to him.

Neither Chesterton nor Eliot can be regarded as a universal humanist. Both of them, notoriously, displayed an anti-Semitism that went beyond what was normal in their age and class. Two of Chesterton's most powerful poems celebrate the military victory of Christian might against the worshippers of Nordic gods and the followers of Muhammad. As for the Stoic belief in reaching out to the furthest corners of the world, Eliot regards 'Stoic' as a dirty word, suitable for the dismissal of obnoxious authors like Nietzsche. The stoical attitude, he tells us, is the reverse of Christian humility. We conclude that if Renaissance humanism is too narrow a system to capture the ideals of Chesterton and Eliot, universalist humanism is too broad.

'Humanism' at the present time is probably most commonly used to refer to secular humanism, that is to say, the refusal of authority to any religious revelation and the denial of the existence of any superhuman beings. Chesterton and Eliot were, of course, the very opposite of humanists in this sense. They fought against materialism and determinism, and insisted that a supernatural element was essential to a good life. The secular humanists were their enemies and prime targets of their attacks: Babbit in the case of Eliot, Wells and Shaw in the case of Chesterton.

However, whether or not it is helpful to call Chesterton and Eliot Christian humanists it is well worth while to make the comparison between them that is suggested by Oser's book. Both came to Christianity comparatively late in life after a long period in what they came to regard as the wilderness of secularism. Both men looked back on their lives up to their conversions as a voyage of discovery which led back to its starting point. Chesterton, Oser reminds us, said, 'I am the man who with the utmost daring discovered what had been discovered before'; while for Eliot 'the end of all our exploring will be to arrive where we started'.

Both men came to see Christianity as providing what was lacking to the humanism of Arnold. Both of them gave a broadly Aristotelian account of human nature, regarding human beings as set off from other animals by the possession of a natural reason that was an ally, not an enemy, of religious faith. This conviction can, I suppose, be called 'humanism', in contrast to the now widespread climate of opinion that sees other animals as members of the same moral community as ourselves. But those who dislike a humanism of this kind prefer to call it 'speciesism'.

There are, of course, important differences between the two writers. Chesterton's nihilistic years have left little trace outside his autobiography, whereas some of Eliot's best poetry was written in his pre-Christian period. *The Waste Land* surely belongs to what Oser sees as the Schopenhauerian strand of modern culture. Even after their conversion the two men favoured different styles of religion: Eliot advocated an austere, ascetic strain of Atlanticist Christianity at some distance from the bibulous Mediterranean bonhomie of the Chesterbelloc.

J. R. R. Tolkien is surely out of place alongside Eliot and Chesterton in this group, and of the three he is the hardest of all to classify as a Christian humanist. He did indeed share with the Erasmians a taste for philological erudition: but it was a Nordic, not a classic, pedantry that he favoured: no *literae humaniores* for him. His massive trilogy never mentions Christianity, and mentions religion hardly at all. The major protagonists in his narratives are not even human beings. Tolkien did indeed once tell a Jesuit friend that *The Lord of the Rings* was 'a fundamentally religious and Catholic work', but this tells us more about the author than about his book. The magical operation of the rings is surely closer to the love philtre of *Tristan und Isolde* than to any Christian sacramentalism.

In his essay on Blake, T. S. Eliot wrote, 'The local divinities of Italy were not wholly exterminated by Christianity, and they were not reduced to the dwarfish fate which fell upon our trolls and pixies. The latter, with the major Saxon deities, were perhaps no great loss in themselves, but they left an empty place.' Blake, Eliot observes, tried to fill this place, but at the cost of 'crankiness and eccentricity'. Undoubtedly Tolkien has amply filled the space left empty, but only, in the eyes of some, at an even greater cost than Blake.

Rather than Tolkien, C. S. Lewis would surely have made a more appropriate third subject for Oser's study. His writings propound many of the doctrines which, appropriately or inappropriately, here go under the name of 'Christian humanism'. A better storyteller than Eliot, and a better critic than Chesterton, he would have added an elegant balance to the trinity of writers.

The Return of Chrisitan Humanism is not an easy book to read. The author takes insufficient care to anchor his anaphoras, and yields too often to the temptation to pirouette. None the less, the book contains lively and insightful paragraphs, and many readers will cheer its more polemical passages. Oser will not lack allies in his attacks on 'bourgeois progressivism', 'Marxist utopianism', 'the postmodern denial of grand narrative', 'politically correct virtues', 'Koran cooing feminists' and 'the czars of diversity'.

Essays in Criticism 59:1, January 2009

Alister McGrath
C. S. Lewis, a Life: Eccentric Genius, Reluctant Prophet
Hodder & Stoughton, 2013

The basic story of C. S. Lewis's life has often been told. Born in Belfast in 1898, he was sent to school at Malvern College, which he hated. Joining University College, Oxford, in 1917, he did not begin his studies there until two years later, in the meantime serving as an infantry officer in France, where he was wounded and then invalided home in May 1918. As a college student he gained a double first in classical letters, followed by a further first-class degree in English. For the greater part of his life, from 1925 to 1954, he was Fellow and Tutor at Magdalen College, Oxford.

During this time Lewis was a spectacularly popular lecturer on medieval and Renaissance literature, filling the largest halls week after week. He also published a number of scholarly academic works culminating with a history of English literature in the sixteenth century which won him election to the British Academy in 1955. In the early 1930s he converted from atheism to Christianity, and went on to publish lively works of popular theology, such as *The Problem of Pain* (1940) and *The Screwtape Letters* (1942). During the war he achieved national fame through a series of talks as 'The Voice of Faith' on the BBC. These talks were collected in the volume *Mere Christianity* (1952), widely regarded as his most successful venture into Christian apologetics.

During the war Lewis wrote three works of science fiction, and after his last major theological work, *Miracles*, had been critically mauled in 1948 he devoted more and more attention to the writing of novels for children – a then unfashionable genre which he helped to make respectable. He created the imaginative world of Narnia, introduced by *The Lion, the Witch and the Wardrobe* in 1950, and further explored in six succeeding novels. In 1955, after long being denied a professorship at Oxford, Lewis became Professor of Medieval and Renaissance English at Cambridge, with a fellowship at Magdalene College.

While a fellow of an Oxford college Lewis lived in a house in Headington, 'The Kilns', with his brother Warnie, and with Jane Moore, the mother of an Oxford friend killed in the Great War. Sometime after Mrs Moore's death in 1951 he entered into a complicated relationship with an American writer, Joy Davidman, whom he eventually married twice, once in a registry office in 1956 and once in a bedside religious ceremony in 1957. Joy helped him with his penultimate book, *The Four Loves*, and her death in 1960 brought forth a poignant expression of mourning in *A Grief Observed*. Lewis himself died in 1963 after a long battle with prostate cancer.

In this diligently researched, densely footnoted and helpfully illustrated biography Alister McGrath has seen it as his task to supplement and correct the work of previous biographers. Some of his revisions of the received narrative will interest only devotees of Lewis who are familiar with earlier biographies. Such, for instance, are the claims that it was in 1930 rather than 1929 that Lewis began to believe in God, and that he came to belief in Christ while being driven to Whipsnade Zoo by car in 1932 rather than when riding to the zoo in a motorbike sidecar in 1931. Such too is the discussion of the correct order in which to read the Narnia novels. Other novelties are of more general interest, such as the discovery that in 1961 Lewis nominated Tolkien for the Nobel Prize in Literature. One of the most attractive features of the book, in fact, is its careful delineation of the rise and decline of the friendship between the two Oxford writers.

It turns out that the previous biography most in need of emendation is that written by Lewis himself – *Surprised by Joy* (1955). Time and again, McGrath has to correct the chronology – as Warnie put it, his brother had a 'life-long inability to keep track of dates'. The proportions devoted to different topics in the autobiography are decidedly odd: for instance three chapters are devoted to berating the boarding schools the author attended, while only scant reference is made to his war service. A quote from a letter Lewis wrote in 1962 to a New York schoolgirl about his schooldays tells us that he 'never hated anything as much, not even the front line trenches in World War I'. To explain the omissions and distortions in the autobiography McGrath offers sympathetic psychological considerations as well as an unhelpful distinction between the order of events in real time and their location in Lewis's inner world.

Another biographer castigated by McGrath is A. N. Wilson, who wrote a life of Lewis in 1990. The main point at issue concerns a famous occasion in 1948 in which Lewis debated, at the Oxford Socratic Club of which he was president, with a young Catholic philosopher, Elizabeth Anscombe. Lewis in his book *Miracles* had attacked what he called 'naturalism', the thesis that there is nothing that exists that is not part of nature. He maintained that naturalism was self-refuting, since if it was true any statement of it would be irrational. Predicates such as 'true' and 'rational' could not be attached to any thought or belief if it was simply the undesigned product of cerebral motions. Anscombe contended that Lewis's argument involved a confusion between reasons and causes: if a weighing machine that spoke one's weight said 'You weigh fifteen stone' that statement could well be true even though produced entirely by mechanical causes.

According to Wilson, this incident signalled a major shift in Lewis's outlook. Defeated in argument, he lost confidence in his ability as a rational apologist for religion, and accordingly shifted to the writing of pro-Christian propaganda in fictional form, such as the chronicles of Narnia. McGrath contests this interpretation, and indeed denies that the debate represented a serious intellectual defeat for Lewis. In rebuttal of the claim that the debate caused a shift in Lewis's literary strategy he can point to the three space-fiction novels already written before the debate, and he is surely right to claim that Wilson goes too far when he claims that the White Witch of Narnia was based on Anscombe. Nonetheless, the debate did show up the limits of Lewis's philosophical talents, and as he later put it himself, Anscombe 'obliterated me as an apologist'. He revised *Miracles* to take account of her argument, but he long bore a grudge against her. As a fellow Christian, he felt, she should have been standing shoulder to shoulder with him in the battle against naturalism, rather than making dents in his own armour.

The final chapter of McGrath's book, entitled 'The Lewis phenomenon', charts the writer's posthumous reputation, particularly in the United States. In the 1960s Lewis almost vanished from view: by the end of the century he had become a cultural icon. Initially, in America, he was read only by Episcopalians, and was condemned by evangelicals as a smoker, a drinker and a liberal. But as barriers between mainstream Protestant denominations began to weaken, the author of *Mere Christianity* began to be admired across the spectrum. Roman Catholics, too, began to link him with Chesterton and Tolkien and to consider him a fellow-traveller. Most surprisingly, we are told, Lewis has now become the patron saint of American evangelicalism. In a centenary article in 1998 its flagship periodical *Christianity Today* declared him 'the Aquinas, the Augustine and the Aesop of contemporary evangelicalism'. Polls of American Christians, McGrath tells us, regularly cite

Mere Christianity as the most influential religious book of the twentieth century.

Fifty years after his death, how should we judge Lewis's contribution to his chosen fields of English literature, Christian apologetics and children's fiction?

Lewis's studies of Milton and Spenser deservedly retain a select group of admirers, but there have been too many changes of fashion in university departments of English for his influence to be at all prominent there. He detested literary theory, and he wrote many passages that are offensive to feminist ears. The Narnia chronicles, of course, are themselves objects of study in courses on children's literature, but favourable and unfavourable judgements about them are often driven by other than literary criteria. The stories are undisputably well told, and can be enjoyed by those quite unaware of their Christian underpinning. Those who do recognise the Christian allusions sometimes find them obtrusive, at times even spoiling the story. But many people, including McGrath, find them impressive precisely as 'an imaginative retelling of the Christian grand narrative'.

Some might deny that the infrastructure of the chronicles is genuinely Christian. In *The Lion, the Witch and the Wardrobe* God is incarnate in the lion Aslan, who dies to atone for a human sin, and rises again. According to many Christians, including Thomas Aquinas, it would be impossible for God to be incarnate in an irrational animal. One might respond – whether or not Lewis would agree – that his Aslan is not in fact a genuine lion, but simply a human being disguised in fur. As Anscombe's teacher Wittgenstein put it, 'If a lion could talk, we could not understand him.'

Lewis once wrote, reporting a night-long conversation with Tolkien, 'The story of Christ is simply a true myth: a myth working on us in the same way as the others, but with this tremendous difference that it *really happened*.' But how do we know that it did really happen? A narrative, however marvellously crafted, cannot certify its own truthfulness. The literary skill of Tolkien does not persuade us that Middle Earth really exists, nor does the genius of Homer make us believe in the gods of Olympus. If we are to be convinced that the Christian master narrative retold in the Narnia books is a true myth, the gifts of the narrator need to be supplemented by those of the apologist.

In his wartime apologetic talks and books Lewis aimed to use reason to convince unbelievers that they should become believers. The 'mere Christianity' to which he sought to introduce people in the book of that name was, he said,

> like a hall out of which doors open into several rooms. If I can bring anyone into that hall I shall have done what I attempted. But it is in the rooms, not in the hall, that there are fires and chairs and meals. The hall is a place to wait in, a place from which they can try the various doors, not a place to live in.

Nowadays, however, Lewis's theological works preach mainly to the converted, to those already living in one or other of the rooms opening off the hall, rather than to those wondering whether to enter the Christian edifice at all.

Lewis's principal apologetic arguments have not worn well. One line of argument he made popular went like this. Jesus said that he was God. Jesus was neither a deceiver nor deceived. Therefore Jesus was indeed God. Mocking the idea that Christ was simply a great moral teacher, Lewis wrote that a man that said the sort of things Jesus said 'would either be a lunatic – on a level with the man who says he is a poached egg – or else he would be the Devil of Hell'. However, nowadays even conservative Scripture scholars think it unlikely that Jesus in his lifetime made any explicit claim to divinity, so that the argument fails to get started.

Another strategy Lewis favoured was the argument from desire. From time to time, he revealed, he experienced a sense of joy, which was a feeling of unsatisfied longing, though more pleasurable than the satisfaction of any other desire. These experiences, he maintained, revealed a need that could only be met through God. 'If I find in myself a desire which no experience in this world can satisfy, the most probable explanation is that I was made for another world.' One might, alternatively, question whether the desire was a rational one, or indeed whether the sensation could fairly be described as a desire at all. To draw a parallel, it would be strange to argue that if an 80-year-old man wishes he was 40 years younger, he must be made for another world in which he actually is 40 years younger.

There remains the argument that naturalism is self-refuting. Despite the rough handling that Lewis's version of it received from Anscombe, versions of this argument remain popular among philosophers. And indeed there are signs that naturalism is collapsing under its own weight. Even self-proclaimed naturalists seem unable to give a clear account of it. Of course, the natural is contrasted with the supernatural; but that contrast by itself will not give us a non-circular account of nature.

At one time it seemed as if a robust and substantive naturalism could be easily stated. This was a conception that thought of the world as being made up of solid, inert, impenetrable and conserved matter – a matter that interacts deterministically and through contact. But twentieth-century physics posited entities and interactions that did not fit the materialist characterisation of reality, and which took science far away from a world of solid, inert, massy material atoms.

Shall we identify naturalism, then, not by its ontology but by its method? Methodological naturalism would be a commitment to employing in inquiry only the methods of the empirical sciences and mathematics. But this would surely be an unjustifiably dogmatic stance. In recent years, it seems, the armoury once deployed so confidently by atheists to demolish belief has been gradually decommissioned: verificationism, materialism, reductionism, physicalism. One is left wondering what remains of naturalism after all these weapons of mass deconstruction have been laid aside.

The Intellectual World of C. S. Lewis reads like an appendix to McGrath's substantive work. The essays it contains revisit and develop themes explored in the biography – the unreliability of *Surprised by Joy*, the concept of myth, the argument from desire and so forth. It is perhaps a pity that this material was not incorporated in the biography to give a fuller picture of Lewis's thought. There can be cases where a subject deserves several independent biographies – it was understandable, for instance, that Ted Heath should write three different books, one about his musical life, one about his life at sea and one about his life in politics. But Lewis's life was a single intellectual life, with the literature, the philosophy and the theology closely interwoven with each other.

In his biography McGrath is candid about the eccentric and less edifying side of his subject's life. Lewis was personally shabby and unkempt, and he let his house get into an unhealthily filthy state. He refused to learn to type or drive a car. He smoked and drank heavily: Tolkien was amused to hear a reference to 'the ascetic Mr Lewis' on a day when he had seen him down three pints of beer at lunchtime.

McGrath quotes Lewis's confession of sado-masochistic tendencies, recording that at a drunken undergraduate dinner in 1917 he went round the guests imploring each to let him 'whip them for the sum of 1s a lash'. The ménage at 'The Kilns' was bizarre, and its true nature was concealed from family and friends. There was, according to McGrath, a sexual as well as a maternal element in Mrs Moore's relations with Lewis, while brother Warnie repeatedly disappeared on alcoholic binges from which he was dried out by Irish nuns.

After Mrs Moore's death, quarrels between her daughter and Lewis's wife about the ownership of 'The Kilns' support the view held by many of Lewis's friends that Joy Davidman was a mercenary gold-digger. The overall picture the biography presents of its hero's relations with women is not an imposing one. After being in thrall for two decades to a manipulative woman some 25 years his senior, Lewis was then entrapped by a manipulative woman 16 years his junior. Undoubtedly he came in the end to love his wife – but at the cost of losing most of his friends.

McGrath is ingenious and persuasive in searching Lewis's writings for clues to his private life. Many of us recall with delight the communications from a senior to a junior devil in *The Screwtape Letters*, with their vivid evocations of the cardinal sins. There is one character who illustrates 'the gluttony of Delicacy'.

> Whatever is offered to her never seems to be quite to her taste. Her requests may be very modest; yet they are never met, and she is never satisfied. '*All* she wants is a cup of tea properly made, or an egg properly boiled, or a slice of bread properly toasted.' Yet neither maid nor family ever seems able to get it right.

McGrath plausibly sees this as indicating Lewis's concern about Mrs Moore's fussiness and fixations at this period. His book contains many similar identifications of clues to the background of the great man's writings.

One of the most famous episodes of Lewis's life was his debate in the 1930s with the Cambridge scholar E. M. W. Tillyard about 'The Personal Heresy'. Tillyard had claimed that

Paradise Lost 'was really about the true state of Milton's mind when he wrote it'. Lewis argued for an impersonal point of view, that literature is about something objective. 'The poet is not a man who asks me to look at *him*; he is a man who says "look at that" and points.'

Frequently, McGrath asks his reader to look in Lewis's writings not for what he had to say, but for what they tell us about his life. In the light of the personal heresy debate, the reader must wonder from time to time what Lewis himself would have thought of this devoted and meticulous biography.

Times Literary Supplement, 19 June 2013

PART SIX

THE DEBATE BETWEEN THEISTS AND NATURALISTS

Introduction

As the twentieth century progressed the differences between the various Churches became less significant than the differences between theists and atheists. Catholics and Protestants and other Christians came to see that the most serious threat to their beliefs and values came not from members of rival Churches, but from those who rejected religion altogether. More and more people became doubtful about the existence of God, and defined themselves as agnostics; others denied his existence outright and espoused atheism.

It is true that many atheists prefer to call themselves 'naturalists'. Naturalism is the belief that there is nothing beyond nature, and that everything that exists is part of nature. Naturalism often goes with a commitment to employing in inquiry only the methods of the empirical sciences and mathematics. It entails a denial that there are any spiritual or supernatural entities that are exempt from the laws governing the natural world. It is not, however, as easy as it may appear to give a clear and consistent account of what is meant by 'nature' and 'natural'. Of course, the natural is contrasted with the supernatural; but that contrast by itself will not give us a non-circular account of nature.

The most cautious atheists restrict themselves to a purely methodological naturalism, a commitment to employing in inquiry only the methods of the empirical sciences. Because science is an ongoing endeavour, and new methods of research are constantly being devised, naturalism of this kind is perforce an open-ended commitment. But naturalists will claim that the limitations it imposes are not vacuous, since new methods in science always have a continuity with, and a dependence on, the corpus of science that each age inherits.

The most fashionable atheists, however, go far beyond this tentative form of naturalism. They claim that the origin and structure of the world and the emergence of human life and human institutions are already in principle fully explained by science, so that no room is left for postulating the existence of activity of any non-natural agent. Their preferred paradigm of explanation is Darwin's account of the origin of species by natural selection.

Neo-Darwinism goes beyond Darwinism in offering to explain the origin of life itself as the product of the chance interaction of non-living materials and forces subject to purely physical laws. It is clear that however successful natural selection may be in explaining the origin of particular species of life, it clearly cannot explain how there came to be such things as species at all. That is to say, it cannot explain how there came to be true breeding populations, since the existence of such populations is one of the premises on which explanations in terms of natural selection rest as their starting point.

Darwin's theory obviously clashes with a literal acceptance of the Bible account of the creation of the world in seven days. Moreover, the length of time that would be necessary for evolution to take place would be immensely longer than the six thousand years which Christian fundamentalists believe to be the age of the universe. But a non-literal interpretation of Genesis was adopted long ago by theologians as orthodox as St Augustine, and few non-fundamentalist Christians today have any difficulty with the idea that the earth may have existed for billions of years. It is wrong to suggest, as is often done, that Darwin disproved the existence of God. For all that Darwin showed, the whole machinery of natural selection may have been part of a Creator's design for the universe. After all, belief that we humans are God's creatures has never been regarded as incompatible with our being the children of our parents; it is no more incompatible with us being, on both sides, descended from the ancestors of the apes.

Natural selection and intelligent design are not incompatible with each other, in the way that natural selection is incompatible with the Genesis story. 'Intelligent design' may be used in political circles as a euphemism for biblical fundamentalism, but in the sheer idea of an extra-cosmic intelligence there is nothing that commits one to a belief in the Judaeo-Christian, or any other, religious revelation. To be sure, discussion of the possibility of such an intelligence does not belong in the science classroom; if it did, the intelligence would not be an extra-cosmic one, but a part of nature. But that is no reason why philosophers should not give it serious consideration.

The most fundamental reason in favour of postulating an extra-cosmic agency of any kind is surely the need to explain the origin of the universe itself. At a time when philosophers and scientists were happy to accept that the universe had existed for ever, there was no question of looking for a cause of its origin, only of looking for an explanation of its nature. But when it is proposed that the universe began at a point of time measurably distant in the past, then it seems perverse simply to shrug one's shoulder and decline to seek any explanation. We would never, in the case of an ordinary existent, tolerate a blithe announcement that there was simply no reason for it coming into existence; and it seems irrational to abandon this principle when the existing thing in question is all-pervasive, like the universe.

The debate between creationists and naturalists is an ongoing one, as is shown by the reviews included in this sixth section. In my view neither the partisans of neo-Darwinism nor the proponents of intelligent design have any solid ground to claim victory. The atheists have failed to provide a convincing account of the origin of life and the universe, while the theists have failed to establish the coherence of the notion of an extra-cosmic intelligence.

Kai Nielsen
Naturalism and Religion
Prometheus Books, 2001

The overall message of this text is clear and simple: naturalism good, religion bad. The message is preached, however, by various methods and in varying registers ranging from slangy abuse to close argument. The book is a bran-tub of essays of different ages and value.

Nielsen's negative stance is clear enough. First, he is an atheist. Belief in an anthropomorphic God is false. Belief in the God of the great monotheistic religions is incoherent. 'For people who have been lucky enough to have a good education, belief in God, I say, should be rejected. And Judaism, Christianity and Islam should, in a world of abundance with well-educated people, become merely cultural-historical artefacts.' Second, he is a disbeliever in an afterlife, whether the bodily resurrection of Christian theology or the spiritual survival of Cartesian dualism. For an intellectually sophisticated and informed person, he tells us, 'none of the faces of immortality provide live options'.

If it is clear what Nielsen is against, it is not quite so clear what he is for, that is to say, what naturalism consists in. We may make, as he does, a distinction between methodological naturalism and cosmological naturalism. Methodological naturalism is a commitment to employing in inquiry only the methods of the empirical sciences and mathematics. Nielsen rejects this: he eschews any claimed hegemony for the scientific method. The naturalism that he supports is cosmological naturalism, which he defines (more than once) in the following way: 'Naturalism denies that there are any spiritual or supernatural realities transcendent to the world or at least that we have sound grounds for believing that there are such realities.' Nature is all: there is nothing that exists that is not a part of nature and there is nothing beyond nature. At this point we look for, and fail to get, a clear and consistent account of what is meant by 'nature' and 'natural'. Of course, the natural is contrasted with the supernatural; but that contrast by itself will not give us a non-circular account of nature.

It is in the case of human beings that Nielsen goes furthest in spelling out what is meant by naturalism. 'Naturalism takes human beings to be complicated, language-using animals (and thus objects) in causal interaction with other physical objects', and naturalism will not postulate 'minds as some private physically indescribable something mysteriously interacting with bodies'. This is clear enough, but so far nothing has been said to distinguish naturalism from (say) Thomism. In the past, the clearest way to delineate naturalism was to identify it with materialism; but Nielsen concedes that developments in microphysics have taken science far away from a world of solid, inert, massy material atoms. However, with regard to middle-sized objects like human beings, Nielsen says, we can be pretty sure that they are observationally identifiable and that their movements are quite deterministically predictable. Here, at last, in determinism we have a thesis that distinguishes Nielsen's naturalism from other non-Cartesian accounts of human beings: but it is a thesis that is highly implausible and is quite unargued for.

One of the most interesting statements of Nielsen's present-day position is his 1998 piece, 'On being a secularist all the way down'. In that essay he defends naturalism, but rejects physicalism on the grounds that human beings are irreducibly social beings, and the human animal is a self-interpreting animal. He also rejects scientism, the belief that physics yields our best approximation of the one true description of the world. To believe this is to assign unreasonable privilege to one language-game above others: in fact, he says, poetry is no more or no less distant than chemistry from 'the truth' or closer or less close to revealing what reality is really like in itself. 'Indeed, we do not know what we are talking about if we speak of "reality in itself" or "ultimate reality".'

On moral issues, Nielsen's current stand is this. We live in a moral wilderness, whose ills are due above all to industrial capitalism. In moral and political reflection we must take our start from the social practices in our common social life and the moral truisms that are deeply embedded in them. We must seek to work our considered moral convictions into a coherent whole, to achieve a 'wide and general reflective equilibrium' that will embrace the assemblage of cultures in the modern world. Here Nielsen acknowledges the influence of Rawls, but the kind of equilibrium he envisages emerging from the reflective process is clearly going to be rather different from the liberal capitalism that Rawls' apparatus is often invoked to justify.

Since Nielsen, unlike many naturalists, is willing to grant non-scientific language-games equal status with the language-game of physics, he may be asked why he does not just accept the language-game of religion on its own terms. He is well aware of the possibility of this challenge, and devotes the final quarter of his book to a careful examination of the writings on religion of Wittgenstein and Wittgensteinian fideists. He detects an incoherence in the Wittgensteinian approach to the topic of religion. On the one hand, religions are metaphysical schemes, and metaphysical schemes are incoherent; on the other hand, religions are forms of life, and it makes no sense to say of a form of life that it is incoherent.

In response to this, Wittgensteinian fideists would reject the claim that religions are metaphysical schemes. Historically, religion and metaphysical cosmology may have been intertwined, but the essence of religion, they would claim, is more a matter of a passionate orientation of one's life. Nielsen – along with many believers – rejects such an account of religion, but in doing so he shows an impressive degree of patience and sympathy with Wittgensteinians such as Malcolm and Rhees.

It is characteristic of these more recent essays of Nielsen that they display an irenic naturalism, far removed from the brash arrogance that characterises many spokesmen for atheism. The temporally different layers of the collection may be seen as milestones along a peace process between philosophy and religion, starting from the positivistic rejection of religious utterances as nonsense and proceeding to an intellectual pluralism that is anxious to make the most of common ground between atheist and theist philosophers.

Nonetheless, Nielsen makes it quite clear that atheism is the bedrock on which his system is built: and the main weakness of the book is its lack of fundamental arguments against the existence of God. This is not inadvertent: Nielsen believes that on the terrain of argument the battle between theism and atheism was won more than a generation ago. Nowadays, he maintains, naturalism is simply taken for granted by the better sort of philosopher. He admits to being bored when, for instance, Swinburne and Mackie go toe-to-toe over which belief system, a secular one or a theistic one, has the better claim to having 'the true cosmology'.

As one puts the book down, one realises that Nielsen occupies a rather lonely position as a philosopher. As an atheist, he leaves behind all believing Jewish, Muslim and Christian philosophers, including Alasdair MacIntyre and Charles Taylor, to whom, on human and social issues, he is often close. In rejecting scientism, he leaves behind his fellow atheists Quine, Smart, Armstrong and Mackie. In rejecting all kinds of physicalism he leaves behind fellow non-reductionist secularists such as

Rorty, Davidson and Dennett. In his hatred for capitalism and sympathy for Marx, he leaves behind right-wing atheists such as Ayn Rand and Antony Flew.

I doubt, however, whether this isolation troubles him. Over a long life he has established and refined his position, and he is always ready with a robust response to critics. On the evidence of this book, he seems to have become a genial and tolerant person, who I am sure is willing to forgive all those others for being out of step.

Times Literary Supplement, 18 January 2002

Alister McGrath with Joanna Collicutt
The Dawkins Delusion? Atheist Fundamentalism and the Denial of the Divine
SPCK, 2007

Alister McGrath and Richard Dawkins both hold doctorates in the life sciences and both are professors at Oxford. In 2004 McGrath, an atheist turned Christian, wrote a study of the work of Dawkins, a Christian turned atheist. Entitled *Dawkins' God: Genes, Memes and the Meaning of Life*, it combined a respectful account of Dawkins' scientific work with a critique of the atheism which has been the background of his writing ever since *The Selfish Gene* of 1976.

In 2006 Dawkins published *The God Delusion*. As McGrath says, this book marks a significant departure. Dawkins is no longer an atheist whose main aim is to make evolutionary biology accessible to the general public: he is now a preacher whose mission is to convert religious readers to atheism. The book has a strident and aggressive tone, and a cavalier attitude to evidence that tells against its thesis that religion is the root of all evil. This has provoked McGrath to write a pamphlet exposing its flaws.

The Dawkins Delusion is credited to both Alister McGrath and Joanna Collicutt McGrath, who is a lecturer in psychology of religion at Heythrop College. But the extent of her contribution is not made clear, and the book is written in the first person singular 'for historical and stylistic reasons'. This makes it difficult to interpret the autobiographical statements in the book. In this review I shall follow the authors' convention and refer to 'McGrath' in the masculine singular.

McGrath says that he is completely baffled by the hostility that Dawkins now displays to religion. But surely two recent phenomena explain the heightened shrillness of Dawkins' atheism. The first is the rise of Christian fundamentalism in the USA, which endangers the teaching of evolutionary science in schools. The second is the rise of Islamic fundamentalism which has spawned extremist groups of people willing to murder thousands of innocent people even at the cost of their own lives.

Of course McGrath is no less horrified than Dawkins by these two developments. But he regards them as largely irrelevant to the evaluation of religion. There can be atheist fundamentalists as well as religious ones, and Dawkins, he claims, shows every sign of being one. Moreover, atheism as well as religion has given rise to massacres, and true religion, as exemplified by Jesus of Nazareth, is hostile to violence.

These points are fairly taken, but I do not think McGrath does justice to the way in which religion, if it does not originate evil, gives it greater power. Those who believe that they have a direct revelation from God regard their sacred texts as trumping whatever science may discover. Those who believe that they are acting out God's will are not going to be deterred by any secular moralising about just and unjust wars. But of course McGrath is right that religion 'transcendentalises' good as well as evil.

McGrath says that much of Dawkins' book is a confused and misleading account of other people's areas of specialisation. He has in mind particularly Dawkins' ventures into historical theology, which is his own field. Oddly enough, it was precisely in this area that it seemed to me that Dawkins was often the more accurate of the two debaters. Let me give a few instances.

McGrath criticises Dawkins' treatment of Aquinas' Five Ways. Dawkins denies that these constitute sound proofs for the existence of God. McGrath agrees that they do not, but maintains that they were never meant to do so. They presuppose faith, he claims, and simply exhibit its coherence with our experience of the world. He is surely in error here. In the *Summa Theologiae* Aquinas states flatly 'that God exists can be proved in five ways', and in the *Summa contra Gentiles* he says that proofs of this kind can convince infidels.

Again, McGrath rebukes Dawkins for maintaining that Jesus did not entertain the idea of taking his gospel to the Gentiles. In rebuttal he cites the story of the good Samaritan and recalls Jesus' gentleness to publicans and sinners, and his cures of non-Jews. But it might have been fair to quote also Jesus' words, 'I am not sent but unto the lost sheep of the house of Israel' (Matthew 15:24).

'Contrary to what Dawkins assumes,' McGrath tells us, 'orthodox Christianity understands Jesus to have been fully human and not omniscient.' No doubt some present-day Christians in good standing deny that Jesus was omniscient, but throughout most Christian centuries it has been taught that Jesus was not only fully human but also fully divine, with all the attributes of divinity. Here it is Dawkins, not McGrath, who is the closer to orthodox Christianity.

These are minor points, though they illustrate that McGrath can be as unfair to Dawkins as Dawkins can be to Christians. A much more serious issue in the debate between the two writers is the nature of faith.

McGrath complains that Dawkins makes no distinction between religion and belief in God, seeing the two of them as two sides of the same coin. In fact, McGrath says, there is a critical distinction between the two. There can be religion without belief in God and there can be belief in God without religious behaviour. Buddhists are cited to illustrate the first case and, less plausibly, evangelicals are held to illustrate the second. Dawkins' failure to make the distinction, we are told, leads him to ignore important religious phenomena such as the emotions which McGrath calls 'hot cognitions'. To which Dawkins would no doubt reply that feelings are no reliable guide to truth.

But if Dawkins fails to make a distinction between religion and belief in God, both McGrath and Dawkins fail to make a distinction between belief in God and faith. Faith is something more than the mere belief that there is a God: it is an assent to a purported revelation from God, communicated through a sacred text or a religious community. It is faith in a creed, not mere belief in God, that is Dawkins' real target in *The God Delusion*. It is the revelations that different religions claim to be communications from God that give rise to the disputes between them and the evils that Dawkins denounces:

> What is really pernicious is the practice of teaching children that faith itself is a virtue. Faith is an evil precisely because it requires no justification and brooks no argument … Suicide bombers do what they do because they really believe what they were taught in their religious schools: that duty to God exceeds all other priorities, and that martyrdom in his service will be rewarded in the gardens of Paradise.

McGrath objects to Dawkins' account of faith: 'It is not a Christian definition of faith, but one that Dawkins has invented to suit his own purposes.' It is, indeed, too much to say that faith requires no justification: many religious people offer arguments not just for belief in God but for their particular creed. It is also excessive to say that faith brooks no argument, if that means that the faithful are unwilling to offer responses to criticisms. Nonetheless, I think that Dawkins is correct to deny that faith is a virtue, for the following reason.

The common characteristic of faith in almost all religious traditions is its irrevocability. A faith which is held tentatively is no true faith. It must be held with the same degree of certainty as knowledge. In some traditions the irrevocability of faith is reinforced by the imposition of the death penalty for apostasy, which is the abandonment of faith. Now the kinds of arguments that believers offer in support of their religion cannot be claimed to have anything like the degree of cogency that would rationally justify the irrevocable commitment of faith. Again, no argument will make a true believer give up his faith, and this is something that he must be resolved on in advance of hearing any argument.

McGrath will no doubt disown such a view of faith. But once again, Dawkins' account is closer to traditional Christianity than McGrath's. The idea that faith is an irrevocable commitment, which goes far beyond any evidence that could be offered in its support, is explicitly stated by Christian thinkers as different from each other as Aquinas, Kierkegaard and Newman. To be sure, it is the degree of commitment involved in faith, rather than its religious object, that is what is really objectionable. Not all fanaticism is religious fanaticism, as the history of Nazism and Stalinism makes abundantly clear.

McGrath is at his most convincing when he is on Dawkins' home patch. He deals briskly and effectively with the principal argument offered in *The God Delusion* against the existence of God. Dawkins points out the antecedent improbability of the existence of beings as complex as humans. Belief in God, he then argues, represents belief in a being whose existence must be even more complex and therefore more improbable. But our own existence, McGrath retorts, shows that something very improbable can happen. The issue is not whether God is probable, but whether he is actual.

This, in my own view, is a question to which no one has given a convincing answer, and the appropriate reaction is one of agnosticism. But I do not agree with Dawkins that all those who believe in God are unreasonable in so doing. Those who claim to *know* that there is a God are making a claim that is not justified; but so too are those who claim to *know* there is no God. But a belief in God, falling short of certainty, is not open to the same objection. A belief may be reasonable, though false, if held with the appropriate degree of caution. As Stephen Jay Gould pointed out, if Darwinism is incompatible with religious belief, then half the world's scientists are stupid.

McGrath's book, sadly, shares some of the vices of *The God Delusion*, and is not free from over-hasty argument and rhetorical padding. But it is hard to dissent from his conclusion that Dawkins has no mandate to speak for the scientific community, and that his recent crusade has done more harm to science than it has to religion. Most people have a greater intellectual and emotional investment in religion than in science; and if they are once convinced that they have to choose between religion and science and cannot have both, it will be science that they will renounce.

Times Literary Supplement, 17 August 2007

John Cornwell
Darwin's Angel: An Angelic Riposte to The
God Delusion
Profile Books, 2007

Since Richard Dawkins' *The God Delusion* was published several responses have appeared. John Cornwell's brief book adopts an ingenious new approach. It takes the form of a series of letters to Dawkins written by his guardian angel – who, it turns out, was previously the guardian angel of Charles Darwin and then of Gregor Mendel. Some readers will find this inverse Screwtape fantasy engaging; others may find it arch. Once the book has got into its stride, however, the angelic machinery fades into the background, providing no more than a peg for the occasional witticism.

Cornwell does indeed adopt a lofty attitude with regard to Dawkins: but it is not the viewpoint of a hovering angel, but rather that of a rooftop sniper. He watches the sentences of *The God Delusion* pass beneath him, watching for some particularly implausible or outrageous one to come into sight. Often his aim is accurate and lethal, as a few instances will illustrate. Cornwell brings out the absurdity of the claim that Mendel became a monk only in order to have a comfortable billet for scientific research. Most readers will find his reading of *The Brothers Karamazov* more sympathetic than Dawkins' reading. Atheist no less than theist philosophers can endorse the claim that Dawkins' 'memes' are mythical entities begotten of false analogies.

But Cornwell's angel often behaves less than angelically. He fails to observe the prime rule of intellectual debate, namely that one should attack an opponent's arguments, not his personality. Dawkins himself is an inveterate violator of this rule. But this offers the angel provocation, not justification.

After many brief, lively exchanges, the reader begins to wonder whether Cornwell is going to face head-on the claim that God is a delusion. The answer is given in the twentieth chapter, 'Does God exist?', which acknowledges a substantial debt to the late Herbert McCabe: 'There is no feature of the universe which indicates that it is God-made. What God accounts for is that the universe is there instead of nothing.' Dawkins denies that God can provide an explanation for the universe. 'Any God capable of designing a universe', he wrote in a passage quoted by Cornwell, 'must be a supremely complex and improbable entity who needs an even bigger explanation than the one he is supposed to provide.' Cornwell points out correctly that theologians have always denied that God was complex. In God there are no parts to come apart, there are no processes that begin, develop and end.

Dawkins offers no argument for his claim that what is complex must be explained by something of at least equal complexity. Perhaps he is tacitly appealing to the principle that 'like can only be caused by like'. But this axiom surely belongs to a long-superannuated physics in which the ultimate principles are the hot and the cold and the wet and the dry, and in which only what is hot heats and only what is wet wets.

Dawkins is right, however, to reject the question, 'Why is there something rather than nothing?' This is a misbegotten query, if only because it is impossible to give sense to 'there is nothing'. It is not the mere existence of the universe that raises the demand for a cause: it is its *coming into* existence. But Dawkins cannot merely shrug off the causal question, since he believes that the universe did come into existence at a point of time measurably distant in the past.

The traditional theologian, on the other hand, faces a formidable difficulty of an opposite kind. The entity that is offered in answer to the causal question about the universe is a simple, necessary, being. It is hard to see how something that is just being, all being, and nothing but being, can be said to be alive, or to be the kind of entity with which one could enter into personal relationships. Cornwell is aware of this problem. He says, 'If we speak of God as having thoughts, or making decisions, or having a strong right arm, or an all-seeing eye, it can only be by way of metaphor.' What is left unclear is whether this is meant to deny what traditional theologians undoubtedly believed, namely that there is literally a divine intellect and a divine will, and that God is literally omniscient and omnipotent.

On the principal issue, whether there is or is not a God with the attributes assigned to him by the three great monotheistic faiths, neither *The God Delusion* nor *Darwin's Angel* provides the reader with sufficient grounds for a reasoned conclusion. On many lesser issues, as I have said, Cornwell scores telling points. But Dawkins, in riposte, might well convict Cornwell of two substantial errors, one philosophical and one theological. The philosophical issue concerns the concepts of purpose and design. Cornwell accuses Dawkins, when he makes use of terms such as 'purpose', 'need', 'welfare', of being inconsistent with his fundamental Darwinism. 'The point of the "blind watchmaker" principle, whereby you earned your reputation as a leading expositor of Darwin's theory of evolution, is that there is no "teleology" in nature – in other words, no grand designer, no purpose; it is blind.' This is to ignore the difference between design and purpose. Design differs from purpose because design is purpose preceded by an idea in somebody's mind. If the world is designed, then there was a precedent idea in the mind of the creator – what, in the Fourth Gospel, is called the *logos* or Word. But one need not believe in such a *logos* in order to recognise purpose in the world.

One of Aristotle's four causes was the final cause, the end, the purpose, the good to be achieved by some action. More than any other philosopher, he emphasised the importance of teleology in the world; but he was no supporter of the argument from design. The budding of a rose and the building of a spider's web were no less teleological than human activities; but Aristotle knew better than to attribute consciousness to roses and spiders. Teleology, for him, was a basic fact about the cosmos, and no extra-cosmic designer was needed to explain it. It was Aquinas, much later, who in his Fifth Way formulated the argument from purpose to design.

Later, Descartes revolutionised philosophy by expunging teleology altogether. He eliminated, outside the human realm, purpose as well as design. With Darwin we return to the position of Aristotle: the world contains purpose but not, outside the human realm, design. Darwin's achievement was to make teleological explanation respectable by offering, in natural selection, a recipe for translating it into a naturalistic explanation that made no call on design.

If Cornwell is philosophically unsound on the topic of teleology, he is surely theologically unsound on the afterlife. What lies beyond the grave, he says, is, even for committed religionists, more a matter of hope than belief. But Christians affirm in their creeds belief in a final judgement, a resurrection of the body and an everlasting life. The only certainty mentioned in Christian obsequies, Cornwell says, 'is that those mourners present will themselves soon follow the same route to mortality'. Has he never heard the words over a grave, 'We commit this body to the ground, earth to earth, ashes to ashes, dust to dust, in sure and certain hope of the resurrection to eternal life'?

The Tablet, 15 September 1997

David Bentley Hart
Atheist Delusions
Yale University Press, 2009

In the ongoing suit of *Secularism vs God* David Bentley Hart is the most able counsel for the defence in recent years. Though confident in the strength of his case, he does not hesitate to abuse the plaintiff's attorneys, and he does so in grand style. Richard Dawkins is guilty of 'rhetorical recklessness'. Christopher Hitchens 'careens drunkenly across the pages' of a book 'that raises the wild non sequitur almost to the level of a dialectical method'. Daniel Dennett's theses are 'sustained by classifications that are entirely arbitrary and fortified by arguments that any attentive reader should notice are wholly circular'.

Hart has the gifts of a good advocate. He writes with clarity and force, and he drives his points home again and again. He exposes his opponents' errors of fact or logic with ruthless precision. He is generous in making concessions on his own side, provided they leave intact his overarching claims. Above all, he has ensured that his brief is modest and manageable.

Thus, no attempt is made to plead in defence of religion, as such. 'Religion in the abstract', Hart says, 'does not actually exist, and almost no one (apart from politicians) would profess any allegiance to it.' This is a sound and fundamental point. The creeds of the major religions are mutually contradictory, so that the one thing we know for certain about religion is that if any religion is true then most religions are false. Hart's client is not religion in general – it is traditional Christianity. It is this, he claims, that has been misunderstood and slandered by its cultured despisers.

Again, Hart concentrates on issues of history rather than philosophy. True, he claims that Dawkins' philosophical arguments are ones that 'a college freshman midway through his first logic course could dismantle in a trice'. However, the claim that Dawkins is philosophically illiterate is based on a theory of Being that would be rejected by many a seasoned professor of philosophy. Hart's own strengths lie elsewhere, so he is wise to concentrate on narrative and invective.

The aim of the first half of the book is to demolish 'the mythology of a secularist age'. Secularists invite us to believe the following story. In the medieval ages of faith, culture stagnated, science languished, wars of religion were routinely waged, witches were burned by inquisitors and Western humanity was enslaved to superstition. The literary remains of antiquity had been consigned to the flames and the achievements of Greek science lay forgotten until Islam restored them to the West. The age of faith was succeeded by an age of reason and enlightenment which gave us the riches of scientific achievement and political liberty, and a new and revolutionary sense of human dignity. The modern separation of Church and State has put an end to the blood-steeped intolerance of religion. Western humanity has at last left its nonage and attained to its majority in science, politics and ethics. 'This is', Hart says, 'a simple and enchanting tale … its sole defect is that it happens to be false in every identifiable detail.'

Six chapters demolish detailed elements of this secularist myth. Chapter Four refutes the allegations that the ancient library of Alexandria was destroyed by Christians and that the pagan philosopher Hypatia was murdered out of hatred for women and learning. Chapter Five shows that far from burning classical texts, Christian monastic librarians preserved them from decay. Chapter Six argues that Greek science had become sterile long before the Christianisation of the Roman Empire. The only innovative physicist of late antiquity, we are told, was the Christian John Philoponus. During the four and a half centuries of its scientific pre-eminence, Islam made 'no more progress than a moderately clever undergraduate today could assimilate in less than a single academic year'. Paying tribute to the Oxford calculators of the fourteenth century, Hart illustrates the continuity between medieval and Renaissance science. Pope Urban VIII's condemnation of Galileo, he claims, was not an index of inherent ecclesiastical hostility to science, but a simple clash of arrogant personalities.

The seventh and eighth chapters defend Christianity from the charges of intolerance and cruelty. The persecution of witches, Hart points out, was an early modern rather than a medieval phenomenon, and the inquisitors of the time did their best to suppress witch-hunts. The rise of modern science and the obsession with sorcery 'were two closely allied manifestations of the development of a new post-Christian sense of human mastery over the world'. In exculpation of the use of torture and the burning of heretics it can be said that the Church was merely following a fashion which was originated by the State. During the so-called Dark Ages the only penalty for misbelief was excommunication, whereas in the heyday of the Holy Roman Empire heresy became a capital crime. 'Violence', Hart says, 'increased in proportion to the degree of sovereignty claimed by the state, and whenever the medieval Church surrendered moral authority to secular power, injustice and cruelty flourished.'

Addressing the responsibility of the Church for warfare, Hart briskly gets the Crusades out of the way. Admitting that they were 'holy wars' – the only ones in Christian history, he maintains – he dismisses them as 'the last gaudy flourish of Western barbarian culture, embellished by the winsome ceremonies of chivalry'. The European wars of the sixteenth and seventeenth centuries are treated at greater length. Here, we learn, 'no prince of the time waged war against another simply on account of his faith'. In its bloodiest days the Thirty Years' War was not a war of religion, but a struggle between two Catholic houses, the Bourbons and the Hapsburgs.

Hart is at his most convincing when he argues that for the sheer scale of its violence the modern period trumps any of the ages of Christian faith.

> The Thirty Years' War, with its appalling toll of civilian casualties, was a scandal to the consciences of the nations of Europe; but midway through the twentieth century … even liberal democracies did not scruple to bomb open cities from the air, or to use incendiary or nuclear devices to incinerate tens of thousands of civilians.

In the second part of the book Hart seeks to replace the secularist myth with a positive account of what he calls 'the Christian revolution' – 'perhaps the only true revolution in the history of the West'. Many of the values prized by modern secularists are, whether they know it or not, inheritances from the early days of Christianity. Pre-Christian cults involved human sacrifice, self-castration and self-mutilation. Pre-Christian society despised the poor and weak and tolerated infanticide; it enjoyed gladiatorial combat, and it was built upon slavery. Only Christianity fostered the concept of a dignity intrinsic to every human soul. Only Christianity built hospitals and almshouses, and taught that charity was the highest virtue.

Well aware that the Christianisation of the Roman Empire did not wipe out the evils of pagan society, Hart is generous in concessions to the opposition. He has no illusions about the great Christian emperors. Constantine was 'a violent, puritanical, ponderous, late Roman brute'. Theodosius was a harsh persecutor of pagans and heretics. Justinian was one 'whom nobody very much liked or likes'. Surprisingly, the one emperor who gets a kind word is Constantine's apostate nephew Julian, who tried to reintroduce paganism: 'Of all the emperors in the Constantinian line Julian alone stands free of any suspicion of bad faith. He was also without question the most estimable and attractive of the lot.'

It is wrong, Hart argues, to see Christianity as invading a joyful pagan milieu of vitality and mirth, and turning the world grey with its breath. Late antiquity was an era of fear and melancholy, and contempt for the body was a leitmotif of many of its thinkers. Christianity was a liberating message, in which the resurrection of Jesus offered hope of the transfiguration of the flesh and the glorification of all creation.

In the present world, Christianity slowly gave greater freedom to the oppressed. The legislation of Constantine and Thedosius II improved the status of women, whether virgins, wives or widows. Christian husbands, unlike pagan ones, could not force their wives to submit to abortion or expose their infants. In the course of Christian history, the foundation of hospitals, leper asylums, almshouses and hostels palliated the lot of the most downtrodden members of society.

Hart cannot deny that the institution of slavery long outlasted Western Europe's conversion to Christianity. With a shrug, he observes that it is no more surprising that some pagan moral values survived in a Christian culture than that some Christian moral values survive in our secular culture today. He can point to imperial edicts ameliorating the lot of slaves, and he can quote a sermon of Gregory of Nyssa as early as 379 that attacked slavery as an institution, denouncing as blasphemous the claim of any human being to own another human being.

In his final plea for the defence, Hart puts to the jury the question, 'When Christianity departs, what is left behind?' The highest ideals of the secular project, he proclaims, are borrowed ideals, and Nietzsche was right that any effort to cast off the

Christian faith while retaining the best elements of Christian morality is doomed to defeat. In an ultimate flourish he dons the robes of opposing counsel.

> To use Richard Dawkins justly famous metaphor (which unfortunately he does not quite grasp is a metaphor), memes like 'human rights' and 'human dignity' may not indefinitely continue to replicate themselves once the Christian 'infinite value of every life' meme has died out.

Let us now abandon the forensic context and ask how accurate is Hart's historical narrative. The set-piece treatments of the iconic events of secularist propaganda – the burning of the Alexandria library, the Spanish Inquisition, the trial of Galileo and so on – are detailed and often convincing. But the book is full of generalisations that spur the reader to look for – and often to find – counter examples. For instance, in expounding the significance of the gospel story of the denial and repentance of Peter, Hart claims that in a pagan world 'Peter, as a rustic, could not possibly have been a worthy object of a well-bred man's sympathy.' To say this is to ignore the existence of a whole genre of classical poetry devoted to the joys and sorrows of rustics, namely pastoral elegy.

Frequently, in order to emphasise the originality of Christianity, Hart devalues the achievements of classical antiquity. Science as we understand it, he claims, depends on Christian underpinning. But if science is the collaborative pursuit of truth about the world by empirical inquiries whose results are structured into a theoretical discipline, then the West's first centre of scientific research was Aristotle's Lyceum.

Hart is not at his best when discussing Aristotle. He cannot have read *The History of Animals* when he calls Albert the Great 'the father of biological field research'. In physics he believes that Aristotle's prime mover was an outermost crystalline sphere, when in fact it was an incorporeal divinity outside the universe. (How Hart would have crowed if he had come across such a howler in Hitchens!) Hart is right that the discoveries of Copernicus, Kepler, Galileo and Newton were not so much a liberation from religious authority as from latter-day Aristotelianism. But the persistence of Aristotle's cosmology for many centuries after its sell-by date was partly due to the religious cultures into which it survived. His works became the possession of 'peoples of the book' – Muslims, Jews and Christians, and accordingly they were treated in the way that sacred texts are treated. That is why many of the greatest minds of the Middle Ages, instead of following Aristotle's example of original investigation, wrote commentaries on his scientific works.

Hart's comparisons between classical and Christian eras are all too often partisan. In order to portray Christianity as more cheerful than paganism he has to downplay the patristic teaching that an eternity of torment awaited the majority of mankind. To claim that the ultimate equality of all humans is an exclusively Christian doctrine he has to ignore the teaching of Stoics such as the slave Epictetus and the emperor Marcus Aurelius. To explain his admiration of Julian the Apostate he has to claim that of all the emperors between Constantine and Theodosius he was the most 'genuinely Christian in sensibility'.

The truth is surely that the institutions and values we cherish, like the works of art and architecture that we prize, are not the exclusive property of any one stage in our long history. Some institutions, like democracy, were invented in the ancient world and others, like universities, date from the Middle Ages. Some values, such as philanthropy, are part of our Judaeo-Christian inheritance, others such as freedom of speech, we owe to the Enlightenment. Some values and institutions can be credited to more recent times, such as the abolition of slavery and the empowerment of women. Surely, we should be grateful to our ancestors, near and distant, for the good things they handed on to us, and we should do our best to eradicate the evils we have inherited from them. But we can also agree with Hart that to regard our own age as blest beyond all others with an overplus of good versus evil is the height of folly.

Times Literary Supplement, 19 February 2010

Edward Feser
The Last Superstition: A Refutation of the New Atheism
St Augustine's Press, 2010

Recent years have seen a proliferation of atheist best-sellers and theist counterblasts. According to the devout, the four horsemen of this contemporary apocalypse are Richard Dawkins, Sam Harris, Daniel Dennett and Christopher Hitchens. Edward Feser's book sets out to give a definitive death blow to all of them at once.

In this good cause he does not hesitate to use the same weapons as his atheist adversaries: tendentious paraphrase, imputation of bad faith, outright insult. Dawkins 'wouldn't know metaphysics from Metamucil' and suffers from a 'Narcissistic Personality Disorder'. Harris is 'a dead ringer for comedian Ben Stiller'. Dennett provides 'a really disgusting spectacle'. Hitchens is 'a *Vanity Fair* boy'. All four of them, in fact, are shallow and sophomoric jackasses. 'If these guys don't believe in purgatory they should read their own books.'

The author defends his polemical style by saying, 'I believe this tone is appropriate, indeed necessary, for the New Atheism derives whatever influence it has far more from its rhetorical force and "sex appeal" than from its very thin intellectual content.' Its rhetoric, he says, must be met with equal and opposite force. But there is no requirement to return evil for evil, and the pursuit of truth is not helped by cheap jibes. Indeed, for British readers, constant references to American chat-show hosts and TV commercials make the chase harder rather than easier.

Fortunately, the book contains far more argument than invective, and in order to keep the reader's attention Feser has no need to descend to vulgar abuse, because he has the rare and enviable gift of making philosophical argument compulsively readable. The book fascinates because of the boldness of its metaphysical claims combined with the denseness of the arguments offered in their support. One of its major merits is to present a forceful revisionist picture of the entire history of Western philosophy.

There is a popular master narrative of the history of philosophy that goes like this. Philosophy was started in the ancient world by Plato and Aristotle, who were not bad philosophers considering how long ago they lived. However, once the Western world became Christian, philosophy went into hibernation for many centuries and saw as its only task to write footnotes to Aristotle. To be sure, some of the scholastic philosophers of the Middle Ages were clever chaps, but they wasted their talents on logical quibbles and pettifogging distinctions. It was only when Aristotle's metaphysics was thrown over in the Renaissance that philosophy got into its stride again and renewed its connection with scientific inquiry. Descartes showed that the way to understand the material universe was to treat it as a conglomeration of purposeless material objects operating according to blind laws: there was no need for Aristotle's final causes. While Descartes was a rationalist, a succession of philosophers writing in English, from Hobbes to Hume, showed that it was sensory experience, not reason, that was the basis of all our knowledge. Kant and his German idealist followers introduced a degree of obfuscation into philosophy, from which continental philosophy has never totally recovered. However, in Britain and America in the twentieth century philosophy re-emerged into the daylight with the logical empiricism of brilliant minds like Freddy Ayer.

Feser, rightly, rejects this entire story. He tells us that abandoning Aristotelianism, as the founders of modern philosophy did, was the single greatest mistake ever made in the entire history of Western thought. He regards the medieval Aristotelian synthesis of St Thomas Aquinas as the high point of philosophy, from which later scholastics such as John Duns Scotus and William Ockham fell away. He devotes a chapter to exhibiting the history of modern philosophy, from Descartes to Kant via the British empiricists, as a story of successive and ever greater intellectual catastrophes. It was the abandonment of Aristotelianism, he claims, which threw up the pseudo-problems that still haunt us: the mind–body problem, the problem of induction, the problem of personal identity, and so on.

In preparation for his thesis, Feser takes the reader through the history of philosophy from the pre-Socratics to Aquinas. He moves at such a steeplechase gallop that an informed reader constantly expects him to be unhorsed at some of the major fences of ancient and medieval metaphysics; but no, he keeps in the saddle despite the obstacles, and he never seriously misleads the reader. He presents fairly and clearly the Aristotelian distinction between actuality and potentiality and its fundamental importance for understanding the world. He expounds Aristotle's doctrine of the four causes – efficient, material, formal and final – and he emphasises the great difference between an Aristotelian efficient cause and causation as modernly conceived as a relationship between events. He places most emphasis on the final cause – the end, the purpose, the good to be achieved by some action or process.

Aristotle, more than any other philosopher, emphasised the importance of teleology in the world. As Feser stresses, Aristotle thought it was a ubiquitous feature of the universe, so that there were kinds of goal-directedness that existed apart from conscious thought and intentions. The budding of a rose and the building of a spider's web were no less teleological than human activities; but Aristotle knew better than to attribute consciousness to roses and spiders.

We should at this point make a distinction between two kinds of teleology: purpose and design. Design differs from purpose because design is purpose preceded by an idea: a thought, or blueprint, in somebody's mind. If the world is designed, then there was a precedent idea in the mind of the creator – what, in the Fourth Gospel, is called the *logos* or Word. Aristotle did not believe that the world was created; for him teleology was a basic fact about the cosmos, and no extra-cosmic designer was needed to explain it.

It was Aquinas who formulated the argument from purpose to design. Things without awareness, he argued in the Fifth Way, do not tend towards a goal unless directed by something with awareness and intelligence, in the way that an arrow is aimed by an archer. The ultimate designer, the arch-archer, is, according to Aquinas, what we call God.

In the early modern era, Descartes sought to revolutionise philosophy by expunging teleology altogether. He eliminated, outside the human realm, purpose as well as design. Final causation, he thought, was a piece of scholastic nonsense. He rejected the explanation of gravity in terms of attraction between bodies, on the grounds that this postulated in inert entities knowledge of a goal or terminus.

With Darwin in the nineteenth century we return to the position of Aristotle: the world contains purpose but not, outside the human realm, design. It is sometimes thought that Darwinism gave the final death blow to teleology; but that, as Feser stresses, is the opposite of the truth. Darwinian scientists have not given up the search for final causes. On the contrary, contemporary biologists are much more adept at discerning the functions of structures and behaviour than their ancient, medieval or Cartesian predecessors. However, Darwin agreed with Aquinas against Aristotle that teleology was not a basic fact, but something needing explanation. His innovation was to offer, in natural selection, a recipe for translating it into a naturalistic explanation that made no call on design. His successors propose to translate final causes into efficient ones – the red teeth and red claws involved in the struggle for survival.

Feser ingeniously argues that this translation is not possible. According to the Darwinian theory, to say that our kidneys have the function of purifying the blood amounts to something like this: those of our ancestors who first developed kidneys (as the result of a random genetic mutation) tended to survive in greater numbers than those without kidneys, because their blood got purified; and this caused the gene for kidneys to get passed on. To say that an organ's function (now) is to do X is therefore shorthand for saying that it was selected for by evolution because its earliest ancestors did X. But this leads to two absurd conclusions: first, that you can't know the function of an organ unless you know its evolutionary history; secondly, that the first kidneys, or whatever, didn't have a function because they hadn't been selected for.

Having rejected the Cartesian elimination of teleology, and the Darwinian reduction of it to efficient causality, Feser opts for Aquinas' view that teleology can only be explained if there is a supreme divine intelligence. With respect to the fourth possible position, that of Aristotle, he is both too lenient and too demanding. He is too lenient in accepting Aristotle's claim for the ubiquity of teleology, too demanding in rejecting Aristotle's idea that teleology is a basic fact of the universe.

The teleological explanation of an action or a process involves three things: that the agent should have a certain tendency to act, that the nature of that activity should be specified by its terminus, not its origin, and that the end state should be beneficial either to the agent or to something intrinsically connected to the agent. Aristotle believed that this type of explanation applied to the motions of inanimate objects no less than to living organisms. He explained the downward motion of heavy bodies by saying that they were seeking their natural place, the place where it was good for them to be. The Newtonian explanation of gravity incorporates the first two elements of teleology, but not the third: there is no suggestion that gravitational attraction is something for the benefit of the bodies involved. If one accepts Newton's physics rather than Aristotle's, there is no reason to think that teleology is ubiquitous.

Feser accepts Aquinas' claim that things without awareness only tend to a goal if directed to it by intelligence. It is impossible, he says, 'for a thing to be directed towards an end unless that end exists in an intellect which directs the thing in question towards it'. But what reason is there to accept this thesis rather than Aristotle's claim that teleology, where it exists, is a basic feature of the universe? Feser's argument is that what does not yet actually exist (e.g. a house) cannot bring about an effect unless it already exists somewhere, and the only place in which it can exist is in someone's intellect (e.g. the architect's). But surely this is to treat final causes as if they were efficient causes: for it is only of such causes that it is true that an effect cannot precede its cause. And the elimination of the difference between efficient and final causes was Feser's great complaint against the Darwinians.

Thus Feser's attempt to use Aquinas' Fifth Way to establish the existence of God fails. Feser also presents dense and plausible versions of the First and Second Way, but each of them, I believe, is ultimately fallacious. There is no space in a review to show this. Feser has a habit, when his argument appears a little thin, of pointing to fuller versions of it in his other books. If I may follow his example, I would refer the reader to my *The Five Ways* in which I have taken 120 pages to point out the flaws in Aquinas' arguments.

Feser believes that the various arguments of Aquinas establish the existence of a God whose essence is to exist. That this is a nonsensical notion was briskly shown many years ago by a philosopher for whom Feser, rightly, has a great admiration. Peter Geach, in *Three Philosophers*, imagines the following dialogue:

> *Theist.*   There is a God.
>
> *Atheist.*   So *you* say: but what sort of being is this God of yours?
>
> *Theist.*   Why, I've just told you! There *is* a God; *that's* what God is!

It is a striking feature of Feser's book that he claims to be basing his contentions entirely on reason and not on faith. Certainly, he never explicitly appeals to any sacred text or religious teacher as an authority. But he makes extensive claims for the powers of reason. Pure reason, he tells us, proves that there is a God and that we have immortal souls. That shows that a miracle like resurrection from the dead is possible. Given that background, the evidence that Jesus rose from the dead is overwhelming. But Jesus claimed to be divine and claimed that his teachings would be confirmed by his resurrection. Hence, reason shows that he really was divine. But he was obviously distinct from the Father to whom he prayed and the Spirit whom he sent. So reason shows the doctrine of the Trinity to be true.

This is to extend the scope of natural reason much further than even Thomas Aquinas was willing to do. While agreeing, in the main, with Feser's revisionist account of the history of philosophy, I would wish personally to question every sentence in the previous paragraph. But Feser has serious reasons for all of his assertions. Unlike many of the other contributors to the recent theism–atheism debate, he is always well worth arguing with. But after as well as before the debate, the default position is surely one of agnosticism. We must confess that where the existence of God is concerned we do not know one way or the other.

Times Literary Supplement, 22 July 2011

Alex Rosenberg
*The Atheist's Guide to Reality: Enjoying Life
without Illusions*
W.W. Norton & Co., 2011

Alvin Plantinga
*Where the Conflict Really Lies: Science,
Religion, and Naturalism*
Oxford University Press, 2011

In his early work *Tractatus Logico-Philosophicus*, Ludwig Wittgenstein wrote, 'The right method of philosophy would be to say nothing except what can be said, that is to say the propositions of natural science.' Regrettably, the sentences that constituted the *Tractatus* itself were not propositions of natural science. In consistency, Wittgenstein had to concede that they were nothing more than nonsense. Peter Geach later nicknamed this line of thought 'Ludwig's Self-Trap'.

Wittgenstein spent the latter part of his life repenting of the claim that only scientific statements made sense. But others were willing to follow him into similar traps. Logical positivists proclaimed the verification principle: meaningful propositions were either analytic or capable of verification or falsification by experience. However, the verification principle itself was neither analytic nor empirical. Accordingly, it had to be meaningless.

Surprisingly, there are still philosophers willing to explore these blind alleys. In *The Atheist's Guide to Reality* Alex Rosenberg asserts repeatedly that physics is the whole truth about reality: the physical facts fix all the facts. But *that there are no facts other than physical facts* is not itself a physical fact. If it is a fact at all, then there is at least one fact that is not a physical fact. If it is not a fact, but a falsehood, then there are facts other than physical facts. The self-trap snaps shut.

In his lively, provocative book Rosenberg presents a philosophy that he describes as scientistic and nihilistic. Both scientism and nihilism, he concedes, are normally regarded as obnoxious. Scientism, according to one standard definition, is 'an exaggerated confidence in the methods of science as the most (or the only) reliable tools of inquiry'. Nihilism, on the other hand, is the thesis that all moral judgements are untenable nonsense. Undaunted by popular disdain, Rosenberg carries a banner for scientism combined with nihilism as the only true philosophy.

The main tenets of this philosophy are bracingly summed up in a series of questions and answers. Is there a God? No. What is the nature of reality? What physics says it is. What is the purpose of the universe? There is none. What is the meaning of life? Ditto. Why am I here? Just dumb luck. Does prayer work? Of course not. Is there a soul? Is it immortal? You must be kidding. Is there free will? Not a chance! What is the difference between right and wrong, good and bad? There is no moral difference between them.

Few readers are likely to agree with all of Rosenberg's answers to his own questions, but different readers will no doubt dissent at different points. An atheist biologist, for instance, may reject the idea that biology is reducible to physics: there is top-down causation as well as bottom-up causation. Physics determines biology, Rosenberg claims. Maybe so, but there is an ambiguity in the word 'determine'. The laws of chess determine every game of chess in the sense that no chess move ever violates those laws; but they do not predict the course of any individual game. Similarly, physics determines biology in the sense that no biological event violates any law of physics; but if the systems biologists are right, events at the higher biological level settle which of many physically possible courses are actually taken.

Others may wish to dissent when it comes to the freedom of the will. To disprove its existence Rosenberg appeals to the well-known experiments of Benjamin Libet. Subjects were asked to push a button at will. It was found that the moment at which they reported taking a conscious decision to push the button was later than the commencement of the brain processes responsible for wrist-flexing. Accordingly, Rosenberg concludes, consciously deciding to do something is not the cause of doing it.

Whether this experiment is relevant to the issue of human freedom depends on a philosophical understanding of what makes an action free. Many philosophers, from Descartes to the present day, have believed that there are interior acts of the will (volitions) whose occurrence makes the difference between voluntary and involuntary actions. On this view, for an action to be voluntary is for it to be preceded and caused by a characteristic internal impression or conscious thought. Now this account has many times been exposed as a grotesque philosophical error – long ago, in anticipation, by Aristotle, and notably in recent times by Gilbert Ryle. What Libet's experiments show is not that we do not have free will, but that the order of events when an experimental subject presses a button is not the one to be expected on the basis of a mistaken philosophical thesis.

One of Rosenberg's more extravagant claims is that nobody ever thinks about anything. Scientism, he says, makes us give up as illusory the notion that when we think our thoughts are about *anything at all*, inside or outside of our minds. His argument goes like this: the mind is identical with the brain, so a thought must be an event in the brain. But no clump of neurons can be *about* anything. Therefore no thought is about anything.

Rosenberg's second premise is undoubtedly true. His first premise, however, involves a category mistake. The brain and the mind are not identical, because the brain is a material object, while the mind is a capacity (or stratified set of capacities). The importance of keeping the categories distinct is highlighted by the absurdity of Rosenberg's conclusion. The absurdity is made manifest by Rosenberg himself in the many passages in which he refers to thoughts about things. Within the space of four pages, for instance, he tells us that we form hypotheses about other people's motives, that we tell stories about art, and that we can acquire correct information about matters that keep us awake at night.

Rosenberg's style is clear and forceful, and in the course of his narrative he has many illuminating things to say. I found particularly interesting, for instance, his discussion of the relation between evolution and entropy, and his claim that the second law of thermodynamics makes reconciliation between theism and Darwinism logically impossible. But long before the end of the book I felt that scientism and nihilism fully deserved their bad name.

It is a striking feature of recent debates about the existence of God that nowadays it is the atheists rather than the theists who write with missionary fervour and a passionate desire to convert the reader. The more defensive stance of theists is well exemplified in Al Plantinga's *Where the Conflict Really Lies*: the book seems aimed not so much to turn nihilists into believers as to reassure Christians that they have nothing to fear from the progress of science.

Plantinga's thesis is that there is superficial conflict but deep concord between science and religion, and superficial concord but deep conflict between science and naturalism. Naturalism denies the existence of God and the immortality of the soul:

a human being is just another animal with a peculiar way of making a living. Famous writers – Dawkins, Dennett, Hitchens and Harris, 'the Four Horsemen of atheism' – would have us believe that naturalism is part of the scientific world-view. Plantinga sets out to prove them wrong: naturalism is not a piece of science, but a metaphysical add-on.

The first question is whether contemporary evolutionary theory is incompatible with Christian belief. The conflict, Plantinga says, is much exaggerated; there is indeed conflict between unguided evolution and Christian belief, but it is no part of evolutionary theory to declare that evolution is in fact unguided. It is perfectly possible both that life has come to be by way of guided natural selection, and that it could not have come to be by way of unguided natural selection.

God's action in the world, we are told, need not be restricted to the setting of initial conditions in the universe or to the overall guidance of evolutionary processes. Neither Newtonian physics nor quantum mechanics rules out the thought that God acts specially in the world, perhaps by way of miracle. Newtonian laws are stated for causally closed systems: they do not state that the physical system in which we live is a closed system, and no system in which God acts specially would be a closed system. The advent of quantum mechanics has made it even harder to find conflict between divine action and current physics.

Theism, Plantinga argues, provides a much more congenial home for science than naturalism does. Historically, it was Christian Europe that fostered modern science. In principle, for science to be possible, the universe has to be stable and regular, and these features have to be accessible to human cognitive powers. There must be a congruence between the truth about the world and our intellectual faculties. Naturalism gives no reason why there should be such a congruence: it can only be a matter of sheer luck. But it is what is to be expected if the universe is the work of a Creator who has made humans in his own image.

Plantinga is at his most persuasive when exhibiting defects in the naturalist world-view and when disarming neo-Darwinist attempts to eliminate intelligent design. He is also properly judicious: he warns us against attaching too great importance to some popular creationist ploys, such as the argument from irreducible complexity and the appeal to the fine-tuning of the universe. He is not at all the kind of theist who will welcome any or every argument in favour of the conclusions to which he is committed.

However, it is not at all clear how the appeal to divine action solves the problems left unexplained by contemporary science. How are we to suppose that God acts in the world? Plantinga accepts a dualist view of human action, and seems to think of God as something like a Cartesian ego on a colossal scale. But we humans are not Cartesian egos: we are rational animals, and we act in the world as material objects among other material objects. If God is simple and immaterial it is hard to see how human action can provide an analogy for, and therefore give meaning to, the notion of divine action.

On one point Rosenberg and Plantinga agree: they think that if human beings are products of unguided natural selection then it is highly improbable that their cognitive faculties are reliable guides to truth. So much the worse for unguided natural selection, concludes Plantinga; so much the worse for our beliefs about the world, concludes Rosenberg.

For my part, I find the common premise quite incredible. To be sure, there is no reason to believe that natural selection would provide us all with equipment for reaching truths of metaphysics or religion, and the history of philosophy and theology suggests that it has not done so. But at any moment I have many much less grand beliefs, about where I am, which and what other animals are nearby, what I can and cannot do unaided, what is good to eat and what is poisonous, which kinds of places and routes are safe and which are not. Unless the overwhelming majority of such of my beliefs are true, and have been since I was a child, I would never have had any hope of survival, let alone of passing on my genes.

Times Literary Supplement, 22 June 2012

Roger Scruton
The Face of God
Continuum, 2012

This book is the published version of the Gifford Lectures of
2010. Scruton begins by describing, and deploring, the current
atheist scientific world-view, according to which everything
happens in accordance with the laws of nature, and those laws
themselves are contingent, neither needing nor getting any
further explanation. He wants us to ask ourselves, 'To what end,
and for what reason, do we live in a law-governed world?'

Neither traditional natural theology, he believes, nor
fashionable arguments from fine-tuning can provide a
satisfactory answer to this question. How then can the
transcendent God of whom philosophers speak be reconciled
with the God who is prayed to by the ordinary believer? The key
is to realise that God is understood not through metaphysical
speculation, but through communion with our fellow human
beings. 'The religious community adapts the view from nowhere
that is God's to the view from somewhere that is ours.'

The 'view from somewhere' is, for Scruton, the identifying
feature of human beings: their first-person perspective on the
world. He emphasises the enormous differences that there are
between humans and other animals. Many people today –
whether animal liberationists or proselytising neo-Darwinians
– have an interest in downplaying these differences. Such
people, Scruton observes, 'all too often end either by describing
us as far simpler than we are, or by describing the lower animals
as far more complex than they are'. He is unimpressed either

by the soldier ant marching into the flames that threaten the anthill or the vampire bat sharing out to others her stocks of blood. Attempts to assimilate human altruism to such activities succeed only by giving the most superficial account of both.

In our concept of human beings, the face has a unique importance. (Animals, Scruton claims, have no concept of the face.) If we try to give an account of human beings solely in terms of scientific objectivity, we will eliminate human action, intention, responsibility, freedom and emotion. What we describe will be a world without a face. 'The face shines in the world of objects with a light that is not of this world – the light of subjectivity.'

What has all this to do with God? Does God have a face? In the third chapter of Exodus God says to Moses, 'Thou canst not see my face, for there shall no man see me and live.' But earlier, when Moses had sought to know God's name, God replied, 'I AM THAT I AM.' Scruton take this as meaning that God is a person, an agent, and an 'I'– he is, in short, everything that in humans is manifested in the face. In fact, the most natural reading of the Hebrew sentence is as a rebuff to Moses, a refusal to reveal the name. But Christian exegetes have always wanted to read more than that into the divine utterance. Whereas Aquinas built from the Mosaic 'I AM' a theory of God as the supreme Being, Scruton now builds a theory of God as the supreme First Person.

To understand what God is, Scruton explains, we have to understand the pronoun 'I' as used by and of human beings. 'I', he tells us, is an expression that refers to a self-conscious and self-referring subject. When he himself says 'I' he is not referring to the Roger Scruton we know and love – that is a mere object, whereas he is referring to a subject. He is well informed, he claims, about that object; indeed, he believes that he is in some mysterious sense identical with it – but it is possible that he could be wrong.

Scruton's account of the human use of 'I' will not convince those who do not believe that the first-person pronoun is a name of anything at all. But a far wider group will object to his account of God as possessing a subjective point of view on the world. '[God] moves in the world, in a somewhere of his own,' he tells us – and then goes on to say that this 'is precisely what sends shivers down the Islamic spine'. Not only Muslims but orthodox Christians may well be affronted by the account here given: belief in the incarnation has always gone hand in hand with an insistence that God, as God, is ubiquitous and eternal and does not view the world as we do from a particular location in space and time.

Before telling us, at the end of his book, how we can come to see the face of God, Scruton discusses the face in art, and the face of the earth in nature and in the built environment. He writes about sex, music and painting with his customary intelligence and sensitivity, and he illustrates his insights with convincing examples. This book, like his others, is full of original and fascinating ideas which range between the persuasive and the preposterous.

In his final chapter Scruton proposes that religion – and especially the Christian religion – answers to a fundamental human need to give thanks, to see the world and our being in it as a gift. God, he claims, is not to be encountered in any self-verifying experience, nor does he provide a causal explanation of the universe. We see the face of God whenever we encounter among human beings suffering and renunciation for the sake of another.

There are many fine observations in this final chapter, but I found it hard to understand what was meant by the 'metaphysical loneliness' for which Scruton thinks religion is the cure. There is, he believes, a terrible separation between a self-conscious being and the world to which he belongs. There is, he says, a fatal fracture – 'the fracture between subject and object that *runs through me*'. Unsympathetic readers may wonder whether the fracture is metaphysical only in the sense that it is an element of Scruton's idiosyncratic metaphysics of the first-person pronoun.

Loneliness is indeed a terrible thing, and one of the benefits of membership of a religious community is that it provides a cure for loneliness. Loneliness, yes – but *metaphysical* loneliness? I am tempted to adopt a diagnosis which Scruton himself has used elsewhere when dismissing the therapeutic claims of psychoanalysis: 'There is no cure, because there is no disease.'

Times Literary Supplement, 14 December 2012

PART SEVEN

MODERN MORAL
THEOLOGY

Introduction

When, in the nineteenth century, many ceased to believe in God it became a serious question whether, after ages in which religion and ethics had been closely linked, morality could survive the demise of belief. Conservative thinkers denied that it could, and denounced atheists as immoralists. Liberal reformers, from Jeremy Bentham onwards, declared that morality was quite independent of religion. We cannot appeal to the will of God to settle whether something is right; we have to know first whether it is right in order to decide whether it is conformable to God's will. Bentham proposed that moral and political systems should be evaluated in accordance with the extent to which they promoted the greatest happiness of the greatest number.

Bentham's utilitarianism remains to this day – with some modifications – the most popular alternative system in opposition to traditional Christian morality. It is not, however, clear what it involves. To be sure, Bentham is steadfast in identifying happiness with pleasure. However, though 'The greatest happiness of the greatest number' is an impressive slogan, when probed it turns out to be riddled with ambiguity. The first question to be raised is 'greatest number of *what?*' Should we add 'voters' or 'citizens' or 'males' or 'human beings' or 'sentient beings'? It makes a huge difference which answer we give. Throughout the two centuries of utilitarianism's history most of its devotees would probably give the answer 'human beings', and this is most likely the answer Bentham himself would have given. In recent years many utilitarians have extended the happiness principle beyond humankind to other sentient beings, claiming that animals have an equal claim with human beings.

It is important to note what is the really significant difference between utilitarianism and other moral systems. We may divide moralists into absolutists and consequentialists. Absolutists believe that there are some kinds of action that are intrinsically wrong, and should never be done, irrespective of any consideration of the consequences. Consequentialists believe that the morality of actions should be judged by their consequences, and that there is no category of act which may not, in special circumstances, be justified by its consequences. Prior to Bentham most philosophers were absolutists, because they believed in a natural law, or natural rights.

Bentham rejected the notion of natural law, on the grounds that no two people could agree what it was. He was scornful of natural rights, believing that real rights could only be conferred by positive law. If there is no natural law and no natural rights, then no class of actions can be ruled out in advance of the consideration of the consequences of such an action in a particular case.

This difference between Bentham and previous moralists is highly significant, as can be easily illustrated. Aristotle, Aquinas and almost all Christian moralists believed that adultery was always wrong. Not so for Bentham: the consequences foreseen by a particular adulterer must be taken into account before making a moral judgement. A believer in natural law, told that some Herod or Nero has killed five thousand citizens guilty of no crime, will say without further ado, 'that was a wicked act'. A thoroughgoing consequentialist, before making such a judgement, must ask further questions. What were the consequences of the massacre? What did the monarch foresee? What would have happened if he had allowed the five thousand to live?

In the twentieth century many philosophers rejected utilitarianism, not because of any abhorrence of consequentialism, but on the basis of various theories of meaning. G. E. Moore, at the beginning of the century, claimed that goodness, the supreme moral value, was a non-natural quality, and utilitarians, by identifying goodness with pleasure, committed a fallacy: the naturalistic fallacy of confusing a non-natural property with a natural one. Later, under the influence of logical positivism, some philosophers began to deny that goodness was any sort of property, natural or non-natural, and to claim that ethical utterances were not statements of fact at all, but simply expressions of emotion. Such emotivists, however, were unable to show in what way logic enters into moral reasoning when we use words like 'because' and 'therefore'.

R. M. Hare, the most famous English moral philosopher in mid-century, was anxious to make room in ethics for logic: a logic of imperatives. He distinguished between prescriptive and descriptive meaning. A descriptive statement is one whose meaning is defined by the factual conditions for its truth. A prescriptive sentence is one which entails, perhaps in conjunction with descriptive statements, at least one imperative. To assent to an imperative is to prescribe action, to tell oneself or others to do this or do that.

Value judgements may contain a word like 'good' or a word like 'ought'. To call something 'good' is to commend it: to call something a good X is to say that it is the kind of X that should be chosen by anyone who wants an X. There will be different criteria for the goodness of Xs and the goodness of Ys, but this does not amount to a difference in the meaning of the word 'good', which is exhausted by its commendatory function. 'Ought' statements – which Hare, following Hume, thought could never be derived from 'is' statements – entail imperatives. Ought sentences, however, are not just prescriptive, but unlike common-or-garden commands they are universalisable.

Hare distinguished between ethics and morals. Ethics is the study of the general features of moral language, of which prescriptivity and universalisability are the most important; moral judgements are prescriptions and prohibitions of specific actions. In principle, ethics is neutral between different and conflicting moral systems. But this does not mean that ethics is practically vacuous: once an understanding of ethics is combined with the desires and beliefs of an actual moral agent, it can lead to concrete and important moral judgements.

In the late 1950s Hare's prescriptivism was subjected to devastating criticism by a number of Oxford colleagues, and as the century progressed philosophers began to focus their attention not so much on the higher-order questions such as the nature of moral language, or the logic of imperatives, but on specific first-order issues such as the rightness or wrongness of particular actions: lying, abortion, torture and euthanasia. Many of the most insightful discussions of these life-and-death issues came from philosophers who wrote from a religious viewpoint without directly invoking any religious authority.

John E. Hare
God and Morality: A Philosophical History
Blackwell, 2007

In this admirably lucid and agreeably readable book John E. Hare, Professor of Philosophical Theology at Yale, emphasises the importance of theology for the understanding of ethical theory and its history. He concentrates on four moralists, one ancient, one medieval, one modern and one contemporary. Each figure illustrates a different ethical focus: one on virtue, one on will, one on duty and one on consequences. The three historical figures selected are Aristotle, Scotus and Kant. Scotus is a philosopher who is unfairly neglected, and in Aristotle and Kant the theological element is unduly downplayed.

In treating of these authors Hare is scholarly without being pedantic and original without being polemical. He has a sharp eye for the foibles of his philosophical contemporaries, but he writes with a gentle humility that enlists the reader's sympathy. He argues convincingly that it is no less odd to avoid theism in the history of Western ethics than it would be in the history of Western art – a field from which he draws many illuminating illustrations.

The final book of Aristotle's *Nicomachean Ethics* holds up the contemplation of the divine as the happiest life and the goal of human existence. A final passage in his *Eudemian Ethics* says that the criterion for best action is 'whatever choice or possession of natural goods – bodily goods, wealth, friends and the like – will most conduce to the contemplation of God'. As Hare points out, modern secular commentators find these passages no less embarrassing than Aristotle's views on women and slavery. They disown the last book of the *Nicomachean Ethics* in favour of the first book, which they interpret as permitting a more inclusive concept of happiness. In the case of the *Eudemian* passage they go so far as to amend the text, without MS warrant, in order to keep God out of it. Hare is surely right to denounce this secularising tendency as a distortion of Aristotle's system.

When we move to the Middle Ages, some readers might have expected to find Aquinas, rather than Scotus, chosen as the medieval representative of moral theory. But Hare's choice is entirely apt. Scotus, not Aquinas, was the great innovator in ethics: it was he who gave the notion of divine law the central position it henceforth enjoyed in Christian moral thinking. Aquinas, like Aristotle, had structured his ethical system not around the concept of law, but around the concept of virtue as the route to self-fulfilment in happiness.

Hare brings out clearly the way in which Scotus' theory leads on to the Kantian ethic of duty. Kant, like Aristotle, has been secularised by his modern admirers. For Kant human beings are ends in themselves, but they are members of a kingdom of ends. Every rational being in making moral choices lays down law for himself and for all his peers; we are all both legislators and subjects. Kant made room for a sovereign who was a legislator but not himself subject to law: this was obviously God. Kant's successors have quietly dropped the sovereign and turned the kingdom of ends into a republic in which no legislator is privileged over any other. In Hare's view, this has destroyed an essential element of the Kantian system.

When Hare comes to choose a twentieth-century representative of consequentialism, he selects for treatment his father, the Oxford philosopher Richard Mervyn Hare (1919–2002).

I know that some will think that exaggerated filial piety has led me to end with my own father. But I needed a utilitarian and I wanted a contemporary or at least near contemporary, and one whose theory I could write about rather than his applications of the theory. What other figure is plausible, given those constraints?

Fair enough – and at this point I should myself declare an interest of a kind. As an undergraduate John Hare was a pupil of mine, and for some years I was a close colleague of his father, when we were both philosophy tutors at Balliol. Richard Hare was one of the most formidable intelligences I have ever encountered. During our years together I do not remember ever once winning an intellectual argument with him.

In any study of twentieth-century Anglophone moral philosophy, R. M. Hare is bound to occupy a prominent place. After positivists had downgraded ethical judgements to little more than expressions of emotion, he reminded the philosophical world that practical and moral thinking had its own genuine logic. Even if his own system attracted few wholehearted disciples, many other influential philosophers – such as Bernard Williams, Alasdair MacIntyre and Philippa Foot – developed their own views in explicit or implicit reaction against that system.

Nonetheless, in this volume R. M. Hare keeps uneasy company with Aristotle, Scotus and Kant. In the case of Aristotle and Kant our author has no difficulty in exhibiting a strong theological element that has been downgraded by secular commentators. But in the published work of R. M. Hare he has to labour to detect any religious element at all.

To be sure, in one of the most interesting sections of the book, the author reveals the existence of an unpublished text of his father's, 'An Essay on Monism', written while a prisoner of war working on the Burma–Thailand railway. This was profoundly religious and argued that without faith in God philosophy can never be a serious occupation, only a game.

R. M. Hare himself, however, never published this youthful essay, and in his later works religion makes only fleeting appearances. There is no entry for 'God' in the index to *The Language of Morals*. What remained of the earlier faith, to judge by the published works, was a conviction that the world was such as to make morality viable, which could perhaps be called faith in Providence. Throughout his life, his son tells us, Hare attended Anglican worship regularly and used to recite the creeds. In my own discussions with him I found it hard to tell how far he accepted the content of those creeds. To those who asked him if he was a Christian, his standard response was 'I don't know. I'll tell you what I believe, and then you tell me whether you count me a Christian or not.'

John Hare would no doubt deny any intention to Christianise his father posthumously, and his quest for a theist underpinning to his ethical system may not convince everybody. However, the history of ethics shows that one should not underestimate the value of philosophical filial piety. After Aristotle's death his son Nicomachus stitched together from various parts of his father's *Nachlass* an anthology, the *Nicomachean Ethics*, which was to become moral philosophy's all-time best-seller.

Times Literary Supplement, 1 October 2007

Richard Harries
*The Re-enchantment of Morality: Wisdom
for a Troubled World*
SPCK, 2008

Lenn E. Goodman
Love Thy Neighbour as Thyself
Oxford University Press, 2008

What is the relation between religion and morality? Can there be morality without religion? If so, is religion a help or a hindrance to leading a morally good life? These issues are widely discussed today and form the leading topic of these two books. Richard Harries, until recently Bishop of Oxford, addresses the questions from a Christian viewpoint; while Lenn Goodman, a philosopher from Vanderbilt University, does so from the viewpoint of Judaism.

The Re-enchantment of Morality is clearly written and well signposted. As a practised and popular preacher, Richard Harries is adept at making a serious point in a light-hearted remark and at illustrating a permanent truth with a topical reference. He has a good eye for a telling quotation and a good ear for a lively anecdote. His writing combines authority with humility, and many of his judgements will commend themselves to Christians and non-Christians alike.

Harries does not believe that morality is a system of divine commands. Things are right or wrong in themselves, and moral judgements are our own responsibility; if we obey God we do so because we see in him supreme goodness, and we must always be in a position to judge whether what is proposed in God's name is holy or wicked. But though it is possible to make valid ethical judgements without religious belief, Christianity adds an extra dimension, an 'enchantment' to the moral life, by presenting it as a response to a gracious God as revealed in the person and teaching of Jesus.

No system of autonomous ethics, we are told, is fully adequate. We cannot base moral theory on our own happiness, à la Aristotle, or on the general happiness, à la Bentham, unless we have a prior, pre-rational, recognition of value and worth. The Kantian emphasis on duty eliminates love from interpersonal relationships and places too much emphasis on the notion of law.

The morality of Jesus, according to Harries, was very different. His teaching did not consist in commands, and when he uttered imperatives, they were often couched in hyperbole. 'He was not', we are told, 'a literalist or a legislator.' Armed with this template for the interpretation of the gospel, Harries explores Jesus' teaching in relation to four drivers of human behaviour: sex, money, power and fame. He applies the message to public policy as well as to private life.

On these topics Harries' conclusions are always sensible and humane. But a secular reader is constantly tempted to ask to what extent they are Christian. On divorce and homosexuality, for instance, his recommendations run counter to apparently plain texts of the Bible and to many centuries of teaching by all the Churches. He would reply that individual items of Scripture and tradition are trumped by the overarching gospel imperative to love our neighbour. But the call to charity was no less known to Christian teachers of earlier ages than to moral theologians of the present century. One cannot help feeling that these developments of liberal thought in the Church are due not so much to deeper reflection on the Bible as to the teaching of secular moralists.

Of course many moral reformers of recent centuries were themselves educated in and influenced by religious beliefs. The interplay of the philosophical and theological components of moral progress is well described in a vivid image of our second book, Lenn Goodman's *Love Thy Neighbour as Thyself*:

> As I see it, the relationship between our idea of God and our conception of other value-laden ideas is properly dialectical, a matter of chimneying. We push off from the sheer rock face of our moral (or aesthetic, or cognitive) values, and back again from our idea of the Absolute, gaining height and a clearer view, if we can, at each pendulum swing between the opposing faces. The vista, if we gain the height to glimpse the monotheist's idea of God as the Source of all good – of light and life, wisdom and forgiveness – changes the air.

Goodman agrees with Harries that there can be ethics without reference to a God. No such reference is needed, he says, in order to forbid torture, mutilation, incest and rape. Moreover, not everything that is held out as God's command, even by sacred texts, can be unquestioningly accepted; Goodman subjects to close scrutiny biblical cruces such as the sacrifice of Isaac and the hewing of Agag. 'The idea of God', he concludes, 'must be disciplined and guided by our moral insights if those insights in turn are ever to be guarded or informed by our idea of God.' The metaphor of the chimney shows that no circularity need be involved here.

However, Goodman maintains, there are seven ways in which monotheism makes a difference in ethics. (1) It insists that our relation to others should be one of love, not merely of justice. (2) It issues absolute as well as conditional moral prohibitions. (3) It justifies self-sacrifice in moral causes. (4) Its ethics is universal, not local. (5) It encourages works of supererogation that go beyond moral obligation. (6) It concerns thoughts as well as deeds. (7) It encourages us to imitate the divine perfection.

Goodman argues for each of these claims and offers copious illustrations of them from the Hebrew Bible, from rabbinic literature and from Jewish philosophers such as Maimonides and Spinoza. (A very helpful appendix gives brief biographies of authors cited, many of whom will be unfamiliar to non-Jewish readers.) These citations offer a special perspective, but the book is in no way a sectarian treatise. It did, after all, begin life as a set of Gifford Lectures on natural theology.

Times Literary Supplement, 22 August 2008

David Albert Jones
The Soul of the Embryo
Continuum, 2004

When did I begin? When does any individual human being begin? At what stage of its development does a human organism become entitled to the moral and legal protection which we give to the life of human adults? Is it at conception, or at birth, or somewhere between the two? In his rich and fascinating book, simultaneously erudite and accessible, David Albert Jones records the answers to this question that have been given by different moral communities across cultures and across centuries. He takes the story from the book of Job and the Hippocratic corpus right up to the Warnock and Harries reports and the Human Reproductive Cloning Act of 2001. He offers closely reasoned arguments for the position he eventually defends, while treating fairly and courteously those he rejects. Though he concentrates on the Christian tradition, his book can be recommended to all those who have a serious interest in the moral issues surrounding abortion, IVF and stem cell research.

The three alternatives – at conception, at birth or between – do not in fact exhaust the possibilities. Plato, and some Jewish and Christian admirers of Plato, thought that individual human persons existed as souls before the conception of the bodies they would eventually inhabit. This idea found expression in the book of Wisdom, where Solomon says, 'I was a boy of happy disposition: I had received a good soul as my lot, or rather, being good, I had entered an undefiled body' (8:19–20). Clement of

Alexandria records an early Christian notion that the soul is introduced by an angel into a suitably purified womb. Jones is surely right to treat such fantasies as having little relevance to any contemporary moral debate.

But in addition to those who thought that the individual soul existed before conception, there have been those who thought that the individual body existed before conception, in the shape of the father's semen. Onan, in Genesis, spilt his seed on the ground; in Jewish tradition this was seen not only as a form of sexual pollution but an offence against life. Aquinas, in the *Summa contra Gentiles*, in a chapter on 'the disordered emission of semen', treats both masturbation and contraception as a crime against humanity, second only to homicide. Such a view is natural in the context of a biological belief that only the male gamete provides the active element in conception, so that the sperm is an early stage of the very same individual as eventually comes to birth. Masturbation is then the same kind of thing, on a minor scale, as the exposure of an infant. The high point of this line of thinking was the bull *Effraenatam* of Pope Sixtus V (1588), which imposed an excommunication, revocable only by the Pope himself, on all forms of contraception as well as on abortion. But the view that masturbation is a poor man's homicide cannot survive the knowledge that both male and female gametes contribute equally to the genetic constitution of the offspring.

At the other extreme are those who maintain that it is not until sometime after birth that human rights arise. In pagan antiquity infanticide was very broadly accepted. Jones quotes a chilling letter from a husband in Alexandria to his wife in first-century Rome: 'If you are delivered of a child before I come home, if it is a boy, keep it, if a girl discard it.' No sharp line was drawn between infanticide and abortion, and as a method of population control abortion was sometimes regarded as inferior to infanticide, since it did not distinguish between healthy and unhealthy offspring.

In our own time a number of secular philosophers have been prepared to defend infanticide of severely deformed and disabled children. They have based their position on a theory of personality that goes back to John Locke. Only persons have rights, and not every human being is a person: only one who, as Locke puts it, 'has reason and reflection, and considers itself as itself, the same thinking thing, in different times and different places'. Very young infants clearly do not possess this degree of self-awareness, and hence, it is argued, they are not persons and do not have an inviolable right to life.

Since such a thesis is far removed from any of the Jewish or Christian traditions recorded in his book, Jones does not spend much time discussing it. Rather, he takes the rejection of infanticide as a starting point for the evaluation of the other positions that he does take seriously. Any argument that is used to justify abortion or IVF or stem cell research must undergo the following test: would the same argument justify infanticide? If so, then it must be rejected.

The central issue, then, is to record, and decide between, the three alternatives from which we began: should we take individual human life as beginning at conception, at birth, or at some point in between? If the correct alternative is the third one, then we must ask further questions. What, in the course of pregnancy, is the crucial moment? Is it the point of formation (when the foetus has acquired distinct organs), or is it the point of quickening (when the movements of the foetus are perceptible to the mother)? Can we identify the moment by specifying a number of days from the beginning of pregnancy?

Some familiar texts from the Bible suggest that we should opt for conception as the beginning of the individual life of the person. 'In sin did my mother conceive me,' sang the Psalmist (51:5). Job cursed not only the day on which he was born but also 'the night that said "there is a man-child conceived"' (3:3). That individual human life begins at conception is a view found in some rabbinic texts, and in the early Christian Church it was held by Tertullian in the West and Gregory of Nyssa in the East. Since 1869 it has been the dominant position among Roman Catholics, but for most of the history of the Catholic Church it was a minority view. As Jones shows clearly, the theologian who first brought it back into favour among Western Christians was Martin Luther.

It has been much less common to regard personality and human rights as beginning only at the moment of birth. But one important rabbinic text allows abortion up to, but not including, the time when a child's head has emerged from the womb. Some Stoics seem to have taught that the human soul was received when a baby drew its first breath, just as it departs when a man draws his last breath.

Through most of the history of Western Europe, however, the majority opinion has been that individual human life begins at some time after conception and before birth. In the terminology that for centuries seemed most natural, the 'ensoulment' of the individual could be dated at a certain period after the intercourse that produced the offspring. Among theologians and canonists in the West 'there was a consensus', Jones tells us, 'that the human soul was directly created by God and that it was infused into the embryo when the form of the body was complete, generally held to be 40 days or thereabouts'. English common law agreed in placing the beginning of personhood between conception and birth, but it took the time of quickening, rather than the time of formation, as marking the time when abortion became homicide.

Thomas Aquinas held a particularly complicated version of this consensus position. For him the first substance independent of the mother is the embryo living a plant life with a vegetative soul. This vegetable substance disappears and is succeeded by a substance with an animal soul, capable of nutrition and sensation. Only at an advanced stage is the rational soul infused by God, turning this animal into a human being. The whole process of development is supervised by the father's semen, which according to Aquinas remained present and active throughout the first 40 days of pregnancy. For this biological narrative Aquinas claimed the authority of Aristotle. According to Jones, however, Aquinas was not only seriously in error about the biological facts, but had also misunderstood Aristotle (who should, he says, be counted among the supporters of the view that human life begins at conception). At this distance of time, it is difficult to see why Aquinas' teaching on this topic should be accorded great respect.

Jones' exhaustive study makes it abundantly clear that there is no such thing as *the* Christian consensus on the timing of the origin of the human individual. There was, indeed, a consensus among all denominations until well into the twentieth century that abortion was sinful, and that late abortion was homicide. There was no agreement whether early abortion was homicide. However, those who denied that it was homicide nonetheless regarded it as wrong because it was the destruction of a potential, if not an actual, human individual. There was again no agreement whether the wrongfulness of early abortion carried over into the destruction of semen prior to any conception. Even within the Roman Church, different popes can be cited in support of each option.

The question whether early abortion is homicide was and is important, because if it is not, then the rights and interests of human beings may legitimately be allowed to override the protection that by common consent should in normal circumstances be extended to the early embryo. The preservation of the life of the mother, the fertilisation of otherwise barren couples, and the furthering of medical research may all, it may be argued, provide reasons to override the embryo's protected status.

This line of argument was found convincing by the Warnock and Harries committees. They made a significant contribution to the debate by offering a new *terminus ante quem* for the origin of individual human life – one which was much earlier in pregnancy than the 40 days set by the pre-Reformation Christian consensus. Experimentation on embryos, they thought, should be impermissible after the fourteenth day. Their reasons were well summarised in the House of Commons by the then Secretary of State for Health, the Rt Hon. Kenneth Clarke:

> A cell that will become a human being – an embryo or conceptus – will do so within fourteen days. If it is not implanted within fourteen days it will never have a birth … The basis for the fourteen-day limit was that it related to the stage of implantation which I have just described, and to the stage at which it is still uncertain whether an embryo will divide into one or more individuals, and thus up to the stage before true individual development has begun. Up to fourteen days that embryo could become one person, two people, or even more.

Jones disagrees with this ethical reasoning. He defends the view, currently the dominant Catholic one, that individual human life begins at conception. An embryo, from the first moment of its existence, has the potential to become a rational human being, and therefore should be allotted full human rights. To be sure, an embryo cannot think or reason or exhibit any of the other activities that define rationality: but neither can a newborn baby. The protection that we afford to infants shows that we accept that it is potentiality, rather than actuality, that determines the conferment of human rights.

In adopting this stance Jones is taking issue with some of his fellow Catholics, such as Anscombe and Ford, who argue, on the same basis as Warnock and Clarke, that individual life cannot begin at a stage when an embryo may well split into a pair of twins. Jones' response to this is that an embryo is an individual living being which has a certain power – that of twinning – which is lost in later life. However, to count embryos is not the same as to count human beings, and in the case of twinning there will be two different human individuals each of whom will be able to trace their life story back to the same embryo, but neither of whom will be the same individual as that embryo.

In arguing for conception as the moment of origin, Jones rightly stresses that before fertilisation we have two entities (two different gametes) and after it we have a single one (one zygote). A moment at which one entity (a single embryo) splits into two entities (two identical twins) is surely equally entitled to be regarded as a defining moment. If Jones defends his position by urging that in the vast majority of cases twinning does not actually take place, he is surely forgetting his own correct emphasis on the ethical importance of potentiality. It is the potentiality of twinning, not its actuality, that gives reason for doubting that an early embryo is an individual human being.

Jones is a skilled and fair-minded advocate for the position that individual life begins at conception. However, in my view, his arguments fail to weaken the case for placing the origin of personhood somewhere around the fourteenth day of pregnancy. But there are two sides to the reasoning that leads to that conclusion. If the course of development of the embryo gives good reason to believe that before the fourteenth day it is not an individual human being, it gives equally good reason to believe that after that time it *is* an individual human being. If so, then late abortion is indeed homicide – and abortion becomes 'late' at an earlier date than was ever dreamt of by Aquinas.

David Fisher
Morality and War: Can War be Just in the Twenty-First Century?
Oxford University Press, 2011

Can a war be just? No, says the pacifist: all war-making is intrinsically immoral. Can a war be unjust? No, says the realist: moral constraints do not apply to the waging of war. Against both pacifists and realists, the theory of the just war says that war may sometimes be morally justified, but only if certain conditions are fulfilled in respect of its inception and conduct.

David Fisher draws on his wide reading in philosophy and history, and his practical experience as a senior official in the Ministry of Defence, to present a lucid exposition and robust defence of the just war tradition. He traces its history from its commencement in the writings of St Augustine, through its development in Aquinas, to its mature exposition in the sixteenth and seventeenth centuries by the Spanish theologians Vitoria and Suarez, and the Dutch jurist Hugo Grotius. He notes its neglect in the era following the Peace of Westphalia, but welcomes its revival in the twentieth century. He applauds the fact that it appears now in the writings not only of theologians and philosophers, but also of policy-makers and service chiefs.

There are two parts to the traditional just war theory. The first lays down the conditions that make it permissible to embark on a war (*jus ad bellum*), the second states the principles that must govern its conduct (*jus in bello*). As stated by Fisher, a war is justified if and only if (1) it is waged by a competent authority, (2) for a just cause, (3) with a right intention, (4) as a last resort. Moreover, (5) the good to be achieved by the war must outweigh the harm it will cause (the principle of proportion). In the course of the war the principle of proportion applies to individual military actions, and there should be no deliberate attacks on non-combatants.

Traditionally, all and only sovereign states were authorities legally competent to make war. In the modern world some have argued that while a sovereign state has the right to fight in self-defence, any other war needs authorisation by the United Nations. Fisher adopts an intermediate position: a humanitarian military intervention may be justified in the absence of a UN resolution if the harm to be averted is grave and immediate. He gives as an example the NATO operation against Serbia to protect the Kosovo Albanians – an operation in whose supervision he was personally involved as FCO adviser in 10 Downing Street.

If a war is to be just at all it must be waged in order to right a wrong done or to prevent an imminent injustice. Two kinds of just cause were recognised by the classical just war theorists. If one's country is attacked, one has the right to defend it in arms. But it can also be legitimate to wage an offensive war: a government may order an attack on another state if that is the only way to remedy a grave injustice to its own people or their allies. Fisher concurs that self-defence is not the only just cause.

What does the requirement of right intention add to the requirement of just cause? Right intention is indeed no more than the intention to rectify the wrong specified in the just cause. But it implies that once the wrong has been rectified the victor should desist from hostilities: the destruction of an enemy society is no legitimate aim of war, nor is the acquisition by the victor of assets of the vanquished, unless by way of compensation for damage inflicted.

It was commonly held that hostilities may be initiated only if there is good hope of victory, since otherwise the recourse to arms will fail to remedy the injustice which provided the initial ground for war. Fisher does not mention this as a separate element of the *jus ad bellum*, but regards it as part of the principle of proportion: in order to assess the likely overall balance of good and harm one will have to take into account the probability of defeat and victory.

Fisher places the just war doctrine within a more general moral framework. He considers currently fashionable moral systems and finds each of them, in isolation, unsatisfactory. Utilitarianism and similar systems are wrong to judge actions solely on the basis of their likely consequences: the internal quality of moral agency must be taken into account as well as its external effects. On the other hand it is wrong to see intention as the only factor to be taken into account in ethical evaluation, as Fisher alleges some moral absolutists do. The virtues, significant in ethics in general, deserve special consideration when we are considering the morality of war-making. It is a merit of the book that it emphasises the importance of the military virtues of obedience, courage, self-control and practical wisdom. But virtue ethics needs help from consequentialism, just as consequentialism does from virtue ethics, and so Fisher develops his own eclectic ethical framework which he calls 'virtuous consequentialism'.

Thus equipped, Fisher addresses a number of concrete issues, beginning with the principle of non-combatant immunity. He treats the principle with respect, and on its basis condemns the Israeli operation in Gaza in January 2009. But he does not treat non-combatant immunity as an absolute principle, arguing that it would have been permissible to shoot down one of the planes about to crash into the Twin Towers on 9/11, killing the innocent passengers as well as the hijackers. It would, I imagine, be open to one who upheld the principle as absolute to reach the same conclusion by treating the deaths as unintended effects of bringing down the plane; but Fisher is unenthusiastic about the principle of double effect.

Fisher takes a similar approach to the issue of torture. Once again, he thinks there is no absolute moral prohibition on torture: it is ethically justified if the only way to discover the location of a nuclear device planted in the middle of New York is to torture the terrorist who planted it. But there is an immense moral presumption against torture, and the practice should never be formally legalised. Fisher applauds President Obama's 2009 ban on coercive interrogation techniques.

The morality of the two Gulf wars is analysed in detail, and conclusions are drawn. On balance, the First Gulf War of 1991 was a just war. But the Second Gulf War, the invasion of Iraq in 2003, failed to meet fully any of the criteria that need to be satisfied before a war can be waged. It was undertaken on doubtful authority, without sufficient just cause and without adequate planning to secure a just outcome. However, though the invasion was unjust, the ensuing operations to restore peace and security in Iraq have, in spite of some disgraceful incidents, been just.

Fisher notes the changes in the nature of warfare since the end of the Cold War. The protean nature of war, he maintains, makes the realist rejection of moral considerations less rather than more plausible. Morality may present the ground for military operations – as in the case of humanitarian intervention – and also furnish a tool for their successful conduct – as in the case of counter-insurgency tactics. As the recent US Counterinsurgency Field Manual states, 'At its core, counterinsurgency is a struggle for the population's support. The protection, welfare, and support of the people are vital to success.'

My only complaint against this admirable book is that some important relevant topics are left out of the picture. We hear much about counter-insurgency, for instance, but almost nothing about insurgency. Fisher tells us 'there may be occasions when a just rebellion may be undertaken against an oppressive state' – but he does not spell out any conditions for a just rebellion. It is worth asking: to what extent do they resemble the conditions for a just war?

The condition of lawful authority clearly cannot be simply carried over to the conditions for just rebellion. If only governments are allowed to wage war, then there cannot be a just rebellion. But there are two elements involved in lawful authority. One is authority and the other is lawfulness. Authority has an importance of its own. It is important that within any warring group there should be a chain of command to enforce discipline, including the discipline of the laws of war. It is important that there should be an authority that is a party to treat with those who wish to bring hostilities to an end.

The need for authority is present in rebellion no less than in war. To be justified in rising in rebellion a group must be sufficiently organised to ensure that its armed struggle consists of more than mere random bursts of violence. This is not, generally, a problematic issue. For the rebels morality and self-interest point the same way. Self-interest urges them to organise as tightly as possible, and if they cannot exercise authority among themselves they cannot hope to present the citizens with a credible alternative government. These two factors commonly ensure that rebellious groups organise themselves under an authority – an Army Council or the like. When setting out the first condition for just rebellion we might say, instead of 'lawful authority', 'credible authority'.

The legitimacy of authority, however, is very relevant to the justice of a just rebellion, but under the heading of just cause. The one just cause for rebellion is that the existing government has forfeited, or has never had, legitimacy. The organisation that rebels has to take as its goal the replacement of an illegitimate government with a legitimate one. The 'credible authority' that we spoke of under the first heading must be, therefore, a potential legitimate authority.

How do existing governments forfeit legitimacy, in a moral as opposed to a constitutional sense? By failing to carry out the main ends of civil government: the protection of the lives of citizens from death and injury, and the provisions of institutions for the secure enjoyment of material conditions of life. This is most clearly the case when the government becomes itself a threat to the life and property of innocent citizens. But the mere breakdown of government, as well as flagrant abuse of power, can justify rebellion.

But while maintaining security of life and property, may not a government cease to govern with the consent of the governed? May not withdrawal of the consent of the governed legitimate rebellion? Here we need to make some distinctions. Clearly the mere fact that a President or Prime Minister may fall below 50 per cent in opinion polls does not justify disaffected citizens in immediately resorting to arms against them. But the matter alters if either of them clings on to power after clearly losing an election. Action by a government that nullifies the constitution from which it derives its power, on a serious scale, and against the wishes of a majority, may indeed justify rebellion.

One of the traditional conditions for just war was hope of victory. Analogous conditions hold for just rebellion. The political goals of the rebels must be realistic. That is, there must be a reasonable chance that the rebellion will be successful and that the successful overthrow of the government will lead to a political situation better than the one that stimulated the rebellion.

Another condition for just rebellion is that – as in warfare – the taking up of arms should be a last resort. That is to say, there must be no alternative method of removing the evil government, or the alternatives must have been tried and failed. If all you have to do to get rid of the government is to wait until the next election and go to the polling booth, then you are not justified in putting gunpowder under both Houses of Parliament.

In rebellion, as in war, we have to distinguish between the title to fight and the rules of fighting: between *ius ad rebellionem* and *ius in rebellione*. In general the rules of combat in rebellion are the same as those in war: most importantly, the innocent are not to be killed, and the harm done must not be out of proportion to the good to be achieved.

But there are two differences, First, the 'innocent' in an ordinary war are all those who are not combatants or their auxiliaries. The civil police are not a legitimate target, only those who are waging war or who are providing others with the means of waging war. But in a justified rebellion, the enemy is not another state waging war; it is a government illegitimately exercising civil coercion. All those who are engaged in so doing are legitimate targets: police, as well as army. This does not of course mean that anyone wearing a government uniform is fair game – the postman would be delivering the mail even if the government was not tyrannical.

A rebel who disregards the conditions for just rebellion, and makes attacks on third parties his means of fighting, by that act becomes a terrorist. It is sometimes said that 'terrorist' is a meaningless word, or at best an emotive expression; one person's terrorist is another person's freedom fighter. But this is not so, if we use words carefully. It is rebellion by immoral means that constitutes terrorism. Rebellion is sometimes justified, terrorism never: even freedom fighters must fight fairly.

Rebellion is not the only topic that Fisher would have done well to discuss: another one is assassination. In discussing non-combatant immunity he notes that the distinction between combatants and non-combatants does not correspond to the distinction between civilian and military, 'since some civilians may be involved in prosecuting the harm – for example, the politicians in charge of the war effort'. If such people are not covered by non-combatant immunity, does that mean that it is legitimate to assassinate them?

Many moralists say that in war it is not permissible to assassinate hostile rulers, even when the ruler is commander in chief of the armed forces. The strongest reason for treating rulers as non-combatants is the need to have someone in authority with power to treat and make peace. In the case of a just rebellion, it may be argued, this does not apply: if the rebellion is justified, then the government is the enemy and its members are legitimate targets.

In the year of the publication of *Morality and War* we have seen the assassination of Osama bin Laden and NATO strikes in support of a rebellion in Libya. Fisher, of course, could not possibly have foreseen these events: but it would have been wonderful to have had his considered opinion, in the abstract, of the justice or injustice of rebellion and assassination.

Times Literary Supplement, 30 September 2011